NO MORE TRAUMA, NO MORE DRAMA 4/22/23

For Sumayyah,

What a wonderful pleasure to make your acquaintance! You have a beautiful spirit & countenance. Always continue to speak your truth & allow your light to shine brightly! I hope these words inspire your continued growth & healing. Please continue to live your life fully 86,400 seconds every single day!! Wishing you exponential peace love & happiness!

NO MORE TRAUMA, NO MORE DRAMA

A Psychologist's Path to Healing

Anthony J. Smith, Ph.D.

Foreword by **Barry Saunders**

Copyright © 2021 by **Alase Center for Enrichment**

All Rights Reserved. No part of this book may be reproduced or transmitted in any form or by any means, electronic or mechanical, including photocopying, recording, or by any information storage and retrieval system, without written permission from the publisher. For more information, contact: Alase Center for Enrichment 6015 Fayetteville Rd. 114 Durham, North Carolina 27713 www.alase.net.

The scanning, uploading and distribution of this book via the Internet or any other means without the permission of the publisher is illegal and punishable by law. Please purchase only authorized print or electronic editions, and do not participate in or encourage electronic piracy of copyright materials. Your support of the authors rights is appreciated.

ISBN: 978-0-578-85563-9

This is a self-help book for adults. Topics covered include history of trauma for African Americans, Impacts of trauma, healing, Positive thinking, healthy living, lifestyles, peace, balance and acceptance,

> Names: Smith, Anthony J. (Psychologist), author. | Saunders, Barry, 1957 Aug. 15- writer of foreword. | Alase Center for Enrichment, issuing body.
>
> Title: No more trauma, no more drama : a psychologist's path to healing / by Anthony J. Smith, Ph.D. ; foreword by Barry Saunders.
>
> Description: Durham, NC : Alase Center for Enrichment, [2021] | Includes bibliographical references and index.
>
> Identifiers: ISBN: 978-0-578-85563-9 (print) | 978-0-578-91843-3 (ebook) | LCCN: 2021910112
>
> Subjects: LCSH: Psychic trauma--Treatment. | Traumatic incident reduction. | Mental healing. | Self-actualization (Psychology) | Self-help techniques. | Psychology, Applied. | Self- management (Psychology) | LCGFT: Self-help publications.
>
> Classification: LCC: RC552.P67 S65 2021 | DDC: 616.85/21--dc23

Edited by ERICA M. PETER
Cover Design by MIKE UGBOGBO
Interior Design by ARC MANOR, LLC. Rockville, MD, USA

Published in the United States of America for Worldwide Distribution

Published by Alase Center For Enrichment
Printed in the United States of America

ACKNOWLEDGMENT

Jack McMillian and Flora Blue McMillian. You held the trauma inside your very bones so that I and your progenitors could one day be free. We willingly accept the baton of change passed down through generations and have been inspired to do our part to create healing. We are thankful to each ancestor on whose shoulders we stand because each one was a necessary brick in the wall of progressive healing and eventual freedom. I honor my grandparents, Robert Smith Sr, Lillie Calloway, and Thelma Moncour, those first known to me who withstood tremendous transgressions to continue the energy and legacy that allows me to exist. I honor and thank my parents, Tommie and Heather Smith, who laid the specific foundation infusing me with the characteristics of discipline, dedication, and excellence of craft that provide the cornerstone for this work that I do. I am an embodiment of your love, life, and sacrifices. For my siblings, Dearta and Tommie, thanks for being my ride or die partners in this thing called life. To my children, Bakari, Mikali, Asha, and Zahara who keep me inspired to do my part to bring healing to our lineages, I thank you for choosing me and trusting the process of change. I know you will continue to contribute to a legacy that we can evolve for many generations to come. You provide for me a mirror with which to see myself and those things that I can do better. Everyone needs a mirror and Glenda Jones you have been a reflection to me, helping me to appreciate loyalty, selflessness, and true friendship. You have helped me to hone the best qualities of myself while simultaneously helping me to refine those rough edges that are constantly in development. As I find those areas that need continued growth and development, I honor the concepts of Yin and Yang, for in that balance is where my love, happiness, and ability to be my best self-resides. Lastly, I am grateful to the Creator for the gifts that allow me to be and for infusing in me the courage to speak truth to power.

CONTENTS

FOREWORD 9

NO MORE TRAUMA NO MORE DRAMA 11

INTRODUCTION 13

PART I:
How did we get here: Understanding the History of Trauma for African Americans in the United States 17

1. KINDLY REMOVE YOUR KNEE FROM MY NECK, PLEASE 19
2. TOWARDS A DEEPER UNDERSTANDING OF TRAUMA 29
3. HISTORICAL PRECEDENTS OF TRAUMA 35
4. HOW HAS TRAUMA IMPACTED US AS A COMMUNITY 47
5. CONTINUED IMPLICATIONS OF TRAUMA 61
6. HOW DID WE GET THIS WAY 67
7. CRAFTING A PATH TOWARDS HEALING 73

PART II:
Behind the Veil: A Personal Example of the Impact of Trauma 79

8. WHY VULNERABILITY IS IMPORTANT TO THE HEALING PROCESS ... 81
9. INDIVIDUAL TRAUMA—The Childhood Years 85
10. COLLECTIVE TRAUMA—The College Years 93
11. INDIVIDUAL TRAUMA—Getting a Ph.D. in Life 107
12. SOCIETAL TRAUMA 177

PART III
Walking the Labyrinth of Healing 189

13. FINDING A PLACE OF PEACE, BALANCE AND ACCEPTANCE......191

14. INSPIRATION 205

15. TRANSFORMATION 217

16. POSITIVE THINKING TO CREATE A NEW REALITY.............. 229

17. THE POWER OF CHANGE................................. 239

18. EQUILIBRIUM 245

19. ALIGNMENT 253

20. CREATING POSITIVE RITUALS............................. 265

21. AUTHENTICITY 275

22. HEALING WITH COUPLES................................ 281

23. HEALING IN CHILDREN/THE ART OF PARENTING 287

24. BLISS.. 297

25. THOUGHTS FOR A FUTURE OF FREEDOM FROM
THE CHAINS OF TRAUMA 301

BIBLIOGRAPHY.. 305

BIOGRAPHY 309

RESOURCES 311

INDEX... 313

FOREWORD

I have been a journalist at newspapers around the country for more than 40 years, and during that time, it has often been necessary for me to try to understand why people do what they do. For nearly half of those years, it has been my good fortune to be able to call upon the professional expertise of Dr. Anthony Smith. His insights into human behavior, psychology, and pathology have been invaluable to me. He brings not just book smarts—of which he has an abundance—but passion, compassion, and sensitivity for people. Those traits and his courage—Dr. Smith is unflinching when it comes to revealing mistakes he has made in his personal life—are evident on each page of this book. His own admitted fallibility, though, is part of the reason he can relate to human imperfection in others and knows what it takes to help them deal with theirs. Nobel Prize-winning author Ernest Hemingway wrote, "The world breaks everyone and afterward many are strong at the broken places." Anyone who reads this book and heeds Dr. Smith's insights will be stronger, too, whether they're broken or not.

Barry Saunders
Publisher,
The Saunders Report

NO MORE TRAUMA NO MORE DRAMA

A Psychologist's Journey to Healing

The Vision:
January 1, 2090 Letter by my great grandson to his brother

Peace bro, it's been a while since we last talked. I hope life has been treating you kindly. Life on this planet is truly amazing. It's an entirely different dimension currently, one that does not keep us tied to the unfair and traumatic past. Currently, in this country, everyone starts from the exact same place and nobody has a head start of several hundred years. The word equity actually has true meaning here. I do not have to lower my abilities to make others comfortable with me. I do not have to change my natural God-given appearance to appease the sensibilities of others who would choose to look down on me for appearing "different." I do not have to switch my word choice and cadence to fit in with others. I think our great grandfather would be proud of the seeds that he and others planted for us to be truly free. And just as he was so grateful for the sacrifices that those who proceeded him in his lineage made, we should be as proud and grateful that we have arrived at this place. If I could talk with him I would ask him, "Do you know what it's like to be unencumbered by thoughts of negativity, nervousness, fear, and apprehension? Constantly worrying about your safety and the possibility that you will be attacked for no reason." If he could answer he might say that this freedom is like a heavy burden lifted that he did not even realize he was carrying, nor did he recognize the immense weight of that tremendous load. We are currently able in the year 2090 to experience life as it should be experienced, a wonderful opportunity to engage with my family, my community, and the environment that surrounds me without worry. Things could not be better for me and life is going extremely well. I am so excited about the opportunities that life has brought my way. It's amazing to think about the challenges that we had earlier in our life where we couldn't have opportunities to be our best selves. Who would have thought that we would both be free to speak our minds and express our opinions with no worry about alienating anyone? The fact that we can tap into the best part of ourselves and be secure about who we are is amazing. Embarking on healing was the best choice I could have possibly made. I wish for everyone to continue in a space of being truly free and uninhibited in a manner that allows us to be our optimal selves. I think it's also wonderful that the residual trauma has been healed. Perhaps, most importantly, we have been given the necessary reparation financially, and with land and resources, to fully atone for the traumatic treatment and history that our ancestors suffered in making this country what it is. There has finally been action that coalesces with the words that are typically freely talked about. Our great grandfather would likely be amazed and shocked at the reform that has taken place in the justice and police systems in our country. What probably seemed impossible to him has actually been created and we no longer have to walk in fear of the police nor worry that justice will not truly be blind and fair. Now we get to live our lives fully 86,400 seconds every day. I am so glad to be in this wonderful place and I honor those wonderful ancestors who have come before us! Ashe!

INTRODUCTION

In doing the work of counseling and therapy over the past 25 years, I have been able to observe mental health concerns in many different people. These have been so tremendous in number and in weight as to lead me to say that were it not for faith and what I have learned about how to promote healing and health, the statistics would be overwhelming. Such circumstances have allowed me to think deeply about and profoundly question the impact that trauma has on the lives of so many people. In some form or fashion, trauma has manifested itself in the lives of most people and has had such a significant impact that it has taken a serious toll on both their ability to live a fulfilled life at the moment and their capacity to enjoy inner peace. This trauma exhibits across many dimensions in the field of mental health. Whether a person is dealing with stress in the workplace, depression, anxiety, parenting, marital issues, blending a family together, grief or just surviving what can be a vicious society, trauma is something that is often at the root of many of these problems. As such I have found myself helping people consider and understand the impact that generational trauma has had on their present situation. It is in this regard that the central theme of this book centers around understanding and moving through trauma so that we can live our optimally healthiest lives.

I came to the writing of this book out of a desire to help people understand the impact of trauma on their lives and assure them there are ways to prevent it from stealing the joy of life. Because it has been my experience that people seem to resonate with stories that influence and inspire change, I have endeavored to share some stories of my own personal experiences that I hope will encourage you to do your own exploration of how trauma has impacted you, and ultimately, to inspire you to engage the internal work to manifest healing. I have had my share of trauma and I have learned to navigate some rough waters to a place of overcoming and restorative calm. Although not an easy process, it has been abundantly useful to myself and those that I serve. I know from experience that we can learn a lot from the lives of others. Even in my practice, I have found that a degree of self-disclosure has been beneficial to those with whom I work. It makes the process real and allows people to appreciate the humanness of us all. I have experienced a significant degree of trauma over the course of my life, some of which remains present in my mind in a consistent way. Other episodes I have managed to move from the forefront of my mind and had not thought about until I was contemplating writing this book. I want to use my experiences with trauma and overcoming trauma to provide for any who are interested in a useful guide from a psychological perspective, a template for understanding personal traumas, thinking about the impact trauma has on our personal lives and confronting it so we can move our lives forward in a healthy manner. To state it differently, I am sharing personal examples with you, the reader, for the purpose of providing a light and potential path to healing. This is something that I think we all can benefit from.

Introduction

As should be evident, these examples are from my perspective and recollection, and others may recall them differently. As a professional psychologist and a person who believes fairness fundamental, I have endeavored to present my stories in a balanced manner. From the aspect of healing,—and facilitating healing is my goal—the details are not as important as understanding the dynamics of trauma and human relationships that many of us go through. These stories offer the reader the opportunity to consider in a larger and different context from his or her own real life the effects and implications of trauma on them individually and subsequently in their intimate relationships. Most importantly, however, this book provides the reader with definitions, encouragement, tools, strategies, and an opportunity to consider living a life free of the insidious impacts of trauma. Since none of us is a hermit, this is done in relationships. I want to urge you not to separate yourself from friends, families, and their loving relationships. They may want to read with you. Most of us are going through some kind of trauma at one time or another in our lives. There is one thing that I know about achieving health and happiness. It is worth all the work of therapy and personal effort it takes to become a compassionate, kind, loving person and thereby allows our relationships to be a reflection of our healing work.

I will make two last points about this process of sharing my story that I believe can be useful. There are many who think talk therapy and counseling are a waste of time. Many have either never had a therapist or had a negative experience with one. I am able to be vulnerable with readers because I not only know personally the importance and the benefits of therapy, but also I have trained and continue to study so that I can help others avoid suffering unnecessary pain and trauma. There are many others who can be available to you if after reading this book you are willing to give therapy a try. My second point goes directly to the issue of trust. There is an implicit trust that occurs when a person comes in for therapy. It is a time of extreme vulnerability, where people are laying bare the many secrets of their lives that they often have not shared with anyone else. For therapy to be successful, there has to be a recognition that the client must unburden themselves if they are going to find any freedom or healing. I do not take this responsibility lightly, this holding space for those that come in at their most naked and exposed state. As with other privileged communication professions such as attorneys, medical professionals, or priests/pastors, these relationships provide the opportunity for unbridled truth. Any reticence for truth and full disclosure limits the ability of one to fully heal and make their life better. The gatekeepers for holding these truths take an ethical pledge to hold the confidence of those we help, and we are mandated by our licenses to do so. For the African American community that comes with a healthy distrust which has been cultivated over centuries of trauma. The importance of this cannot be understated. It is in that spirit that I am allowing myself to be vulnerable, shifting the role to one who is trusting that the audience will appreciate the purpose and the scope of which I am utilizing my life as an example of how to understand and work through trauma. For I cannot ask of others what I am unwilling to do myself. The writer, Audre Lorde, reminds us "it is not difference which immobilizes us, but silence." I am breaking my silence because I have a story to tell about lessons learned. I have knowledge to share, and some truths to speak. In this way—with this book—I am inviting you as an individual member of this reading audience to join me in a process and on a journey that can lead to growth and for which I am offering you this light.

PART I

**How did we get here:
Understanding the history of trauma for
African Americans in the United States**

CHAPTER 1

KINDLY REMOVE YOUR KNEE FROM MY NECK, PLEASE

On May 25th, 2020, an incident transpired that stunned the entire world and instantaneously became etched into the psyche and consciousness of all who witnessed this moment. We all watched as the life of George Floyd was slowly and painstakingly sucked away while his neck was under the knee of a Minneapolis police officer, Derek Chauvin. The apparent casualness and lack of remorse at the event that was occurring appeared to awaken for many a sense of disbelief that human life could be regarded with so little concern. For the African American community, this event was not a new reality and, in fact, has become something that is accepted as a part of life, this daily and constant barrage of traumatic events large and small. However, for those who have not been impacted by the discriminatory practices of the police at large in this country, this senseless killing appeared to touch something in the moral fiber of their souls that would not allow them to proceed with business as usual. With the force and strength of a rocket launch, this incident catapulted into the homes and lives of people worldwide and made it impossible for anyone to pretend that they did not observe what they observed. We would all have to confront and deal with the manifestation of what we had now been privy to whether we wanted to or not, even in the midst of a worldwide pandemic that had slowed the pace and interaction of life around the globe. The life values that most people profess to believe were now being confronted with the reality of the actions that were being observed. We say that everyone is afforded justice but is that what we just watched? We say that we value life but was this demonstrated in this incident? We say that the police are there to protect and serve but were either of these things actually happening? These and more questions were being forced upon us even if we did not want to consider them. An easy justification or rationalization was nowhere to be found, although there were some who pressed to find some sliver of justification despite what they had witnessed. Everyone had beheld this traumatic event, and it pulled at the core of our souls and caused an intense sense of anger, frustration, sadness, and hopelessness. These are the fruits of the insidiousness of trauma, the legacy of which for those in the African American community are as deep and long as the birth of this nation. The symbolic nature of the knee on the neck of George Floyd is only a microcosm of the legacy that the African American community has had to negotiate with the knee of this country on the necks of the African American community. And this interaction where the lives of George Floyd, the store owner, the cops involved, and those that witnessed the event live, all flowed to a point of convergence that would forever change this world.

Like everyone else, I struggled to accept the reality of what had occurred in our community yet again and in such a heinous manner. As an African American psychologist, I found myself in the midst of two worlds, struggling to manage my own emotions while also being a repository for those that come to me to unburden themselves with the various issues that they are dealing with. In the days following this incident, in practically every therapy session, individuals spent at least some time emoting and discussing the surplus of feelings that were present. Many were forlorn and hopeless that things would ever change. Many were despondent at the incessant feeling of being unable to do anything and feeling victimized. And so very many were just plain exhausted. In the midst of this, I was tasked with assisting people with this struggle of understanding something that is not really understandable. I came to a realization that I wanted to offer something that could help with moving us out of a place of being consumed by trauma and provide some avenues for healing the angst that we all felt.

One of the projects that I had engaged to help underscore the importance of mental health in the African American community was to create a podcast that focused on this issue, Black Folks Do Therapy. I decided, days after the murder of George Floyd, to contact my colleague who is a psychologist in Minneapolis and interview him for my podcast to discuss on a broader level the impact of this situation for those in the city of Minneapolis as well as for those in the African American community at large. I saw it as a way for us to provide some psychological relief while offering healing interventions that people could use to better cope and manage through the situation. My colleague shared something that was ultimately quite insightful and surprising in terms of the impact of these traumas on his own life. As we convened the topic, he related an incident from his childhood, that being the murder of Emmett Till in 1955, and how this murder actually took place in his community in Mississippi when he was seven years old. I never know what will come out as I interview people, but to say that I was surprised at the immediate connection between the murder of Emmett Till and the murder of George Floyd would be an understatement.

The fact that he could be within miles of both of these incidents was uncanny. Yet at the same time, it possibly speaks to the reality of the continued proliferation of injustice wherever we are, even now in 2020. In further describing the trauma associated with these situations, he relayed how at the time of the murder of Emmett Till, the fear was palpable within the families in his community, so much so that they were taught to hide whenever white people would come around. He described being told by his elders to run into ditches or hide out in the fields when they saw cars and people that they did not recognize, as they were concerned for their safety and did not know what might happen at the hands of angry white people. It was a part of their reality of life that the adults in his community had taught the children that this is what they needed to do to stay safe during this and other situations. On a broader level, there were all types of admonitions and rules about how to conduct oneself and behavior that became as natural to those living in the African American community as breathing. These standards for living had been passed down through generations and continue to be passed down currently in contemporary society. Most African Americans know this as "the talk" where adults teach their children how to behave should they encounter the police, shrinking themselves and making no sudden movements to avoid being assaulted or killed. Even those African Americans who have achieved some degree of "status or financial independence" are still subject to the necessity of comporting themselves in a manner that is not natural. In essence, in order to manage these situations and get through life, we are taught how to survive as opposed to focusing on how to thrive.

For myself, having visited the African American museum in Washington DC and seeing the exhibit of Emmett Till, this was something that I recognized as historical. Yet here I was talking with someone who not only lived during the time that Emmett Till was horrendously murdered having been tortured, disfigured, shot in the head, and tied with barbed wire to a large metal fan before being pushed into the river. He was actually living in the community that this assault and murder occurred at that time. Of course, somewhere in the back of my mind, I knew that my colleague would have been alive at the time of this incident based on his age, but having him discuss his real-life experience in the community conveyed that reality in a way that was astonishing. It brought home the realization that this was really not that long ago. It also raises several other questions that lurk below the surface for many, but that we do not necessarily give voice to such as how does one engage the mental gymnastics necessary to deal with this early childhood trauma and make sense of it into adulthood. These events are having a traumatic impact on the psyche of those experiencing them and the need to survive is normalizing behavior that is quite abnormal. How does one teach their family, their children, their friends how to just be in life, wanting like others to live the American dream? Are the choices that are made to shrink to the margins of life in themselves traumatic or do they just become adaptations to the way life is? These are questions worthy of further deeper analysis as we delve into the much broader impact of trauma and the manner in which it affects us all.

After concluding my conversation with my colleague in Minneapolis, I continued to ponder the significant relevance of trauma in my life and its broader, generational impact on the African American community. This caused me to reflect back to the initial departure point for my having an interest in helping people to move through trauma, an experience, and a history that occurred in my own family. You see, if we think about it, everyone in the African American community has a story, a connection to a story, a lived experience that speaks to witnessing or receiving some aspect of trauma. I am just a representative sample in this regard. In November 2013, at the funeral of an uncle, I met a set of cousins that I had not been acquainted with previously. My father is from a large family and had a total of nine siblings that we grew up knowing and interacting with. However, they had another older sibling who had been taken away from the family as a toddler, and this incident was not discussed much within the family. Eventually, she was found many years later and ultimately was able to make it back into the fold of the family. As I interacted with my newfound cousins, we had an immediate connection and they insisted that I come to visit and connect with them in Atlanta. I assured them that I would do this at some point, and we vowed to keep in contact and continue to get to know each other. Approximately one year later, I had occasion to be traveling through Atlanta and contacted them about us getting together. They insisted that I stay with them and they would host me and so I agreed and arrangements were made. On the second day of the visit we put some food on the grill and sat outside on the patio reminiscing and conversing about life. My two cousins began to describe their childhood and what it was like growing up for them.

I listened to them discuss the difficulties around growing up impoverished in New York City, in an abusive household with no significant family around to assist them with the struggles that they faced. Their mother, who would be my oldest aunt, was to their knowledge an only child and married to an abusive man who eventually left them and established another family mere blocks away. Despite having this other family, her father also returned whenever he wanted and interacted with his wife who felt obligated to continue to engage with him as this was in line with the teachings of their strict Pentecostal church. They discussed many incidents where they would awaken to fighting and screaming, seeing their mother being dragged down the stairs, all types of injuries occurring, and furniture or household materials being damaged. Often, they would be in situations where they were unsure of what they would eat for their meals. In one incident my cousin described waking up to her mother crying and going out to sit on the stoop. Friends of the family came by and asked where their mother was, and she replied that she was inside crying. When they went in to investigate, her mother told them that she was crying because she did not know what she would feed the children that day. The friends ended up going to the store and bringing groceries that would allow them to solve this problem for the moment. My cousin describes another incident where she, at the age of 7, was with her mother running errands and they needed to take the bus back home. The price for the bus was 35 cents but her mother only had 34 cents and so put my cousin on the bus as she walked up and down asking anyone for a penny. She states that no one was able to offer this penny and she eventually asked the bus driver if he would allow her to get by without it and he allowed it. My cousin described being absolutely terrified that her mother would not be allowed on the bus and she would have been stuck on the bus alone and unsure of where to get off and how to walk home by herself. The memory of this seemingly small incident still haunts her and underscores the impact of situations in our life that we may not consider to be traumatic at first glance. Clearly, for her, this incident left an indelible mark and still haunts her to this day.

They described other incidents, being whipped with extension cords and having to go to school with whelps on their bodies, being put in positions where older men would try to assault them, and being teased relentlessly by other children because of their style of dress due to being Pentecostal, which for the girls meant wearing dresses even in the brutal winters. Through all this time they never considered that they had an entire family somewhere that they could have been connected to and received help from. Eventually, they moved to Alabama where things were slower and there was more family from their father and grandmother's family that could help them. It was during this time that cracks in the foundation of their family story began to occur. Their mother who thought she was an only child, had cousins who would make sly comments to my cousins about their grandmother not really being their grandmother. These comments seemed to come during times of anger, so no one really gave them much validity. However, one day my uncle, who had apparently known about them for some time, had been looking for his sister and showed up at their house unexpectedly and introduced himself. His aunt had kept a picture of their mother as a baby, and he had seen this picture and been given the history of his sister. As a result, he was determined that he would one day find her. He was ultimately able to track her down through an informal network of churches and families and soon brought his other siblings along to meet them. We have endeavored to make up for lost time and my long-lost aunt and cousins have since been integrated into the fabric of a family. This has proven to be a blessing in so many ways, even while decrying the fact that they missed so much valuable time with family that can never be reclaimed.

In describing the trauma, one cousin is most sad about her mother that presumed only child, who suffered so much and in so many different ways. It is speculated that her mother was sent away with the woman who she came to know as her mother because her biological mother gave birth to her as a teenager and was unable to adequately care for her. Although my cousins are able to appreciate that the choices made at that time were not done with any ill intent, it still bothers them that now three generations of the family have been impacted by this single decision. One lamented that she wished that those who made that decision would have considered the impact this would have on those that come down the line in the family. She was able to see that this decision has impacted her children and grandchildren currently. This is quite prescient and something that I will return to later on in this book. Suffice to say that a consideration for the healing of generational trauma will have to include having a keen outlook and plan of action for what the future looks like, and a specific plan of action for how to achieve this. One wondered if her father would have continued to be so abusive if he had known that there were other men in the family, brothers of her mother who could serve in a protective role of some capacity. These are all speculative considerations that illustrate the complexities inherent in this particular series of trauma.

Later that evening, we moved to discuss the current issues in the extended family and the difficulties that continue to be present that span a range of fighting, alcohol abuse, and poor impulse control and decision making, amongst others. They described many of the behaviors as dysfunctional, but I offered a different observation in that how could they be any more functional than what they had been taught. They were in many cases doing the best they could with what they had. Any of us could look at the choices and situations of our lives and recognize opportunities that we could have chosen differently. In some regards, the beauty of life unfolding is that one can never predict the exact outcome of the choices we make every day. We all are left with the reflection of ourselves as we consider how to live our lives in the most optimal manner.

I find it amazing that many of the siblings have proved themselves to be capable of being as accomplished as they are in the face of such difficult traumatic circumstances. We must also ponder the heights that could have been reached without the hurdles of the traumatic situations that they were forced to navigate. There were many other incidents that would further illustrate the complexities of trauma that this family endured. In short, though, there are effects that are continuing to be experienced currently. This illustrates that the downgrowth and reach of trauma does not stop with the individual impacted at the moment. There is a residual effect that can flow into those that come after us, impacting choices and opportunities for change. As can be seen in the various situations highlighted thus far, the tenacious reach of trauma is quite pervasive. I think that we all can benefit from considering the impact that trauma has on us individually, within our families, and ultimately within our communities.

CHAPTER 2

TOWARDS A DEEPER UNDERSTANDING OF TRAUMA

So what is trauma? The concept of trauma is a relatively broad concept that has garnered a lot of attention recently. Much discourse has occurred about the collective types of trauma and the impact these traumas have had on individuals, communities, and ultimately our world. As with any situation, the identification of the challenges that trauma presents is relatively easy. The harder, more challenging aspect as it relates to trauma revolves around what we do in a practical sense to move ourselves forward in a healthy and positive manner once the difficulty has been identified.

It can be argued that no one escapes life without experiencing some form of trauma. Of course, some people experience more or different types of trauma than others. It is virtually impossible for anyone to escape life without having some level of experience with a version of trauma, and this is exponentially heightened in the African American community. Some families or groups experience more trauma than others. Some cultures experience more trauma than others. The African American community has experienced a consistent barrage of trauma, beginning with the inception of the United States of America. This trauma manifests on many different levels, and, in some cases, has become so present that we have habituated to the effects of this trauma, and as a result move through life in an unconscious manner, responding to events and issues in ways that have been passed down for generations. As a result, much attention has been given to the things that are problematic in our community. More attention is needed for the practical application of what will bring about healing.

Before delving into the topic at hand, it is important to provide a quick baseline summary of how we conceptualize trauma. A precise definition of trauma is given by Merriam-Webster's dictionary which states that trauma is: 1. Any physical damage to the body caused by violence or accident 2. An emotional wound or shock often having long-lasting effects and lastly 3. A disordered psychic or behavioral state resulting from severe mental or emotional stress or physical injury.[1] The premise here is that one has been impacted by some outside source in a manner that causes pain or emotional stress resulting in a long-term difficulty. In short, in regards to mental health, trauma can be thought of as any type of abuse, neglect, or violence that is enacted on a person or that a person witnesses.

In the field of psychology, we utilize the Diagnostic and Statistical Manual[2] as the primary tool for understanding and diagnosing different mental health conditions. Trauma is covered as a category and most people are familiar with the concept of Posttraumatic stress disorder. Posttraumatic stress disorder identifies the various outcomes of what happens to

---

1 "Trauma." Merriam-Webster.com 2021 https://www.merriam-webster.com (8 May 2011).

2 American Psychiatric Association: Diagnostic and Statistical Manual of Mental Disorders, Fifth Edition, Arlington, VA, American Psychiatric Association, 2013

a person who has experienced trauma. The outcomes of the trauma can show up in many different forms, the most popular among these being depression and anxiety in a classic sense. However, other symptoms or outcomes of trauma include nightmares, flashbacks, low self-esteem, lack of confidence, irritability, reckless or self-destructive behavior, and difficulty concentrating. More intense reactions can lead to alcohol or drug abuse, sleeping too much or too little, overeating, gambling, sexual acting out, and, in extreme cases, feeling detached from one's body or surroundings in a surreal sense. Even if we do not endorse any of these symptoms, it is quite likely that we know someone that does. It is important to state that I would propose that we would not allow ourselves to focus on the "diagnosing" aspect of understanding this concept, particularly as in this book we will focus more on healing, but it is necessary to provide this as a baseline for understanding the information we will be covering.

In addition to understanding the definition of trauma, it is also important to recognize that there can be different levels in terms of the intensity of the trauma. Acute trauma describes a situation where there is a specific event that causes a reaction resulting in any of the previously discussed outcomes. Chronic trauma involves repeated and consistent exposure to a traumatic event that causes an undue amount of stress and anxiety as a result. Complex trauma builds the intensity even more as there are now multiple sources of trauma which exists for extended and consistent periods of time. So in considering these brief explanations of trauma, would you say that you have been impacted by trauma? Have you considered whether these trauma(s) still have an effect on you? Is this something that you have ever considered, and do you know how to manage the outcomes of the trauma? We will consider these questions and more as we explore this topic.

We can see that there are distinct characteristics that comprise a definition of trauma. Once the core definition is understood; however, we can see how this trauma can exist across a number of different dimensions. For instance, there can be family trauma where the family is confronted with managing a major issue such as a car accident taking the life of two of its members. Financial trauma can result when one member of a couple is unexpectedly laid off and is out of work for over a year resulting in the family losing their home and having an automobile repossessed. Sexual trauma can result when a woman or man is raped or molested as a child and does not have an outlet for discussing the resulting pain and difficulties this causes them. Natural disasters cause trauma as in the case of a family watching their house destroyed in a hurricane, earthquake, or fire and being unable to retrieve any of their lifelong possessions. How people respond to and interpret any of these situations can vary dramatically depending on their life perspective. This does not mean that they have not experienced trauma though, even if it appears that it is not having an impact anymore. Each of these issues happens for people in general, but the impact is exponentially heightened when members of marginalized populations have to negotiate these traumas in addition to the layers of racism and oppression that exist. The couple who have lost their family members having to also deal with an insensitive and racist police officer who takes an extended time to release information necessary for the death certificate. The doctor at the hospital who ignores or diminishes the trauma that a woman comes in with regarding a rape, especially if she accuses someone who presents as white. The family who is dealing with the insurance company that delays and takes their time processing the claim that allows them to have adequate housing and sustenance while their home is being rebuilt. These things happen quite frequently, and though many African Americans adapt and attempt to move through these situations, the buildup of stress continues, often unseen, and spills out in negative ways that can cause further stressors to arise. For example, consider that the depression and anxiety that comes with the unknown situation of when the money for the claim will come in can lead to overeating and a poor diet which can then cause high blood pressure and lead to a heart attack. This heart attack might not have occurred if the person were treated in a way commensurate with the respect and care that is afforded to those in the white community.

When these types of situations happen, we are impacted immensely. Because there are so many ways that trauma can present and it often can be normalized, many people do not realize that they have been impacted. Often, we do not grasp the full scope of the intensity of the episode and because our society does not adequately deal with difficult situations, the resulting mental health issues are often then pushed to the side as we are left to institute platitudes such as "it's all in God's hands/will" or "the worst is behind us and it will get better" or "toughen up." On the whole, we do not know how to allow ourselves to feel and experience the pain and navigate the healing process in a patient and compassionate manner. We have been psychologically "trained" to accept and respond to trauma in a manner that is not healthy and does not yield healing. Again we are taught to survive rather than thrive. The numbing that occurs after yet another police shooting of an innocent and unarmed African American person is an example of this trained response. We say things like "this would never have happened to a white person" or "if this were a white neighborhood, things would be different." Some aspect of this thinking continues to show up and becomes an automatic response to the trauma, an unconscious method for coping and trying to make sense of that which can never make sense.

What happens to us when we experience trauma? In my years of working with and observing people, there are so many responses to consider. Depression may present within a person as they are dissatisfied and unhappy with life and the circumstances they find themselves dealing with. Seeing no opportunity for change or ability to move from their present space, lethargy might set in. For others, anxiety about something negative occurring to them or a loved one renders them unable to find peace, as a constant and nagging worry pervades their mindset. Feeling a need to reduce the anxiety or depression we may try to escape these feelings and thus look to numb our emotions through drugs or alcohol. Being unable to understand or tap into our emotions we may look for relief from these feelings through indiscriminate casual sex, or verbally or physically abusive relationships. All of these and more present as the unhealthy answers to trauma and we must understand this before we can do the work necessary to heal ourselves from these negatives. As we are able to understand the colossal monster of trauma that encompasses us, we can deliver the appropriate remedy to render this monster ineffective, and thus provide a clear pathway for healthy living.

CHAPTER 3

HISTORICAL PRECEDENTS OF TRAUMA

To Ask a Question

There have been many civilizations that have enslaved others and waged wars for a variety of selfish reasons in the history of the world. However, the legacy of the institute of slavery in the United States stands out in its particular cruelty, and this approach has left an indelible mark on African people worldwide. This legacy stretches through generations and across cultures all around the globe. It is important to understand the philosophy of those who had in their mind the purpose of subjugating others to work for their benefit, and in the process dehumanizing them to allow this atrocity to make sense in their minds.

One of my favorite things to do is look at old pictures. I like to imagine what the people in the pictures were thinking and what their life was like. I explore what the expression on their face communicates. I like to ponder what were their dreams and aspirations. What were their fears and what were they hiding deep within their soul? What traumas had they endured and how had they developed the fortitude to persevere despite unwieldy odds. Where did they stuff their pain and how did this impact the manner in which they related to others in their family? What did they pass on to their children and what patterns still exist?

I was able to do this with the oldest pictures in my family after my father's first cousin blessed me with her wealth of family research she had done for our family over the years. Of particular importance were the documents that delineated the furthest we could trace back the origins of our family line. In this document, the will of the person who had my ancestors enslaved, their descriptions and the cost associated with them were items that stood out to me. As I thought about what it was like for them to be sold and bartered with a price on their head and unable to do anything about it, I considered what the amount was that had been determined to be their worth. Jack McMillan, the oldest in my family lineage was deemed to be worth $1000. Holding for inflation that would equate to $34,157 today. His life was valued at $34,157. Ponder this for a moment and reflect on what you think your life is worth. What value do you come up with? How do you value the life of others? Do you think some lives are worth more than others? Could this be at least one reason why even if on a subconscious level, Black life is valued with such little regard by the police and many in the white community? How do we even put a value on life? Clearly, this placement of value is done as we observe the various payouts that come when one who has been improperly imprisoned is exonerated or when a civil suit is paid to the family of one killed by the police. If we do a comparison of who gets killed and how much they are given, disparities are glaringly evident.

1851 ESTATE AND WILL OF DANIEL MCMILLAN

1851 ESTATE AND WILL OF DANIEL MCMILLAN

The McMillan Estate was actually recorded in the Probate office of Clayton County, Alabama. Based on the information contained in Daniel McMillan's Estate and Will of 1851, it appears that Susan (McMillan) Christian and her entire family were sold, and then separated among the slave owners, the McMillan family. Edited and translated by Hermetta E. Williams.

THE STATE OF ALABAMA AND BARBOUR COUNTY*

Be it remembered that a Probate Court by and held in and for said Barbour county on the 10th day of State of Alabama of January, 1853 present & presiding, W.R. Barbour County Cowen Judge of said Court, we the undersigned commissioners appointed by the Judge of the probate are to divide the slaves of the Estate of **Daniel McMillan**. Daniel McMillan of this county left a deed. After having been duly qualified, we have divided the estate, first giving the widow of said deceased one-fifth of his slaves. The widow's lot consisting of **WILLIS** valued at five hundred & fifty dollars; and **JANNET** valued at four hundred dollars; and **SARAH** valued at three hundred and fifty dollars. The widow's lot amounts to thirteen hundred dollars, her part being fifteen hundred and fifteen dollars Lot No. 3, [Pays] to the widow two hundred and fifteen dollars.

Charles McMillan Lot No. 1 **JACK** valued at one-thousand dollars and each share after the widow's one-fifth having been taken from said slaves amounting to twelve hundred and twelve dollars.

The fifth Lot is to [pay] to the first lot two hundred & twelve & twelve dollars [**Finlay McMillan**, Lot 2 **MINGO** valued at Nine hundred and fifty dollars, and to be paid by fourth Lot two hundred and thirty eight dollars, and by Lot No. five one dollar, and also by lot No. [3] three, twenty-three dollars.

John McMillan, Lot No. 3 **DAVID**, valued at five hundred and fifty dollars being valued at five hundred and fifty Dollars. Also, Lot No. 3 pays to the widow, two hundred and fifteen dollars and to Lot No. 2, twenty three dollars.

Edward McMillan Lot No. four receives HANNAH, valued at seven hundred and seventy-five dollars and SOLOMON valued at six hundred and seventy-five dollars, while Lot No. 4 pays to Lot No. 2, two hundred and thirty-eight dollars.

[Fairly] McMillan Receives the fifty Lot consisting of SUSAN, a girl, valued at seven hundred and twenty-five dollars and [Tip], a boy, valued at seven hundred dollars. Lot No. 5 pays to Lot No. 1, two hundred and twelve dollars, and also pays to Lot No. 2 one-dollars, this December the 30th 1852. The under signed Commissioners: **AH KING, HINCKLEY GREEN AND DANIEL CALAWAY,**

For Barbour County, I, H. Pipkin, a Justice of the Peace in and for said county and state, I do hereby certify that the above commissioners were duly qualified by me, and that the above Estate was assigned before me given under my hand and Seal this December 30, 1852. (Signed) Haywood Pipkin (seal), a Justice of the Peace ordered that the Report of the Commissioners appointed by the court to divide the negro sale of the Estate of **Daniel McMillan**.

Name of persons and the value price:

Willis -- $550]
Jannet -- $400] ----------(Widow)
Sarah -- $350]

Jack -- $1,000   (Charles McMillan (Lot. No. 1))

David -- $550   (John (Lot No. 3))

Hannah -- $750]---------- (Edward McMillan (Lot No. 4))
Solomon -- $650]

Susan -- $725]
Tip -- $700]   (Fairlay (Lot No. 5))

Mingo -- $950   (Finley (Lot 2))

Historical Precedents of Trauma

ORIGINAL DEED OF DANIEL MCMILLAN

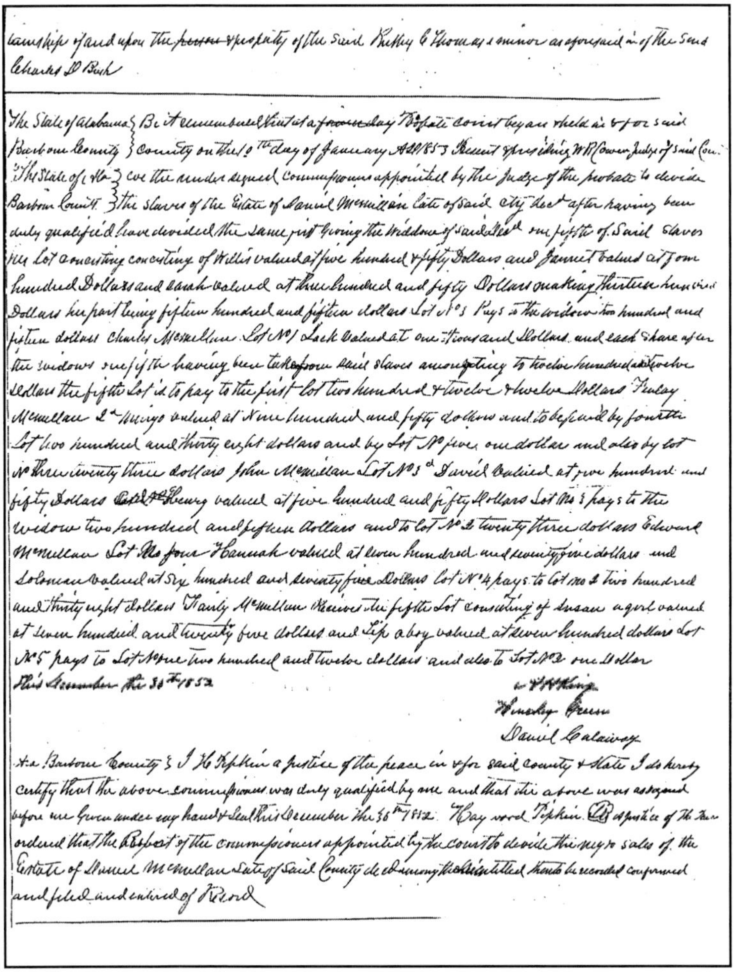

[Handwritten document, partially legible]

township of and upon the persons & property of the said Kitty C Thomas a minor as aforesaid in of the said Charles D Bush

The State of Alabama } Be it remembered that at a [former] day Probate court began & held in & for said Barbour County } County on the 10th day of January A.D. 1853 Present & presiding W R Cowen Judge of said Cou. The State of Ala } We the undersigned commissioners appointed by the Judge of the probate to divide Barbour County } the slaves of the Estate of Daniel McMillan late of said city dec'd after having been duly qualified have divided the same just giving the widow of said dec'd one fifth of said slaves her lot consisting consisting of Willis valued at five hundred & fifty dollars and Janniet valued at Tom hundred Dollars and Sarah valued at three hundred and fifty Dollars making thirteen hundred Dollars her part being fifteen hundred and fifteen dollars Lot No 1 Jack valued at one thousand dollars and each share of the widows one fifth having been taken from said slaves amounting to twelve hundred & twelve dollars the fifth Lot i'd to pay to the first lot two hundred & twelve & twelve Dollars Finley McMillan 2d Mingo valued at Nine hundred and fifty dollars and to be paid by fourth Lot two hundred and thirty eight dollars and by Lot No five one dollar and also by lot No three twenty three dollars John McMillan Lot No 3d David valued at five hundred and fifty Dollars Old & Henry valued at five hundred and fifty Dollars Lot No 3 pays to the widow two hundred and fifteen dollars and to lot No 2 twenty three dollars Edward McMillan Lot No four Hannah valued at eleven hundred and seventy five dollars and Solomon valued at Six hundred and seventy five Dollars Lot No 4 pays to lot No 3 two hundred and thirty eight dollars Hardy McMillan Receives the fifth Lot consisting of Susan a girl valued at seven hundred and twenty five dollars and Lip a boy valued at eleven hundred dollars Lot No 5 pays to Lot No one two hundred and twelve dollars and also to Lot No 2 one dollar this December the 30th 1852

W H Hings
Winsley Green
Daniel Calaway

the Barbour County } I H Tipkin a justice of the peace in & for said county & State I do hereby certify that the above commissioners was duly qualified by one and that the above was assigned before me Given under my hand & Seal this December the 30 1852. Hay wood Tipkin [ ] a justice of the [ ] ordered that the Report of the commissioners appointed by the court to divide the negro sales of the Estate of Daniel McMillan late of said County dec [ ] hereto be recorded confirmed and filed and entered of Record

There are so many things that have been perpetrated on those in the African American community that consists of trauma. We have to begin, of course, with the institute of slavery. This was not a system unique to the United States, however, the level of debauchery that was instituted by those in charge of this country reached levels not previously seen. The thought and treatment of humans of African descent as less than human, even while engaging with them in the most intimate ways was quite unique to the United States. Rationalizations and justifications for this behavior abound and still persist by some currently. Yet no one can argue the heinousness of the violent and barbaric actions.

As we delve into a discussion of some of the specifics of the trauma imposed on enslaved Africans, be aware that some may find this information traumatic. Consider some of the types of torture that were instituted on enslaved Africans which caused a level of trauma that sought to break the spirits of those that were enslaved. According to the historian John Blassingame[3], Africans were captured in their native home and put in chains while being made to trek hundreds of miles to the dungeon on the coast that would hold them until it was time to be loaded on the boat and taken to America. Having been to this dungeon, I can attest to the grotesque nature of this structure and the torture that would have been sustained by those enslaved there during this time. Even after all these years, the energy, smell, and trauma of the situation can be felt. Imagine being chained in the dungeon, unable to move, having to urine and defecate on yourself in extreme heat with no relief. From there, being placed on a ship, some making the decision to jump to their death rather than risk going to a foreign place bound for slavery. Consider further what it

---

3   John W. Blassingame, The Slave Commuity: Plantation Life in the Antebellum South (New York: Oxford University Press, 1979)

was like to be chained on a ship for upwards of 3 months packed tightly amongst others and having to lie in your feces, vomit, or sickness, again with no relief.

Upon arriving in America, the most obvious and popular form of trauma that most think of involves the whippings that took place with lashes that cut through the skin and could last for extended time periods[4]. Observing the pictures of the aftermath of these incidents does little to really capture the extent of the pain involved as often after the beatings were completed the entire back of the enslaved Africans would be covered in blood. Additionally, they might have an astringent applied to inflict even more pain. What does it feel like to be tied faced down so that you could not move and whipped for thirty minutes?

Arguably one of the most painful traumatic practices during this time revolved around the separation of families[5]. The slave auction was a place of inhumane treatment on a range of levels. Enslaved Africans had no agency over their bodies and could be poked, prodded, and analyzed in the most intimate manner with no recourse. Additionally, mothers and fathers being separated from the children they birthed, siblings being broken up, families decimated with no regard for the traumatic impact this had on their wellbeing. Immense depression and a sense of apathy would not be uncommon given these circumstances. The trauma faced from these circumstances was certainly unbearable. I have wondered what did it feel like to watch your child

---

4   Anthony Gene Carey, Sold Down the River: Slavery in the Lower Chattahoochee Valley of Alabama and Georgia (Tuscalusa, AL: University of Alabama Press, 2011)
      Robert H Gumestad, A troublesome Comerce: The Transformation of the Interstate Slave Trade (Baton Rouge, LA: Louisiana State University Press, 2003)

5   James Benson Sellers, Slavery in Alabama (Tuscaloosa, AL: University of Alabama Press, 1950)

taken from your arms and sold away to a person in a state hundreds of miles away, knowing you would never see them again? Simultaneously, I have wondered what was it like to be 6 years old and taken away from your parents never to see them again? The psychological turmoil resulting from these situations would have to be unbearable. And yet they survived somehow, a testament to a greater force within willing them forward despite the trauma.

The sexual exploitation of enslaved Africans also caused a tremendous psychological trauma, the effects of which would be practically impossible to heal from[6]. African American women and men were raped, mutilated, and forced to withstand all manners of egregious sexual behaviors inflicted upon them. At the whim of those in power, sexual activity was forced no matter how they felt in the moment. Questions again arise as to what did it feel like to have no control over your body, standing naked and being poked and prodded into every orifice in your body? What was it like as a woman to have no agency over your body and have to submit to whatever horrible act perpetrated upon you willingly with no resistance? This might seem unthinkable to many in today's society and yet it is woven into the DNA of those whose lineage traced back to these horrific acts.

Racial terror lynchings are another area of significant trauma that has impacted the African American community[7]. Used as a means for torture and keeping people in their place through terror, this process took the lives of many enslaved Africans in an unjustifiable manner. Following emancipation and continuing through World War II, terror lynchings were utilized to maintain power and control after slavery

---

6   Michael Tadman, Speculators and Slaves: Masters, Traders and Slaves in the Old South (Madison, WI: University of Wisconsin Press, 1989)

7   Lisa Cardyn, Sexualized Racism/Gendered Violence: Outraging the Body Politic in the Reconstruction South

Historical Precedents of Trauma

was abolished[8]. Situations were fabricated frequently to justify the terror lynchings and the smallest infraction could lead to an uproar. When reading of the accounts of these lynchings, it is unfathomable to think that lives were lost for the most mundane issues one could think of, and many lives were taken after being incorrectly identified as the supposed perpetrator of said crime. It is difficult for my mind to consider that thousands of people could watch a human burn to death or be hung from a tree twisting in the wind while those responsible take pictures smiling for postcards. Many of those in the African American community learned to make themselves small so as not to arouse any angst amongst the dominant population. But there were always those who were willing to fight against the injustices of this situation. In addition to the lynchings, techniques for abuse included whipping their genitals, genital mutilation and castration. I would suggest that the clear widespread trauma brought about by these events has produced a lasting impact on the African American community that continues in many regards today. It is not difficult to connect the palpable fear that I have when a police car is behind me to the historical legacy of trauma imposed by the actions of racial terror lynchings. Compounding the trauma I wonder about the thoughts and feelings of the people who had to cut down a person that had been recently lynched or burned? How was an understanding of these heinous acts communicated to the children of the community and what type of mental trauma did they suffer as a result of these traumatic episodes?

The Jim Crow era brought about a slight shift in the manner in which trauma was perpetrated on the African American community. Legal policies were enacted that would ensure and allow white communities to legally traumatize and take

---

8   Stewart E. Tolnay and E. M. Beck, A Festival of Violence: An analysis of Southern Lynchings, 1882-1930

advantage of those deemed below them[9]. The Supreme Court was instrumental in providing the policy backbone that gave credence for the traumatic behaviors enacted by those engaging in them to continue[10]. Whether refusing to protect African Americans from domestic terrorism or authorizing the separate but equal doctrine, the highest court in the land was certainly complicit in encouraging the trauma inflicted upon the African American community by the laws that it passed or did not pass.

As a result of the inaction and lack of support from the Supreme Court, African Americans had to deal with a range of traumas that led some to migrate north and west in search of better opportunities.[11] Many African American families had become sharecroppers after emancipation from slavery and found themselves in a perpetual cycle of work and debt. This unfair arrangement where the families would work land owned by whites in exchange for meager housing and small crops did not allow for the families to grow out of this arrangement. Coupled with the unscrupulous accounting of the landowners, these families would never be able to pay off their debt and remain locked in servitude. Those that protested or attempted to vote would be evicted, beaten, or worse.

Freedom riders attempted to bring equality and an end to racial segregation beginning in 1961 and they were terrorized in a number of ways[12]. Buses were bombed and white terrorists

---

9   Kari Frederickson, The Dixiecrat Revolt and the End of the Solid South, 1932-1968 (Chapel Hill: UNC Press, 2001)

10 Michael J. Klarman, From Jim Crow to Civil Rights: The Supreme Court and the Struggle for Racial Equality (New York: Oxford University Press, 2004)

11 The Wealth of Other Suns: The Epic Study of America's Great Migration (New York: Random House, 2010)

12 Noelle Matteson, The Freedom Rides and Alabama: A Guide to Key Events and Places, Context, and Impact (Montgomery: NewSouth Books, 2011)

attacked those that dared to stand up for their rights, causing a range of injuries and bloodshed. Much damage was done physically and to the property of African Americans in the community who supported these freedom riders and vowed to continue the process to equality. Mobs of whites rioted and vandalized in an attempt to intimidate and suppress the march to freedom.

The Civil Rights protests and advancements continued to be met with resistance and vitriol. In looking at the picture of a young girl and her friend being escorted by her mother to integrate and elementary school, the fear and questioning on her face for why this is happening is quite telling. What lasting impact did the hatred and vitriol that she received have on her overall development and sense of self? How did this impact the psyche and self-esteem of those who were on the front lines as children carrying the weight of an entire culture on their tiny shoulders? Has she been able to make peace with being thrown into such a hostile environment when she was just a young child, emotionally incapable of understanding and processing the wealth of feelings that this situation would have produced? In another picture, young Donna Jean Barksdale sits alone in her classroom in Hoxie Arkansas in 1955, one of 21 students to integrate the schools. The sadness of this young student jumps out of the picture and grabs me as I look at it. The psychological trauma of being the other, the outcast is intense, and I wonder about how she managed this time. How did this impact her interaction and relationships with others moving forward? Did it cause her to retreat within herself feeling unprotected and unsure? Did she become more vocal and willing to fight as she was forced to be strong? There is no right answer and however things turned out, it is clear that she was impacted tremendously by these experiences. Thinking of this underscores that there were many people who made extensive sacrifices to fight and create a better place, willing themselves to be part of the collateral damage that would ensure a better life for those that came after them. We should always be grateful for them and their sacrifice.

A thorough assessment of these historical traumas is beyond the scope of this book, and indeed is an area that many historical scholars have addressed on its own in much detail. However, it is important to touch on these areas as we work to make a connection between the history and the current manifestations of trauma. This is because as with a weed we have to attack the problem at its root and not just cut off the top or it will return and continue to be a problem. So we must understand the history of how we got here so that we can correctly diagnose what we need to do to move forward in a truly healthy manner.

CHAPTER 4

HOW HAS TRAUMA IMPACTED US AS A COMMUNITY

Keep my business out them streets!

How many people have heard this refrain in some capacity in their childhood? In our culture we have been taught to hide things when it comes to the often dysfunctional or inappropriate behaviors that exist within the walls of our homes. On the one hand, parents do not want the things that they are doing that they intuitively know they should not be doing to get out to others for fear of judgment and admonition about what is occurring. Parents might also be embarrassed to admit that they are engaging in behaviors that others might not find to be socially acceptable.

On the other hand, there is also a protective mechanism in this admonition as the information utilized by those outside of the culture has the potential to be dangerous and cause serious problems. Two African American psychiatrists, Grier and Cobbs in their seminal book Black Rage[13] described cultural paranoia as a healthy and normal response by Black people to the trauma that is inflicted upon them by the dominant culture. They propose that it is quite

---

13   Grier, W. H., & Cobbs, P. M. (1968). Black rage. New York: Basic Books.

natural for Black people to have a response that hides the true thoughts and feelings from the outside world because they do not know how this information might be utilized in a manner that yields negative outcomes. Additionally, they note that the rage that manifests as a result of being placed in situations that are unfair should only be expected as these feelings have to go somewhere. A person treated unfairly has to do something with their emotions, and rage is a natural outlet for these emotions.

In 1984, an African American psychologist Charles Ridley[14] used this concept of paranoia to describe the reluctance of African American clients to fully open up and disclose in sessions with a therapist of a different race. He argued that this paranoia was generated by a healthy mistrust, and further validated when people were not accepted and believed by someone from outside of the culture. In an effort to protect themselves, sensitive information was thus not revealed. This complicates the ability to fully and completely address the issues one presents with. Arthur Whaley[15], another African American psychologist built on this line of thinking and removed the stigma that can be associated with paranoia, shifting the dynamic to mistrust which is the root of the problem. Since that time measurements have been created to assess the level of mistrust present for African Americans in dealing with other cultures in these types of settings.

It is important to understand the history and the progression of how we have arrived at a certain place, why we think about things in a particular fashion or do things in a certain manner. The fear and distrust evident in the refrain "keep my business out the street" has an etiology that makes sense when

---

14   Ridley, C. R. (1984). Clinical treatment of the nondisclosing Black client: A therapeutic paradox. American Psychologist, 39, 1234-1244.

15   Whaley, A. L. (1998b). Cross-cultural perspective on paranoia: A focus on the Black American experience. Psychiatric Quarterly, 69, 325-343.

we consider the historical antecedents from where it evolved. It makes sense for there to be a level of distrust in mental health services given this traumatic history. However, we are currently in an era where quality, culturally responsive mental health services for African Americans is on the rise with African American psychologists who are a part of the community and culturally competent in understanding and addressing this trauma in a healthy and culturally relevant manner.

Additionally, we have evidence of the benefits of mental health treatment that we are shown through the risks that are being taken by prominent African Americans who are courageously making their own struggles with mental illness public[16]. By sharing their personal stories, and thereby increasing awareness and acceptance, the stigma that surrounds therapeutic intervention among the African American community is diminishing. Thus, a new generation is invited to manage age-old struggles related to chronic mental health diagnoses of various levels of severity and to manage the real life challenges associated with building healthy relationships and marriages, resolving conflict, overcoming addictions, managing stress, and navigating major life changes. We are now in a better position than in the past to take action and embrace and enjoy better mental health and should do so willingly.

Understanding the etiology of the stigma attached to mental health services in the Black community, allows us to appreciate the mindset this produces. "I'm not crazy," "I'm not going to tell my business," "I'm not laying on anybody's couch," are some of the sentiments expressed in this regard. There are historical and cultural reasons that explain the legitimate concerns that underlie these sentiments. However, as we have evolved, there are now people who not

---

16 Whitten, L. (2020). Stigma matters: An African American psychology professor comes out of the mental illness closet. Psychological Services.

only understand and appreciate the previous reluctance to engage in mental health treatment but who also know how to work with the African American community to produce positive healthy results in a safe and pleasant environment, while simultaneously addressing and mitigating the stigma that exists for people seeking mental health treatment. We have been able to witness a recent trend toward beginning to openly talk about the issues related to mental health in the African American community and normalizing seeing a mental health professional. Recently, Charlemagne the God, a popular morning talk show host who has written two books that discuss his mental health challenges, allowed his psychology session to be televised. This was done so that people can observe what actually happens in therapy and was a brave groundbreaking effort to undo some of the barriers that have been legitimately erected over time. Through his efforts, he is able to model the appropriateness of an African American man receiving help and assistance to see himself and work through the issues that are plaguing him. In another example, Metta World Peace, formerly known as Ron Artest, a former star in the National Basketball Association has also openly discussed his mental health challenges and his efforts to confront them. He was known for years to have issues with anger and for much of his time in the NBA led the league in technical fouls received due to an inability to manage his anger. He was often involved in fights and, most infamously, what has come to be known as the "Malice in the Palace" brawl between his then team, the Indiana Pacers, and the Detroit Pistons. The resulting punishments from the fight, in that case, ended up costing him over $5 million and the loss of an entire season and playing time. He has been public in speaking about the impact the trauma of his childhood has had on his life and the resultant anger, and in this regard can be a model for others in recognizing the need to engage therapy to help heal the emotional wounds of the past.

These are important conversations because, for too long, many of these issues have been glossed over, covered up, or avoided all together. There are historical precedents for this, of course. Our parents and grandparents used to warn us to "keep your business in the house" or "keep my business off the street." It is important to understand that this admonition was often a matter of life or death and rose primarily out of a desire to protect the family from any negative consequences from the majority community. In the book Medical Apartheid by Harriet Washington, she discusses many incidents of callous, painful, life-threatening research done in the name of science that used African Americans as the primary subject[17]. Most people are familiar with the US Public Health Service Syphilis Study at Tuskegee where innocent Black men diagnosed with syphilis were denied medication which could have easily eased their suffering and/or prolonged their life. Unknowingly and without their consent, they were being used as guinea pigs in the name of medical advancement. The fact that the United States government would sanction such behavior creates the mindset employed by the community to, in fact, "keep our business out of the street." We see this mindset even now in 2021 as we deal with the Covid-19 virus that has caused a worldwide pandemic. Many African Americans are reluctant to take the vaccine due to a historical mistrust related to situations like what happened at Tuskegee. Medical Apartheid comprehensively outlines many more instances where members of the African American community were taken advantage of that, in some cases, were even more egregious. When one understands the

---

17 Harriet Washington, (2006) Medical Apartheid: The Dark History of Medical Experimentation on Black Americans from colonial times to the present, New York, Doubleday.

manner in which the African American community has been repeatedly marginalized and taken advantage of in the name of science, it becomes understandable that there was a lot of value in putting forth the mantra of "keeping your business out the street" as there were many foreseeable risks involved with seeking treatment from a system that had proven itself to be untrustworthy at best, and flat out predatory in its worst and most insidious incarnation.

So we will now gain an understanding of how trauma is something that impacts us across several different dimensions. There is a historical component of trauma in the way the trauma gets passed down and there is also a current component of trauma in the things that we experience in real time and impact us at the moment. We will first consider some historical examples and the outgrowth of potential difficulties that arise as a result of a traumatic situation.

In the novel Glorious, the author Bernice McFadden does a wonderful job illustrating how one episode of trauma can impact a family for their entire lives, and we can speculate about how this trauma can be passed down for generations[18]. Although this is a novel, the story is one that has occurred in history hundreds if not thousands of times and is something that resonates for most African Americans. In the story which takes place in 1910, a young girl is abducted on her way home by three white teenagers who rape her. She struggles home and is met by her father and sister who notice that she has been abused and is bleeding. Her sister and father go down to the sheriff in an attempt to have justice served, and the sheriff treats the father with a sense of indifference and disdain that is quite belittling. He refuses to even make eye contact with the father and dismisses the claims of what happened to his daughter as untruth. Even when the father states that she had strands of the boy's hair still in her hands and bite marks on

---

18   Bernice McFadden, (2010) Glorious Brooklyn, NY: Akashic Books

her breast, the sheriff still refuses to make a report and bring about justice. The daughter gets upset about not only what happened, but watching her father be reduced to a small boy, unable to do anything to protect his family. The husband, unable to reconcile his inability to get justice for his daughter ends up having an affair with a much younger woman, an apparent attempt to drown out his sorrows. When the mother finds out about the affair, she ultimately ends up dying of heartache. The son when he finds out about his father's affair ends up attempting to fight his father, and as a result of this and his festering rage at the injustice related to the rape of his sister, he is sent away to the North for his own safety. The son was unable to repress his anger in a way that his behavior would be acceptable to the white people in the town. Finally, the daughter, feeling a sense of sadness and anger, does not accept the new young wife that her father brings into the home after the death of her mother, and engages in what her father considers rebellious behavior that ultimately forces her to leave as well.

In this short scenario, we are able to see the tentacles of trauma from one isolated incident reach out and have an impact that touches an entire family at that moment, and we can speculate for generations to come. As we look at this from a psychological perspective, the most obvious trauma is to the victim herself who does not speak anymore and is a broken shell of herself for the foreseeable future. Her bright light has been extinguished and the dreams that she may have had for her life have been shattered. She will likely have a hard time interacting in relationships, and even if she does, this trauma may keep her from fully embracing intimacy, instead showing an inability to trust the partner that she is with. If she has children, she is likely to be overprotective of them due to the attack she suffered through, and as a result, not allow them to explore the world in a way most children are able to. Her overprotectiveness may cause frustration for the children and create a pattern of behavior that is codependent. She may also continue to suffer anytime they are out of her sight with an intense level of anxiety, worrying about their return to safety. We can next consider the sister who accompanied her father and watched him attempt to be a man and stand up for his family but was unable to do this because of the systems that are in place. Not understanding the nuances of these structures and knowing that justice needs to be served, her anger and rage at her father and the system can ultimately cause her extreme problems. Her ability to respect her father and eventually men, in general, is likely impacted, and she could develop a mindset that men, in general, are not to be trusted nor depended on for anything serious. Additionally, she has observed her heartbroken mother give up her fight and will to live, and this has to have an impact on how she sees herself as a woman. She may decide that she will always fight for herself and never allow herself to be in a subservient position, or she might internalize and mimic the characteristics of the woman that her mother displayed. The father unable to adequately defend his family and having his manhood questioned implicitly has an inward feeling of disgust and hate for himself at his inability to stand up to the system that surrounds and oppresses him. He has no outlets to express this and would not know how to allow for this expression even if he did have an outlet and thus turns to another younger woman to help boost his self-esteem. It would not be far-fetched to think that he would engage in an extreme use of alcohol to numb his feelings and take away the memories of the pain of seeing his daughter brutally raped in that manner. Going a step further, we could also see him becoming abusive and taking out his inability to fight on those who surround him that he has "control" over, his family. Finally, the brother watching his revered father shrink right before his eyes loses respect for him and his seeming inability to fight for his family. This might cause him to be consumed in anger and this anger will likely manifest in all of the relationships that he engages in moving forward. Seemingly, small slights can turn into large issues that cause him to fight. He might have difficulty maintaining relationships and friendships. Unable to understand his pain and frustration and without a release for these negative emotions he could engage in some negative numbing behavior such as gambling, drugs, or alcohol to bring him a sense of comfort.

When we consider the possibilities of the way trauma impacts each of these four individuals separately, it really helps us to appreciate how one single incident can cause tremendous problems that last a lifetime. Thinking about how each of these people will interact with their children, grandchildren, and extended family, we can certainly realize that patterns of behavior that are being put into place by the manner in which each of them chooses to interact with others. These resulting patterns that get passed down are often not thought about in terms of where they evolved from. Certainly, most families do not have the capability to be introspective enough to understand why they do the things that they do and why the dynamics that exist in their family have come to be. It is not hard to consider the time that this took place and extrapolate that each person would likely have kept their feelings to themselves and not had an avenue or outlet for processing their feelings in a healthy manner. In looking at these situations thoroughly, we can better understand how certain things have been passed down which will then enable us to do the work to create new patterns of behavior and interaction.

What do you feel when you think about the pain connected to this family? Are there situations in your life that you can remember that bring up similar issues? Can you recall situations where you have been unfairly treated or have observed justice not being served? Are you able to consider and appreciate how your own situations have impacted you and your choices in life? These are things we must consider if we are going to move towards a place of healing that allows us to free ourselves from these patterns of trauma.

Let's consider another example from history, a true story this time that occurred in Omaha Nebraska during the infamous Red Summer of race riots that occurred across the United States in 1919[19]. Summarizing what occurred, a 19-year-old white woman, Agnes Loebeck, accused a 41-year-old black man, Willie Brown, of raping her. As alluded to in the past discussion on the history of trauma, this is an often engaged technique that has been used by whites repeatedly over the years in various shapes and fashions to essentially reign terror onto African Americans who dared to "rise above their station," or "get out of their place." Incidentally, this approach has evolved and currently exists in today's lexicon as "white women's tears" and is embodied by such incidents as what occurred in Central Park in May of 2020[20]. In this situation, if not for a videotaped recording of the incident, the blatant lies told by Amy Cooper could have resulted in the death of the African American man who had politely asked her to follow the rules of the park and leash her dog. She raised her voice at him and approached him in a confrontational manner, but when calling the police, portrayed herself as a victim, a tactic that could have resulted in the death of this man given the reality of police violence perpetrated on African American men in this country. His videotape ultimately exonerated him and allowed Amy Cooper to be

---

19 Cameron McWhirter 201 Red Summer: The Summer of 1919 and the Awakening of Black America, St. Martin's Press, New York.

20 Stewart, Nikita (May 30, 2020). "The White Dog Walker and #LivingWhileBlack in New York City." The New York Times.

held accountable and ultimately fired from her job. However, the innocent bystander should never have been placed in this position, to begin with, having to prove his innocence in a situation he did not cause.

However, back in 1919, this technique enabled a rationalization for whites to find "justice" for an actual or alleged offense by any means necessary. In this case, a mob of white men estimated between 5 and 15,000 descended upon the jail to enact "justice" upon Mr. Brown. An attempt was made by the sheriff to fight them off, but they ultimately set fire to the jail and were able to get custody of Mr. Brown. They proceeded to hang him on a light post and peppered his body with gunshots. Now it would seem to any reasonable person to be pretty clear that he died at some point during this process, pretty early on one would suspect. Yet the rage and anger that was displayed in continuing to mutilate his body was beyond any moral comprehension. After shooting his body up and burning it thoroughly they then decided to tie the body to the back of a car and drive it through the city. Of course, I am vastly unable to adequately express in words the amount of terror, fear, and pain inflicted on not only Mr. Brown but the entire African American community during this event. However, I would encourage you to attempt to visualize the scene playing out and imagine the feelings and other sensations of the people that lived through this event in 1919 to appreciate the utter atrociousness of this one event of many like it in American history.

The purpose of revisiting this incident is not to stay in this place of anger and trauma as it is in the past and we cannot do anything about changing what happened. However, the lingering intense psychological impact of this event is not always adequately considered, and in the rare case it is given a voice, is quickly minimized. What happened to the family of Mr. Brown and how did they process this incredible tragedy? How did they allow their minds to try to make sense of something that did not make sense? What impact did this have on the way they decided to comport themselves as they dealt with the white community moving forward? What did they teach their children and family about this event and what their response to it should be? What got passed down through the generations about this situation and how they should understand it and respond to situations in the future? It is not hard for me as a psychologist to draw conclusions about the manner in which people were scarred from this incident, likely for the remainder of their lives. Something as simple as the smell of smoke or seeing a fire burning out of control could elicit flashbacks and feelings associated with that traumatic day. They might have had horrible dreams that did not allow them to sleep peacefully. In attempting to make sense of something that cannot make sense they may have accepted the belief that this was their destined lot in life, and they will receive a reward for their suffering later in heaven. This could create a low self-esteem and a sense of unworthiness that becomes the family tradition as we can only teach what we know.

Another level of trauma that comes out of the previous two examples can be found in another reason that families during this time felt the need to keep their conversations and opinions about what happened very quiet and within the walls of the family. In talking with people who have lived through the trauma of a lynching in their community, they express that in their household they would have to whisper about their thoughts and feelings in fear that someone might be walking by the house and overhear the conversation[21]. This could then cause problems for them in the sense that if this information about their dissatisfaction at the trauma that occurred were to become known, they could be the next

---

21   Leon Litwack, Trouble in mind: Black Southerners in the age of Jim Crow 1998 Alfred A Knopf, New York.

targeted for being too "uppity." This perpetual fear was commonplace and as much a part of the fabric of life as breathing. It is not difficult to draw a connection to other historical trauma related to the fear that someone would report an enslaved African who was attempting to flee the confines of slavery. They not only had to worry about the overseers who were watching them, but they also had to be worried about any other enslaved Africans that would turn them in for their desire to be free. Trauma on multiple levels. This was the way that things were done throughout the need to stay focused on what was happening.

Ultimately, I am attempting to help bridge the connection between the historical trauma and the current trauma that we experienced. If we can appreciate from whence we have come and how we got here, we could do the work to overcome the issues we are currently faced with and move to a true place of healing. Additionally, using new keys available to us to unlock our emotional baggage presents us with pathways to overcoming and creating new realities steeped in healthy interactions.

CHAPTER 5

CONTINUED IMPLICATIONS OF TRAUMA

We frequently hear those from the dominant culture suggesting that we should get over it and not allow something that has seemingly been gone for years to currently impact us. They push aside the thought that the things that their ancestors did have any degree of impact currently. Of course, this is patently false and there exists a myriad number of ways to explain how this manifests.

This lack of compassion and understanding can be seen in the callous behavior on the part of some individuals who thought it would be a smart and witty thing to create a George Floyd challenge, where they mocked his death by recreating this gruesome and traumatic scene with friends. Someone actually decided this would be a good idea and followed through with creating viral infamy. If we understand the manner in which things are passed down generationally, this should not be surprising. It is my belief that the people and mindset who would engage in this current behavior, are the likely descendants of those who would smile and pose for pictures after the horrendous lynching of a man. The socialization that allowed them to overcome the dissonance they may have felt with watching the death of a human being and lacking any empathy has been taught and passed down for generations.

Every time we watch yet another video of an African American person getting killed or being mistreated, a message is sent to our subconscious that reinforces lessons learned about where we belong in society and how we are valued. The anger and rage that is felt can never be acted upon fully though as the consequences for this enactment ultimately prove to be too much. So instead, even when expressed, the energies only go so far, and for most people, there is a repression that eludes awareness.

What are some outcomes of trauma that are problematic?

1. Anxiousness—Anxiety results from trauma when the thought of a catastrophic event occurring produces feelings of worry. The tension that results from worrying can manifest in a number of ways. Excessive crying and fear about the event happening can be present. In addition, the individual may have difficulty focusing and concentrating, spending an excessive amount of time ruminating about an occurrence of trauma. Many African Americans report having a fear that results from a police officer coming behind them in traffic. Even though no crime has been committed, the presence of this officer coupled with the knowledge of negative interactions with people in the community in the past combines to drive a sense of anxiety.

2. Repressed anger—The accumulated feelings of anger that manifest in individuals who have watched injustice for extended periods of time can cause significant problems if not addressed appropriately. Like a balloon that can only take so much air most

of us can only allow our feelings to percolate and manifest for so long until something has to give. If we do not have positive means of releasing this anger, it can fester inside and cause high blood pressure, an aneurysm, or a stroke. Additionally, this pent-up anger can result in a sudden need to release that anger for a seemingly insignificant thing. This becomes the proverbial "straw that broke the camel's back" where the camel can carry 200 pounds but at 200.0001 pounds the camel falls down. A little straw has seemingly broken the camel. A person dealing with the accumulated anger of years of watching injustice that equals 200 pounds over a lifetime can suddenly have a coworker make a comment that on any other day would have been overlooked but as it comes in the space similar to the straw, it causes that person to snap and lash out in a way that ultimately results in their job loss, arrest or worse.

3. Difficulty asking for help—In this area, individuals who have been impacted feel that they are not able to adequately request help from those who might be able to provide it. They may be dealing with the residual shock of the traumatic event and unable to adequately feel worthy of asking for and receiving help. The shock further causes a sense of hopelessness as the person may rationalize that they deserved whatever happened to them. They may also feel a **sense of shame for being in the position, even though** they are there through no fault of their own. The inability to ask for help is also problematic in that we may not want to be told no or we do not want to owe someone for what they have given us. An implicit pull to respond in kind often occurs when someone does something for us. We feel the need to

reciprocate, and the guilt of owing someone limits how we might engage.

4. Fear of being judged—When the person asks for help they may feel that they are putting themselves in a vulnerable position that allows others to observe the difficulties that they are facing. Many people do not like to have others see them at their most vulnerable as they are subjected to the judgment of other people. This judgment is a really fickle thing that has a way of creeping into our thoughts at any time. As humans, we often make these snap judgments during the course of the day without taking into account details and circumstances that would change our outlook of the situation. It is therefore important for us to get to a place where we are not overly concerned with what people think of us as these thoughts are not anything that we can control. The fear of being judged enacts a protective mechanism that keeps us from allowing any vulnerability to arise. As a way to appreciate the capriciousness of judgment, consider an example of sitting in a restaurant enjoying a meal with your family. You are excited to see each other because you have not had time to interact recently and are just looking forward to a good time together. After you place your order and the food is brought out, you notice that the waiter has made several big mistakes and people have the wrong items, some of which even prepared incorrectly. This inconvenience frustrates you and in addition, the waiter appears to be nonchalant in his response to correcting this situation. You request to see a manager now having gotten angry at being inconvenienced. When the manager comes over and you explain the situation he apologizes profusely and informs you that the waiter just found out earlier that

morning that his mother has terminal cancer and has been given two weeks to live. He further states that his mother lives 2000 miles away and the waiter is worried about how he will be able to make this trip to see his mother before she passes. What do you think happens to your feelings at this moment? For most people, a wave of compassion would likely overcome them, and the anger that was profound moments before is suddenly reduced and replaced with a sense of concern instead. We would have made a judgment about the carelessness of this waiter in completing the order and ascribe all types of attributes to him that are not necessarily true. At that moment we were not concerned about what is going on with the waiter we were only concerned with getting our meal appropriately. Of course, we should be concerned with getting our meal correct but the point is to illustrate how easy it is for us to cast judgment on a relatively benign situation even though we may not want to be or consider ourselves to be judgmental. Returning to the issue of avoiding judgment, it becomes easy to see why most people would not want to put themselves in a potentially compromising position where they are on the receiving end of this judgment. Most people do not like to be thought of in a harsh or unflattering manner. We only want to present the positive aspects of ourselves to the world, and this pull can be so strong that it keeps us from asking for the help that we need.

These are just some of the possible things that might be implications of trauma that we should be aware of and think about how it is impacting ourselves and others. Ideally, this allows for further thought about how trauma impacts us and considers positive things we can do to move forward.

CHAPTER 6

HOW DID WE GET THIS WAY

From the time we are born, we are receiving information and cues that dictate to us how and what we should be. A 6-month-old infant is able to understand when it is time to eat and what she should do to get the attention of the parents to feed her. At 9 months she is able to understand that a cry elicits one response from her mother and a different response from her father and is able to utilize this cry appropriately to get what she wants from the mother but because the father will not respond does not engage this around him. My father likes to tell a story about how I would engage this process as a child approaching the age of 1. According to my father, when I wanted something from my mother that she was not wanting to give me, such as a cookie, I would hold my breath in a fit which would rattle her and she would eventually give in and let me have what I wanted not wanting me to hurt myself. Interestingly enough, I only engaged in this behavior when my father was not at home. One day he was home and I did not know it and I started up with this behavior. He came out of his room and grabbed me with his hands over my mouth and nose not allowing me to breathe.

Sounds horrible, but he did this long enough for a message to be communicated to me that this was not acceptable and I should not engage in this behavior anymore because there would be a consequence. Needless to say, I stopped doing this behavior, but the point of the example is that I knew to act this way with my mother but never did this behavior around my father because something had been communicated to my brain that I could not get away with this behavior with him. I did not even know how to talk at that point so could not sit down and explain why I would make these choices. Yet I clearly engaged in this behavior so I intuitively understood something that had been communicated at that point in my young life.

So we all have a cumulative set of experiences that color who we are and have become, how we think about things, what we do and enjoy. Some of who we are entails our personality and this part is likely fixed. If I am an introvert by nature it is unlikely that I am going to be able to do enough retraining to make myself the life of the party. Not impossible but unlikely. The other part of ourselves is based on our socialization, how we have been taught and molded to be a certain way. If you think about things that you do that are like your parents, this point becomes clear. Our cadence in our speech, our mannerisms, our perspectives on life, our value system, the manner in which we treat people are all the result of these early interactions, and how our brain encodes this information to create who we are. Essentially, to use a computer analogy, our hard drive was delivered with an operating system or personality and then programmed with various applications and themes that make it run.

Trauma produces a corrupt file that needs to be replaced or healed. The abject nature of trauma is unnatural to the human mind and although there have been things that we have done to allow ourselves to cope, it is still not an occurrence that is natural and consistent with being our best selves. Understanding this allows us to embark upon the process of reprogramming the corrupt file and replacing it with files that will allow for optimal operation. This reprogramming for us involves remapping our brain with information that allows us to tap into our internal genius and be our true authentic selves without fear. My shortcut for all of this is the concept of aligning our actions and our values, a concept I referred to previously and to which I will discuss in more detail in the healing section of the book.

Taking into account all of the experiences that have made the life of an individual, we can see that we have been influenced and shaped depending on the nature of these experiences. **We all have seminal events that have occurred that** we remember vividly as they impacted us in such a profound manner. The same event occurring in a family might only be remembered by one individual and for the others was just another day in a multitude of days where nothing important stood out.

As an example, I can remember two events, one collective and one individual, that introduced me to trauma and racism as a young elementary school student. At that point, I do not believe I had the awareness or sophistication to fully understand the vestiges of racism. My parents made a conscious decision to keep me sheltered from this and so although I knew there were differences, it did not weigh heavily on me. However, in December 1979, Arthur McDuffie, an African American man who was a Marine and insurance salesman was murdered by six Miami police officers after a high speed chase[22]. The officers beat him so badly that according to the medical examiner "his skull was cracked like an egg using long, heavy blunt objects." The officers fabricated evidence

---

22 Lardner, G (1980 May 21) McDuffie Death: It seemed to be open-shut case. Washington Post.

surrounding the incident and what had occurred, including initially having the position that Arthur McDuffie had fallen off of his motorcycle, but their lies ultimately did not hold up in the face of the evidence. Despite the overwhelming evidence, an all-white jury acquitted all of the officers after less than 3 hours of deliberation on May 17th, setting off three days of insurrection that resulted in 18 deaths, hundreds of injuries, and over 100 million dollars of damage. During this time, I remember the adults in my life having a subdued degree of anger about the events as the "Christian way" was to be in a space of forgiveness. However, the events playing out on the news and as we drove through the streets of the city presented a different reality. I remember my father having to flash his lights in solidarity in order to avoid any attacks on us. We could see the outcome of the anger that was resonating throughout the community at the injustice that had occurred. This incident likely heightened my own sense of racism and its deleterious impact on me as I moved toward my individual episode with racism. The trauma of this incident impacted the entire African American community and many were filled with anger and rage as a result.

    I was moved to a predominantly white elementary school for the 6th grade, ostensibly to give me the opportunity for a better education. I do not recollect if this would have been the case, but I do know that I did not feel comfortable in that environment. One particular teacher made some comments one day that did not feel right to me and some of my African American classmates. We knew that what he had said was racist but did not have the words or wisdom to combat it. Instead I just made the statement that it was racist and he asked me to explain how. I could not and was made to feel embarrassed. Reflecting on this as an adult, he would have realized that I did not have the capacity to challenge what he was saying and even doing to us, sometimes in subtle ways, but I intuitively knew and knew that he knew as well. The trauma of isolation and being singled out definitely impacted my self-confidence and belief in myself, something that I would have to work to overcome.

I encourage you to reflect on your own life experiences and the impact they have had on how you understand your life. We are all the accumulation of our experiences, good and bad, and the understanding of the impact of these experiences can go a long way to helping us attain and maintain a space of healing.

CHAPTER 7

CRAFTING A PATH TOWARDS HEALING

Serendipity has been present in my life in many ways that are quite amazing to consider. When I had the encounter with my cousins who expressed their own history of trauma, they inadvertently gave a boost to this present work. As we wrapped up our conversations and they remarked how helpful it was to discuss, release and gain a healthy perspective about their lives, they suggested that the entire family needed to benefit from the things that I had shared with them. As they were in charge of planning our next family reunion six months from that point, they insisted that I do a workshop for the family at that time, to which I agreed.

As I left the next day to begin my drive back to my home in Durham North Carolina I was considering what I would listen to during the drive to keep me company. I spend a lot of time listening to audiobooks, podcasts, news, or music, so I always have options. I often will download things that I want to get to someday so always have a lot of options that interest me. As I considered the list of books that I had downloaded into my account I decided to listen to a book that I had downloaded many months before. I had been reading a lot of the work of Bernice McFadden and decided to listen to her book that I mentioned previously, Glorious. The first ten minutes of the book, the summation of which I referred to earlier, provided the foundation for framing the conversation about trauma in a way that was nothing short of genius. The symbolic representation of the impact one event can have in shaping the lives of the parties involved would prove to be a strong grounding force in helping people to appreciate and understand the impact of trauma and the long-term ramifications of trauma. Her ability to help the reader feel and see the emotions of the situation as if they were there allowed people to reflect on their own lives and the way historical trauma might manifest for them. I knew right away the direction that my presentation would take, and it would be easy to build around this foundation. A few months later I was able to present this information to my family at the reunion as they had requested and indeed it had a profound impact. The excerpt generated a lot of lively discussion and emotional reactions, something I have since experienced on a number of occasions when I present on this matter. It was as if a veil had been lifted that allowed people to go beyond and understand the impact that various traumatic events had on their own lives.

I had not expected the impact that I received from the presentation, and this caused me to consider expanding the work and presenting it at my national conference for the Association of Black Psychologists. Again as with my family, this information was well received and helped expand the conversation of multigenerational trauma and the impact this has on those we work with as clinicians. Other mental health professionals were able to recognize the benefit of utilizing historical stories to draw a connection to current trauma and the work took off. I was also able to receive feedback that provided other concepts that I was able to consider and incorporate into this work.

Which brings me to the current space of writing this book to help people on a larger scale to understand and appreciate how trauma impacts their life. Because it has been my experience that people seem to resonate with stories which impact and inspires change, I have endeavored to share stories of my own personal experiences with trauma and my ability to navigate and overcome this trauma. We can learn a lot from the lives of others, and I have found that a degree of self-disclosure has been beneficial to those that I work with. It makes the process real and allows people to appreciate the humanness of us all. I have experienced a significant degree of trauma over the course of my life, some of which remains present in my mind in a consistent way. Other episodes I have managed to move from the forefront of my mind and had not thought about until I was contemplating writing this book. I want to use my experiences with trauma to provide a template for understanding your own personal traumas and thinking about how they impact your life. It has been my observation that when working with people, sharing with them practical examples of real life situations can help them to process how their own personal situations impact their lives. In the times that I have shared aspects of my life and the ability to utilize various techniques to bring about healing, I have received feedback affirming the usefulness of this self-disclosure. It is in this manner that I will share these personal examples with the purpose of providing a light and potential template for healing.

As should be evident, these examples are from my perspective and recollection, and life as I recall it. I can only speak from my perspective, and when I do discuss these issues, I always work to present them in a balanced manner. However, it is indeed the case that the one telling the story will be telling the story from their point of view. From the aspect of healing, the details are not as important as understanding the dynamics of trauma and human relationships that many of us go through. The story is told mainly so that one could consider in a larger context real life implications of trauma on an individual. As with the prior mentioned shorter examples, we are able to draw connections that we otherwise might not have been able to do. Our society is at a place where ego and the need to present a beautiful, well-manicured picture dominate socially. The proliferation of social media has only added to this phenomenon as everyone is working to present the perfect persona. The paradox in this is that many of the very people who work so hard to put forth a sterling image are often quite unhappy with their lives. I know that there are many who hold onto things that they dare not tell another for fear of judgment. They keep these events, self-doubts, and other incriminating issues close to their heart, not wanting anyone to glimpse these broken places. As a result of these perspectives, we often do not have the courage to admit our internal issues to ourselves let alone to everyone else, and this is the area that I would like to place the emphasis on as we move forward. For if we can recognize that everyone has a past, a history, a veritable lifetime movie story and this is actually a fundamental aspect of life, we can then let go of this need to present this "perfect" image to the world. The paradox in this is that we are all perfect as we are, even as we are striving to improve and be perfect. We all have things to learn, evolve, and grow from in life, and this I believe is a fundamental purpose of our lives. I have come to believe that we all have issues to work through as we walk our path in life. What seems to be a struggle for you may be an easy proposition for another and vice versa. This is likely where the saying "the grass is always greener on the other side" originates.

So I share these experiences in a space of vulnerability overcoming the ego and need to present a polished perfect picture. The blemishes are real as is the pain that was suffered.

These examples are offered simply so that you might think about your own life experiences and how your own experiences may have impacted you in ways you have not previously considered. My personal healing continues to be an ongoing process but one that I can say has me at a place of peace. It is my desire to help everyone find their place of peace, no longer tormented by unspoken ghosts of the past. Those willing to do the work can find this peace and it is my hope that these words can assist in some small way with that process. Ultimately, I have had to do and continue to engage the healing work necessary to get me through these experiences and to a place of healthy living. It is true that we all have to engage in this process of healing to be our optimal selves. It is clear to me that there are some simple things that we can do to embark upon the path to healing ourselves once we are made aware of them.

PART II

**Behind the Veil:
A Personal Example of the Impact of Trauma**

CHAPTER 8

__ WHY VULNERABILITY IS IMPORTANT TO THE HEALING PROCESS __

I have observed trauma on many levels during my life. Personally, I have had to navigate a minefield of various traumatic situations. On a larger level, I have watched my community suffer through traumatic events inflicted on it by the dominant community. I have studied the historical traumas perpetrated by the larger society. As a psychologist, my interest in healing converged with an understanding of observing this trauma. It is quite clear to me: we cannot be fully healed unless we deal with the source of our trauma. We all have a story. We repeat this story over and over to ourselves and if not aware, become the story. We really do not think about how much we tell our story repeatedly and the impact this has. In reviewing my notes and recordings for writing this book, I was struck by things that I had recorded myself saying or that I had written earlier in my life were almost verbatim to what I had come up with in writing this book. It became clear to me the importance of appreciating the nature and relevance of the events that occur in our lives and their subsequent impact in shaping our lives but not becoming enslaved to the narrative. Our experiences are not us, they do not define who we are. None of us are the cumulative effects of our mistakes or missteps. These experiences and traumas are things that happened to us and we can free ourselves from their grip on us. As we understand this we can move to a place of forgiveness for ourselves and then for others. This allows us to accept our stories without any sense of attachment.

For as long as I can remember, I have felt a deep connection to nature and the spiritual essence of life. Intuitive messages from Spirit have guided my life, and have assisted me on my journey as a psychologist, helping me to tap into the various issues that confront those that I work with. The work that I do comes naturally to me, and I do and have done it consistently in one form or another on a daily basis. Since middle school, I have been a person that friends can talk to for advice and guidance about a variety of things. Over time this gift has been augmented by developing the skill of listening. Listening to the things said and unsaid, searching for the underlying meanings in the things left unsaid that point to the untapped solutions for the problems being faced. Ultimately, this process is further enhanced by the aspect of critical thinking, the willingness to ask yet another question, refusing to settle, or accepting the status quo.

Where did this intuitive wisdom evolve from I have come to ponder as I have considered the evolution of my work. I remember listening to the wisdom of the adults in my life at a very young age when my peers would discard this information as the folly of disconnected adulthood, the adults being over the hill or out of touch with reality. This developmental stage of life is one we all move through and in and of itself is not a bad thing. We cannot know what we do not know until we know it. So I listened to adults say to me countless times, "Enjoy your time in school and don't rush to be an adult because you have the rest of your life to work." It occurred to me that these adults, who had no connection to each other, could not all be wrong. So while my friends rushed to the traditional milestones of 16 and driving, 21 and drinking, obtaining the seeming independence brought on by a job, car, or house, I took my time and soaked up my years in high school, college, and graduate school. In fact, I believe that I may have had more fun in graduate school than most people would believe, all while managing to finish my program without any significant setbacks or blockages that many of my peers had to deal with. There has to be joy amidst the trauma after all for balance.

Upon receiving my Ph.D. I felt that I was prepared to go forth and help heal the world. Ah, the folly of youth. Little did I know that I was entering into a more important doctorate program, more difficult than I would ever imagine, that being the doctorate of life. My advisor foreshadowed this many times, although I could not appreciate it then. "Smith, it's a damn shame that you will have a Ph.D. at 26 and you don't have any life experience" my advisor would often say as we would laugh and joke about it. I would come to realize that life was also there laughing and looking at what loomed ahead for me.

It is important for me to say that where I have evolved to currently is that I have an absolutely incredible life and I love the place that I am in currently in my life. There is nothing in my life that I would change, and I have come to a place of being secure in who I am and knowing that each of my experiences have been building blocks in my process of becoming. But trust me, there was a whole lot of pain, suffering, frustration, apathy, and plain old just not wanting to be here anymore previously. There were days where I questioned my existence in this life and I really did not want to go on. I could not face another negative thing and did not want to deal with what life was bringing me. I thought that no one would even miss my presence anyway, so what did it matter.

Eventually, I was able to put these negative feelings aside and persevere to a place of peace and happiness. But there was a process of important work involved, the steps of which we will delve into later.

We will divide this discussion of trauma into three different categories: personal trauma which are those specific situations that happened to me directly and individually, collective trauma which are traumas that happened to me as a part of a group of other people but which I was still personally impacted by, and societal trauma which are those larger incidents that impact society as a whole and me individually. In the latter two categories, it is important to remember that what affects one person may not affect another person in a similar way, so we will all have to determine for ourselves how we have been impacted by things on a collective or societal level.

CHAPTER 9

INDIVIDUAL TRAUMA

The Childhood Years

As with most African American families, discipline played a large part in my life growing up. My parents being young parents and me being the first-born they had to figure out what this thing called parenting was. Unfortunately, we do not have a manual that is passed out at the hospital for people to review and understand what they need to do to raise a child. Most of us the world over primarily do what our parents did with some exceptions where we do the exact opposite. I believe that my parents were always intent on helping their children develop to be the best possible people they could be. Their parents had raised them in a similar way with similar values and expectations. And their parents had done the same for them and so on and so on. As it relates to me, my parents had an expectation that they would prepare us to evolve in life in ways that they had not been able to attain. I would say that they were quite successful in achieving this goal. So much so that they have served as de facto parents for dozens of other children over the course of my life and still continue to serve in this role with grandchildren and great grandchildren. My mother understands how to prepare a child for school even though she never had any formal training to do this. By the time my siblings and I made it to the 1st grade we were several grades ahead of our peers and as a result, placed in gifted programs. As an aside, I remember I initially thought that I would be getting a gift when they told me that I would be in this program and it was quite upsetting for me to find that there would be no gift coming. I actually found being in those programs to be an inconvenience as it separated me from my peers and made me stand out as a better or smarter. This was not the ideal place to be for a young African American kid just trying to fit in and survive. I did not have a strong sense of self as a child and did not like being teased at all. I tried to make myself fit in with everyone around me and not stand out, especially as it related to intelligence. As a result, I learned to minimize my intelligence so that I could better fit in with my classmates. I did not give a good effort on many of my assignments in the gifted program and ultimately halfheartedly made it through the program all the way through 9th grade. In retrospect had I understood and appreciated what that opportunity could prepare me for, and had the requisite reinforcement of self-confidence, this opportunity could have allowed me to evolve at a different pace and potentially could have brought other opportunities that I may have missed out on. Things still turned out well as it is, but knowing what I know now I recognize missed opportunities that I can now assist others with.

My parents got the hang of parenting and became quite good at it. Discipline was a key element, and they ran a tight household with no room for any departure from the expectations. If we did venture away from what was expected, we could be sure to find ourselves facing punishment that would not be fun. Two such situations stand out as particularly impressionable moments in my life. There are not many other moments that I really remember as it relates to discipline but these occasions remain etched in my memory and have ultimately impacted decisions and choices that I have made as it relates to discipline.

With the first incident it was a Sunday afternoon, and we were on our break from church. Growing up in a Pentecostal church meant that this was an all-day occurrence on Sundays. Because my father was the Sunday school superintendent it meant that the day was that much longer. We would be up by 7 so that he could go take the church bus to pick up children who were coming for Sunday school that day. After he finished his route we would arrive at the church and prepare for the beginning of Sunday school. Sunday school would last for an hour and then we would have a 30-minute break before the start of church. Church could go on for three hours if we were lucky, otherwise longer. I always wished that we would be lucky. After church he would drop people off and then we would head home for dinner. After dinner was over, we would return to church for Sunday evening service preceded by a youth for Christ meeting. Like I said, it was an all-day excursion. At any rate on this particular Sunday after finishing dinner and getting ready to head back to church I was in the kitchen getting my allotted cup of juice after having finished my meal. I had poured my juice and was drinking it down and had my hand on the bottle getting ready to put it back in the refrigerator after I finished my drink. I remember it was an orange, half gallon juice bottle, the kind that we would get from Farm Stores. The sugar intake must have been off the chart. I digress. As I was finishing the last few drops my dad came into the kitchen and observing what he thought was me trying to get more juice, wrapped me upside my head with his knuckles proclaiming that I should not be getting more juice. I tried to explain to him that I was not getting more juice and he told me to shut up because I was lying. Of course, I had to shut up because if there is anything we know back then with Black parents it is that you do not speak back to your parents, at least if you expect to live. But I remember the feeling of unfairness that I was not able to explain the truth of the matter, and his assumption about what occurred stood as valid. In this case, it was not the pain of the situation that proved to be traumatic for me, it was the inability to express myself, to prove my innocence. I believe this is why such a simple event has remained etched in my memory when no one else in my family can remember it. I believe we all have these seminal incidents that have occurred for us that we remember but no one else can. Things that stand out for us as important or that made such an impression on our lives that it impacts what and how we do and how we live our lives. This theme of me being punished for something that I did not do would come to surface many more times in my life, and eventually, I would have to examine the significance of this.

Looking at the generational progression of this type of incident, a similar thing happened with my son when he was approximately 6 years old. We were at a family reunion in Alabama and at the banquet, I had him and his younger sister, and we were in line at the buffet table to make our plates for dinner. The line was long, and I asked them to stand quietly while I made their plates. They were playing around and ended up bumping into the person in front of us and I yelled at my son saying, "didn't I tell you to be still!" He tried to inform me that it was not him but his sister that was the problem and I told him to be quiet and be still as I was frustrated and focused on getting the plates made as quickly as possible so we could sit down and eat. This caused him to be sad about being accused of something that he had not done similar to what had happened to me. As we went to sit down, I thought about my previous incident and it dawned on me that he was probably right, and I was doing the same thing that was done to me. At that moment I decided to correct it and told him the story I relayed earlier about something similar happening to me as a child. I let him know that parents are not always correct, and we make mistakes sometimes. I further shared that I was sorry for engaging with him in that manner and accusing him of something that he did not do. I was happy to engage in behavior that would be important in changing a generational pattern that had existed in our family and did not allow my ego as a parent to get in the way of this.

The second significant incident regarding punishment occurred on a Saturday afternoon. As stated previously, my parents like most in my community had no problems with engaging in physical punishment, and in fact, they had been raised in the era of picking their own switches. My grandmother had me do this a few times earlier in my life. On this particular day, my mother was upset that I had gotten into a fight with my brother and proceeded to administer the whipping of the year. My mother had pretty good arm strength, I imagine she might have thrown a mean fastball in the majors. And her accuracy was unprecedented. As she began beating me something in my brain came up with the crazy idea that I should run. This was ridiculous for a number of reasons: one our house was only so big so there was only so far for me to go, and two eventually, I was going to get caught and suffer even worse consequences than if I just took the pain to begin with, as my running would make her even madder than she already was. Logic was not working for me at this time and as I made my break around the table the belt came flying towards my eye and made direct contact. I hit the ground and she continued beating me as I lay there. After the beating was over she recognized the swelling from my eye and put aloe on it and she talked to me about how I should not have ran. As I write this I found this logic amusing in that who would not run from pain. It makes me think of a book written by my dissertation advisor, Dr. Robert Guthrie, "Even the Rat Was White," where he discussed the ridiculousness of this diagnosis that was given to enslaved Africans who dared to run away from slavery[23]. Drapetomania was the name of the mental diagnosis developed by Dr. Samuel Cartwright, and yet another example of the racism inherent in those making decisions from a position of power that elevates themselves while lowering those that are subjugated. Although not coming from this same mindset, the thought of not avoiding pain made me think just how ludicrous are some of the things we engage in as parents that have been passed down to us, that can ultimately prove traumatic. We tell our children not to cry or we going to give them something to cry about, but the children are in pain because we have already given them something to cry about. We are teaching a stifling of emotions that if we really consider it are merely the seeds planted to what turns out to be stunted emotional availability in adulthood. Coupled with what we teach young boys about being a man and never let anybody see you cry and shaking it off when it hurts, we can see a veritable recipe for an eventual inability to tap into emotions. A popular example I have dealt with is a couple having difficulty with communication because the husband refuses to be vulnerable and express his true emotions, while the wife is wanting to have this level of intimacy that true honesty would bring. We will need to continue bringing light to the traumatic impact of these behaviors so that we might change and engage in healthier choices. I want to reiterate that my parents were no different than most of their peers and the predominant thinking in the culture at that time. They could not do anything different because they did not know anything different, and in fact, they did not do some of the more painful punishments that

---

23 Guthrie, Robert V. Even The Rat Was White : a Historical View of Psychology. Boston, MA :Pearson/Allyn and Bacon, 2004

Individual Trauma

their parents did, so progress was being made. We still have more progress to go and recognition and acknowledgment of the areas of weakness are essential keys to healing.

As I progressed into high school, I would encounter my next significant episode of personal trauma, which involved having my face burned and suffering excruciating pain as a result. I was driving my first car, a Ford Fairmont for which I worked multiple jobs and saved money to purchase for $800. Years later my dad informed me that he put some additional money with it, but at the time I believed that I had utilized my hard-earned money for this purchase, and I was very proud of this car. It was an older car but serviceable as many of my high school friends could attest to as we put many miles on it riding all over Miami. Over time the car developed a slight leak in the radiator, and because of this, I would have to routinely stop to add water to keep the radiator from malfunctioning. This particular morning on the way to school I stopped to pick up my best friend at his home. While waiting for him to come out I lifted my hood to open my radiator and add water as I had done many times before, assuming that the light being on indicated that it was time for this. Yet when I opened the cap, I was met with a force unlike anything I even remotely thought was possible. There was a rush of tremendously hot water right into my face, and I hit the ground feeling the most piercing pain I have ever felt in my life. The ambulance came and they had to tend to my face in the bathroom. I remember thinking that I would hyperventilate and die in the bathtub. I did not want to go out like this. Ultimately, I was taken to the emergency room and given treatment. I was released that day and begin the process of healing. My pictures for my senior year were taken with my face having splotches from the burns. You can imagine that at a time when a teenager is highly impacted by image and fitting in with the crowd that having to manage what I, at the time, considered a deformed face would be an intense challenge. Feeling self-conscious and pitied by those who observed me, I attempted to shrink myself until I could heal. This seems to be a theme in my life, shrinking myself. Some of my senior pictures were taken when I still bore the scars of the incident on my face. There were many events I was unable to participate in.

Eventually, the scabs from my face crusted and began to fall away as the healing process advanced. Part of the healing required that my face regain its color, which took some months to fully happen. I remember being depressed during this time as it took some of the shine out of my senior year. Ultimately, I made a full recovery which was quite remarkable given that I suffered such remarkable burns, but I do not remember being so grateful at the time, instead being self-absorbed about the negatives of the situation. I have been able to use this event to describe the emotional healing process that we go through after being faced with some emotional pain, grief, or loss. Similar to the process of the sores feeling raw initially and being tender to the touch before eventually developing a scab, our emotional wounds have a similar healing process. Next, the scabs will fall away and the color will return. If we pick at the scabs too soon in the healing process, we will see bleeding return and the healing process is delayed. Emotionally, we can imagine a similar thing is happening with our heart as we attempt to recover from emotional pain. As we move into the third part of the book and our discussion on healing there will be more to say about this process. My recovery from this situation enabled me to move quickly into the next chapter of my life, which brought me to an era of dealing with collective trauma that I was not at all prepared for.

CHAPTER 10

COLLECTIVE TRAUMA

The College Years

Attending college at the University of Notre Dame was another in a long list of being in the right place at the right time situations. I knew practically nothing about Notre Dame and had not given this university any serious thought. Having taken the PSAT, a standardized achievement test that gave an indication of how well you would do on the SAT, a number of colleges were writing me based on my scores. I had received a partial scholarship to attend the University of Florida and was content to go there. I even had a roommate arranged, a friend of mine from high school. I was pretty set and then my father suggested I talk to his manager at Roadway where he was a truck driver. His manager had attended West Point and had a broader view about things related to college that my father could not give me. I do not remember everything we discussed or for how long we talked, but what I do remember is that he suggested that if these prestigious schools were contacting me, I should apply because it can open up doors that other schools might not be able to open up. As an impressionable teenager, this sounded reasonable and so I applied to several of these schools. When the acceptance letter came, we were all quite excited. Although it would be an extremely heavy lift financially compared to going to my state school, my parents decided that we would somehow make it work. I still cannot clearly say how I managed to make it through that four years of college, as we were scraping every semester and pleading with the financial aid office to try to manage the debt. At any rate, I now had to consider leaving sunny Miami and headed to cold South Bend, Indiana, a place near enough to Lake Michigan to receive the lake effect snow that can make for a long winter. I was going to a school that I had never even visited, 1300 miles away. There was no virtual visiting during this time either, so I had no sense of what was ahead of me.

After deciding to attend following my acceptance, I was then fortunate to be selected for a summer program for aspiring medical and engineering students prior to beginning our freshman year. There were 16 of us selected for this program and everything was paid for. This happened quickly and we did not have much time to think about it, so my parents put me on a plane headed to South Bend and I was off on my journey away from home. I actually had to leave high school a week early and fly back for graduation before returning to finish out the summer program, that's how fast things moved. This was my mother's only time crying as I boarded the flight, which connected in Chicago. I arrived in South Bend, collected my things, and hailed a taxi to take me to campus. I had a mixture of excitement, nervousness, and indeed fear as we drove towards the campus and this new environment for me. I remember driving down the street, approaching campus, and seeing the famed golden dome, wondering what I had gotten myself into. As we pulled up and begin to unload, my resident assistant met me and took me to my room in Morrissey Hall. I was amazed at the vastness of the campus and the idea of a golden dome. The amount of money that surrounded me was immense, and I was now around people who had access to wealth, something that I had not experienced before. As a result, I had very little appreciation for the nature of what I was embarking upon and the challenges that would result. Clearly, I had the raw talent to succeed in this environment but would need to sync this up with how to apply this talent in a manner that would yield success.

 My first three semesters were absolute disasters academically. Attending our freshman orientation, our dean of freshman studies indicated in a talk that we should be spending 50 hours a week studying outside of class time with no hint of exaggeration. Doing the quick math this equated to 7 hours a day, including the weekends and I also had a work-study job that required a commitment of 20 hours a week. What the heck was this guy talking about, I wondered. Despite the overwhelming challenge of meeting this guideline I proceeded to engage in a process to make this happen. If I was not studying 50 hours a week it was very close to that. I was spending most of my time on the weekends in the library doing work. Despite all the time that I was engaging in studying I was not seeing a return on my investment when it came to my grades. Because I had not engaged in good study habits in high school where everything came easy to me and I could get by with doing half-assed work, I was now attempting to figure out on the fly how to bolster my study skills and participate on a level with my peers. By the end of my third semester, I was starting to find a flow but still only had a dismal 1.8 grade point average to show for it. If I did not turn things around, I would not be able to stay at this institution any longer. Fortunately, things finally clicked with me now integrating all that I learned about myself, how to retain information and present it in a way that it could be received in a polished manner. I now was able to make the dean's list and completed a miraculous turnaround. Yet the difficulties that I faced worrying about my grades and comparing myself to my classmates definitely had an effect on me that was traumatic in terms of my sense of self and my abilities. I had a roommate who would only study the night before the exam all night and he was making A's while I was failing. The amount of effort that we were expending was not correlated with the grades and I found this to be quite demoralizing.

The trauma of not being able to compete and fit in with my peers really impacted my self-esteem, and I found myself heartbroken and crying many nights. This is a story shared by many of my colleagues in various ways. Of course, there were some of my colleagues who did have the access to resources and who might have had parents who had college degrees, but I do not know if this was the majority. It was easy for us to get into a comparative analysis with the white students on campus and this impacted my self-esteem and self-confidence as it did many of my peers, and we discussed the inequities often. As an aside, one of the hidden blessings of being one of few in a vastly oppressive environment was the support that we were forced to provide each other that created some truly wonderful friendships that might not occur in other places. I am proud of my peers who, like I, have been able to survive in spite of not having the level of access that many of the larger university community were able to avail themselves. The fact that we could survive in the least supportive environment really makes me wonder what would happen if the opportunities from birth were truly equal. That is what I am working for in the future.

At any rate, I was competing with people who had been at the top of their class and were used to being the best at everything. They had the best resources and had been appropriately groomed for this atmosphere. Many had parents who had also attended the university and so were quite steeped in the tradition of Notre Dame and higher education. To say this was an advantage for them would be understating the obvious drastically. My parents, through no fault of their own, had not been afforded the opportunity to attend college and did not have the access to resources that their white counterparts had been privy to utilizing. This is not a complaint but rather points out the inherent advantages built into a system designed to reward whiteness and limit blackness. Something so minute as being able to utilize the resources of your parent who is an executive at a Fortune 500 company to obtain summer internships working in the corporate world as opposed to my working loading trucks at RPS provide further advantages for skill building and creating professional connections that will last a lifetime. For a young student unable to appreciate the complexities of this reality it is easy to fall into a place of perpetual less than, a trauma that often is not discussed let alone noticed. Looking back on it, this is a significant point in terms of my shrinking myself and having less self-confidence about who I was and how well I can be.

In addition, not only was I being challenged with keeping my grades up but I was also faced with the difficulty of managing financially. Every semester seemed like a challenge to come up with the money to remain at school. I was on a first name basis with the woman in financial aid and we always had to come up with a viable plan to remain at school. I could not explain to you how we were actually able to make it through as it really defies logic. My parents were also under stress to try to scrape together what they really did not have to keep me going. Of course, this is what our community has always done, work to push our loved ones forward, making sacrifices that may not even be seen immediately. Staying in a place of gratitude honors those who make the sacrifices and also keeps us in a place of humility for the path laid by those who go before us.

As if these two challenges were not enough, I was also forced to deal with inherent overt and covert racism that permeated the campus. Affronts large and small were evident in many interactions and it put me in a position of having to be on guard often. One such slight that occurred would be when I would be asked if I played football. There was an implicit assumption made that because I was African American I had to be an athlete. Did I mention that I'm 5'8 and at the time weighed all of 140 pounds on my best day. Even the kicker on the football team was larger than me so this made no rational sense for this assumption to be made. Of course, many of my peers were also on the receiving end of these types of questions, and it became a running joke amongst us how many times we had been asked that question. It was as if the question could be utilized as a way to keep us "in our place" in a subtle non-threatening kind of way. These types of microaggressions wreak havoc in the minds of those on the receiving end, particularly when we have not been adequately prepared to understand and deal with them. The resulting trauma again creates feelings of doubt about who we are and what we are capable of accomplishing. These are issues that those in the majority at the university never had to worry about or even consider. Even if engaged in the conversation about a certain microaggression, most white people would not be able to identify with or understand said aggression.

I interviewed several classmates while writing this book to get their perspective on the issue of managing trauma while a student at Notre Dame to give a sense of the collective nature of this trauma. One expressed the dichotomy between being recruited and invited to campus while in high school and then arriving on campus to find things quite unlike the experience of the minority recruitment weekend. The thinking of Notre Dame being a family for all soon began to take shape as a family for all except us. Interestingly, my friend pointed out that these same fans who idolized and adored the African American athletes during the season saw them as enemies during the annual student run Bookstore Basketball tournament, a staple of tradition at Notre Dame. Many athletes were heckled and called all types of nasty and negative names during this time, something I found perplexing at the time, but over time have come to see this mentality as the athlete as a performer for our benefit, only when they want it. It goes without saying that there are certainly exceptions to this, but the overwhelming experience was one consumed in the energy of racism.

Other instances of having to deal with racism and boorish behavior described by my classmates include being told that we were only there because they made exceptions for our test scores, but giving no discussion to the "legacy" admits whose parents had attended or could afford to donate significant amounts of money to get their children admitted. One particularly appalling incident involved a Black history dinner where someone had the bright idea to serve fried chicken, watermelon, and bologna sandwiches. This really happened. Some gatekeepers in charge of making decisions thought that this would be a good way to celebrate Black history. These types of experiences became the norm and we developed a sense of understanding that this was our reality and we would have to just survive through it, a concept many of us adopted. There was a constant undercurrent of institutional racism that made the abnormal normal, creating trauma for those impacted. After witnessing so many of these episodes one becomes immune to it and then comes to engage in a way that limits the hurt and protects the spirit.

Another particular traumatic episode came at the end of my junior year at Notre Dame and showed that trauma can even be imposed by those who supposedly mean well. The week leading up to the graduation of the senior class was particularly stressful and as one of our classmates lost her father that week. As I mentioned, our closeness facilitated by our small numbers meant that everyone rallied around to support her through this time. So things were already fraught with an energy of support during a difficult time and a collective hug and support were offered and felt by everyone. I had remained to support my friends and provide help during the intimate Black Graduation ceremony. Bill Cosby had been selected to address the graduates at Notre Dame this year and he was asked to make a special trip to address the African American graduates at the traditional Black graduate ceremony. The Cosby Show and A Different World had been standard weekly viewing that were part of our collective healing, and we were all excited for this appearance. It quickly devolved into a spectacle of an event that proved traumatic on so many levels.

When it was time for him to speak, Bill Cosby began talking about the necessity of students maintaining better grades than this class had ended up with. A curious beginning to a celebratory graduation discussion and certainly not the typical "you have your entire life ahead of you, the world is your oyster, make the most of it" perfunctory remarks we assumed would be made interspersed with some Cosby witticisms. At one point he asked if there were any single mothers among the crowd and asked them to stand. He then chose one and asked who her son was. We all wondered where this was going. The person chosen happened to be one of the football players and Bill Cosby asked him what his grade point average was. When he replied 2.5 Cosby began to excoriate him telling him that his GPA was unacceptable and the only thing he should have been committed to do while in college was get decent grades. The student was also a football player and attempted to explain that he was an athlete with a very challenging schedule and that he had done the best that he could. Bill Cosby would not let up and continued to press this point even as the football player was in tears from the sudden unexpected embarrassment. The energy had shifted dramatically, and another classmate, one of the student leaders running the ceremony, came off the stage and challenged Cosby suggesting that he had no right to speak to the students in the way that he had, particularly since his life was not so perfect. He had approached the stage yelling at Cosby and had to be pulled away by his parents in an attempt to restore any semblance of order. At this point, no one wanted to hear anything else Cosby had to say as what was supposed to be a celebration of a crowning achievement had devolved into a horrible display of self-hate. Some of the parents supported the premise of Cosby not understanding and appreciating the pressure associated with trying to survive on an overtly hostile campus. One of my graduating classmates described that she felt disrespected at a time we should have been honored. At the main graduation, a different Bill Cosby appeared, eager to regain his role as a showman for the overwhelmingly white audience. The change in his behavior and attitude was lost on none of the students and turned a joyful day into an anticlimactic day full of sadness. It is likely that Cosby did not appreciate the level of hurt and pain that he left in his wake that day. What was just another day for him that he may not even remember is indelibly etched into the minds of the students that were there that day. Many of us never watched anything with him in it again after being completely enamored with his shows throughout college. I wish he could see these students that he thought were not up to par and the progression to the positions they hold in the world now. I am very proud to say that every one of my classmates that I keep up with is killing the game in their respective fields. CEOs, doctors, dentists, lawyers, business owners, financial analysts, politicians, judges, you name it.

What Cosby did not take into account was the strength and perseverance cultivated by existing in such a hostile environment. The bonds that we were forced to create to support each other imbued in us the strength to not only make it but to be the absolute best at what we do. Words can be more harmful and painful than a lash at times and the damage done to the psyches of young aspiring students was not considered. This is why it is important that we choose our words carefully and be cognizant of the manner in which they are being received by those on the other end of the communication.

    The systemic racism evident at this University and others like it have to be considered from a top-down perspective. If the administrations of these organizations really wanted things to change, they would tomorrow. This is likely no different in many places where people would rather discuss the problem than implement solutions to actually eliminate the problem. In the legal community, they would say patterns and practices. If we look at the patterns and practices of the University, we would have to say they are committed to maintaining the status quo as many of the same issues discussed among students of color on campus today are the same as they were 30 years ago, causing the same degree of trauma. Here is a clue: If you hear an organization talking about a task force to address an issue you can be sure that this is code for we have to talk about this to give the appearance that we care and will do something different. We are committed to diversity, they say but in 30 years there has been no significant change in numbers or policies. Talking with students while on campus last year, some of the same issues still prevail. Why is this the case and what can be done about it? Does anyone really want to do anything about it? It continues to happen because those at the top do not say this is not acceptable. Incidentally this is the same mindset that perpetuated the scandal with pedophile priests being moved from parish to parish by an administration who knew that they were molesting young boys. What is the mindset of the person who made the decision that they would just move the priest somewhere else to continue working, knowing that they had molested a child?? We would have to conclude that he did not care about the children being molested as his actions suggest this. We would have to conclude that he would not have allowed his children to be traumatized in this manner. I believe that those who allow the perpetuation of trauma know that it is happening but choose not to do anything to bring about substantial change. The reasons can be monetary or status-driven but ultimately, it is a moral failing in that the actions are in no way consistent with the very values that they are teaching others. This hypocrisy is quite telling and, in my mind, indefensible.

Just one week after writing about this, I came across the post by a current student where he videotaped an incident that he was involved in on campus. In the incident, as he was entering the Chapel a security guard came up to where he was and asked him to remove his hat. This security guard did not give the student an opportunity to get comfortable in his seat and get to the place where he would have removed his hat, and although bothered he did not consider it to be a big deal until he noticed two white students walk in right past the same security guard with their hats on and they did not receive admonition he had received. Those students were never asked to remove their hats and this bothered the African American student so much that a week later he returned to the Chapel to let the security guard know that his behavior was racist and not acceptable. He videotaped this encounter and interestingly a white classmate of his saw his video and asked why he felt the need to record the security guard without asking his permission. His focus on the videotaping, which has become a default protective measure as his word and experience can be rendered invalid, as opposed to the offense that occurred, speaks volumes to the different perspectives that exist for those who are the victims of racism versus those who never have to experience this type of treatment. If one thinks that this incident was an exception a quick visit to the Instagram site Black at Notre Dame will reveal many other similar incidents happening right now that speaks to the same level of racism in traumatic experiences that were happening 30 years ago. As the lead post on that site says "while we appreciate the public statement prayers and peace walks we expect substantial change that will positively impact the culture and experience for black students faculty and staff." To which I can only say good luck with that. Looking at the circumstances and energy that is evident on the campus, it is clear to me that this sentiment is embedded into the fabric of Notre Dame, despite those that would like to believe otherwise about this wonderful Catholic University. It is laughable to think that even within the most sacred aspects of this university where the values of Christ are supposed to be practiced, the prevailing sentiment for many African American students faculty and staff is one of hypocrisy, resulting in the collective trauma of being unheard and isolated.

While I was in school there, the issues that were prevalent on campus required some level of response, and many of us would organize and attempt to take on an unbeatable foe in systemic inequity and racism. Perhaps the largest outpouring in this regard centered around an effort on behalf of students of color on campus to demand respect and resources for our communities. This resulted in us having a sit-in and taking over the administration building, demanding for things to improve. Many of us risked graduation, at the time just months away for me, but felt it necessary to make this stand to bring about justice. At the end of the protest, slight concessions were made that were quickly wiped away. It is not an accident that the largest class of African American students was during this time and the percentage has not gone above the 3% that it was during that time since that time. Values and actions.

Current tuition and fees at the University currently stand at $57,000, which means that $228,000 will get you a Notre Dame degree if you are able to finish in 4 years. Absent a scholarship, this rules out many from this opportunity. Of course, there are other options for school, but again if we consider access to resources and opportunities to connect to circles that give entry to investment capital, for instance, it becomes clear that African American students continue to be marginalized and left to figure things out alone. Although discussing Notre Dame, it should go without saying that many of these issues can be seen at other predominantly white universities throughout the country.

Many of my classmates have refused to return to the University and still remember a lot of the traumas of having been there. Others have pushed it to the side and moved forward being active members of the Black Alumni Association and proudly supporting the University. And there are some who probably are in the middle as well, still harboring resentment but finding a way to appreciate the benefits of attending the University. Although everyone would not characterize the experience as traumatic there are certainly those that would, including myself, and this thus makes the perfect example of appreciating that we are all impacted by things differently. There are some similarities in the collective response and yet we are not a monolith and the variations in experience and the variables that make up the individual ultimately determine the response that one engages.

For me dealing with the trauma of the events of these years allowed me to have a fresh perspective when it came to parenting and breaking this pattern of trauma with my children. There are certain things that I have been able to provide for them that allowed them to come in and compete with their peers on a totally different level than I was able to. For instance, I am proud to say that my son was able to attend one of the top universities in the country, major in biology, and make the Dean's list from the first semester onward. He was further able to matriculate to a graduate program studying prosthetics in a very competitive field in which he is easily excelling. My daughter has received a full scholarship to a university and continues to make the Dean's list every semester. For me, this shows that there is a difference in experience when the opportunities and understanding more approximate equality. The opportunity to break patterns of trauma that allow them to see themselves in a manner that allows them to exude confidence and an awareness of who they are so that they are not intimidated in the least. There are still other elements that they have to deal with in terms of racism and microaggressions, but the trauma of feeling less than is not present. I understand the formula for success now and have been able to convey this to my children and some other students as well. For a while, I created and conducted a Saturday academy focused on critical thinking and teaching our youth how to position themselves to be successful in the world. Many of those skills learned through the adversity of being in a traumatic space can now benefit others that I come in contact with, and I know that this is the case for many of my classmates as well who have done similar things with their children and other youth, turning a negative into a positive.

CHAPTER 11

INDIVIDUAL TRAUMA

Getting a Ph.D. in Life

ACT I

I have been married 3 times. Each of the first two times I knew within hours of interacting with them that I was going to marry them. On the third occasion, it might have taken a week. I have come to appreciate and understand that each marriage is unique and has its own essence ensconced in the relationship. They were all necessary experiences on my journey of becoming. And yet they each in their own way produced a degree of trauma for myself and possibly for them as well. I can only offer my perspective here, for the purpose of discussing the impact on me.

My first marriage was to a wonderfully bright and intelligent woman whom I met prior to my last year in graduate school. She was an undergraduate with one more semester to graduation. We began dating when she invited me over one day and were together every day from that point. I had only dated one person seriously during my time in graduate school when we began dating, and we eventually found that we had a mutual friend who had attempted to match us previously but we had both ultimately declined. The relationship was wonderful during the initial honeymoon period. We got along well and discussed our wide-eyed dreams of taking on the world. At some point around month four, we had our first argument. I, being one that eschews conflict, found this to be difficult. She appeared to be better suited to arguing. I would hold a grudge and stop talking for days after an argument. She could argue and then seamlessly move to discussing dinner plans if she were not intent on holding a grudge herself. We started a pattern of conflict that never lessened during our time together. Despite the conflict and given our love for each other, I proposed to her on the anniversary of our first year together. I was moving across the country for my internship year to complete my doctorate and wanted her to come but with a commitment for our future together. We made plans to get married two years later, which would give us time to work on our issues and solidify our relationship.

During the two years, we continued to fluctuate up and down. The arguments persisted in retrospect about really silly things that were based on ego. However, we were very young and likely could have used more individual seasoning in our maturity prior to deciding to spend our lives together. I fully support Frances Cress Welsing's position that anyone should not get married until at least the age of 30 so that we give ourselves an opportunity to fully mature[24]. When I think back to myself at 25 now, I shake my head at my lack of maturity. I also have to keep in perspective that I was just 25 and so can only have the maturity that one has at that age. I have since learned in more depth the degree that my actions contributed to the problems even though, at the time, I thought she was the issue. Because, after all, I was an aspiring professional African American man who could cook, clean, provide, and parent. Who would not want me? That arrogance though not displayed in a brash overtly loud manner, nevertheless, was

---

24   Frances Cress Welsing (1991) The Isis Papers, Chicago, Third World Press.

there in a quiet condescending way and was ultimately problematic. It took my engaging the process of self-understanding in a much deeper manner that allowed me to ultimately see myself in a totally different way, which allowed for this level of growth. More on that to follow.

Approximately 6 months before we were scheduled to get married we reached a point where we decided that the conflict was too much for both of us and we should go our separate ways. We had "broken up" several times before in the relationship but this time took on a different energy. Highlighting this decision and making it concrete with our families we began making plans in this regard. One thing that was a definite plus in our relationship was our passion for each other. After two weeks apart we made up and as a result of the intimacy involved in making up, we now had a son on the way. Now that we were pregnant the energy shifted and we decided to really commit to staying together and go through with the wedding date that had been previously set. With this timing in place, we got married and 6 weeks later our son arrived, a whole month and a half early.

When our son was approximately 9 months old, trauma visited in the form of his being diagnosed with intussusception, a blockage of his intestines. The thought of having a major operation performed on a young infant produced an immeasurable amount of stress, and for a young couple it was quite difficult to deal with this emotionally. For me, at that time unable to fully access my feelings, I went through the process detached and trying to support my wife who has always been much more in touch with her feelings than me. Being so young and out of touch with my emotions, I had no clear understanding of how to successfully and in a healthy manner support my wife and deal with the emotions of potentially losing my child. If you can envision a young infant attached to multiple tubes, connected to a machine helping him to breathe and live, and his parents wondering and worrying if he will be healed and come through this situation, you can maybe feel the range of emotions we were experiencing. We ultimately made it through a successful surgery, and my son was able to thrive and have a healthy childhood, but the trauma of seeing your defenseless child, hooked to monitors and dealing with pain and being uncomfortable, had an obvious impact on the relationship and on me in ways I did not fully understand. My son could have easily died and I understood that an infant having such an invasive surgery was not a good thing, and yet I did not feel comfortable appearing "weak" and as though I could not handle the pressure of this. Where had I learned that I could not show emotions in a situation that was obviously laden with emotions. As mentioned previously, I have come to understand the manner in which boys and men are socialized in our society with admonitions of "suck it up," "brush it off" or "don't act like a girl." For African American boys these admonitions take on another level of significance as there are expectations foisted upon these young boys that suggest that they have to grow up sooner than others, unable to enjoy the natural development of being a child. How many young boys are told that they have to be the man of the house when they cannot even mow the lawn correctly let alone manage a bank account. These types of sentiments likely contributed to my own inability to appreciate the impact that the trauma of seeing my son in peril was having on me internally. I would have to engage in a process of self-reflection to work through these issues and move to a healthier place where I could access my emotions from a true position of strength, but this would take time and much work. It is also interesting in retrospect that I did not seek help for this traumatic situation, and honestly, I do not know if it ever even entered my mind as a consideration.

Another area of challenge for me in the relationship centered around fidelity to the marriage. Growing up I had distinct sets of right and wrong, likely impacted by my Pentecostal upbringing. With my father being an assistant pastor in the church and my mother being a missionary and Sunday school teacher I grew up attending church several times a week and knowing the Bible inside and out. A large part of me was very fearful of what could happen if I did not follow the values that we were being taught in church. As a result, I think that this kept me from doing things early on like cheating on my girlfriend. I remember thinking that guys who did this were not good and could not understand why they would not appreciate the person that they were with. This mentality lasted through the point of my relationship with my first wife. As we began dating I was very content and had no interest in anyone else. However, once I was in the relationship there were many people who were suddenly interested in me who had not previously been interested. Initially, I fought off this attempt to engage and stayed true to my relationship. Eventually, as we moved past the honeymoon phase and began having conflict, I began to rationalize having a sexual relationship with another person. The first time this happened we had an argument where she broke up with me. We had engaged in a number of these arguments previously and I knew that we would end up back together in a matter of days. However, a young lady had been flirting with me, and because we were technically "broken up," I rationalized this as an opportunity to engage with her. I hooked up with the other woman and did what people do and sure enough, a few days later ended up back with my girlfriend. I justified my behavior by saying to myself that technically I did not cheat on her because she had broken up with me. But there was no real justification. I knew we would be getting back together and if she had done a similar thing, I would have had a problem with it. I was wrong but unwilling to accept my wrongness at this time.

This began my foray into a slippery slope of behavior that would come to define my next few years. In the next three years prior to us getting married several other opportunities presented themselves and I found similar means of rationalization for justifying my behavior and choice to engage with these women. Eventually, it reached the place where my justification became, we are constantly fighting, and I am not getting my needs met. This juvenile rationalization was something that I would soon have to take accountability for. I never talked about my indiscretions with these other women, and I was never discovered, but I knew what I was doing was wrong, and ultimately that was important as I was surely not living according to the values which I would profess to believe. I believed that the women that I engaged with would have never discussed what had occurred and felt that I would take this information to my grave. I did not yet have the wisdom to appreciate that life has a way of writing chapters that I could not even envision. This is the folly of youth. Little did I realize that the boomerang of life was on its way back to me in full force and would literally put me on my back.

I will never forget December 31, 1999. This was the day that I found out that my wife had an affair and was the first time in my life that I had ever experienced depression to the degree that I suffered. This is not a novel occurrence for most people. Infidelity is a significant part of our lives as humans and for instance, there are many songs that point this out. Johnnie Taylor's Whose Making Love and Shirley Murdock's As We Lay come to mind amongst many. Prior to this point, even with my training as a psychologist, I believed that people could shake off depression if they really wanted to. This experience taught me that it was nowhere near that easy. I found myself crying every day and unable to eat or sleep. I could not do what I had done so often in the past, fighting through it and moving forward. I was depressed. I didn't want to believe that MY wife would do this to me. I had not yet come to understand the fallacy of ownership in relationship, her being her own person as I am my own person. Love being two people making a decision to come together and share love. Instead, I was in the space of trying to control what is uncontrollable and did not recognize the role ego played in my feelings. Additionally, it resonated with me that what was occurring was essentially what I believed in terms of karma. Logically, even though she did not know about my multiple indiscretions, I knew that I had not been faithful, and so it did not make sense that I would be upset with her for her indiscretion. Despite this logic twirling around in my brain, I remained upset and at times I exploited the guilt she felt about this situation. One could say that it was my actions that triggered her affair. Thinking about me as a man during that time, it is likely that if I had given her the attention and nurturing necessary for a healthy relationship, it's unlikely she would have stepped out. When neglected the opportunity for someone else to fill the void manifests. For me, I had finally had an experience that pierced the veil of emotions and allowed me to understand the depths of depression. I traumatized myself further, ruminating about the situation and what had happened, wanting answers to questions that could bring me no relief or serve any real purpose other than trying to soothe my wounded ego. It would take some time before I was able to do the necessary work to understand and appreciate my role and make choices to carry myself differently. After much discussion, back and forth, we ultimately decided to stay together and to figure out how to heal. In the pattern that defined our relationship we once again found the way back to each other and ultimately conceived our second child. My continuation on the path to feeling was only beginning though.

This next pregnancy proved to be a challenging one from early on and added more layers of trauma to what we were already beginning to experience. As if nearly losing one child was not enough, we would be faced with this prospect yet again with the arrival of our second child. This pregnancy with my first daughter was a high-risk pregnancy, and my wife ended up on bed rest very early on in the pregnancy due to her condition. After being on bed rest for months our daughter still came six weeks early but healthy. Within the first week of going home she had an episode where she stopped breathing and we had to have the paramedics called to resuscitate her. In retrospect, this was just foreshadowing an episode that was to come a few months later when our daughter was diagnosed with Respiratory Syncytial Virus (RSV). After the diagnosis, we endured a tough night at home with our daughter and that morning my wife was told to bring her in to see the pediatrician. My wife took her to the pediatrician, and during the office visit, our daughter stopped breathing. She was described as turning blue from a lack of oxygen and was placed on a ventilator to help her breathe as she was transported to the hospital. I remember receiving the call from my wife that they were headed to the hospital and our daughter had stopped breathing. I was on my way to work and after I got off the phone with her I called one of my good friends and told her the news. She said to me, "Anthony, what are you feeling right now?" I remember thinking that an odd question because I did not know what I was feeling. I remember the traffic light and the cross-section of the street I was on at the precise moment when we were having this conversation, that's how vivid the memory is. Yet, I was clearly not in touch with my feelings and the ability to tap into my emotions at this time. The experience was still a rational one and my mind was trying to make sense of the possibility of my daughter dying. My daughter was rushed to the hospital where they had to again resuscitate her. She was hospitalized for several days and again watching an even younger infant this time struggle to live and thrive was difficult to work through. We were witnessing our infant daughter being attached to all manner of tubes and machines to keep her alive with no assurance that this, in fact, would be successful. Another child that we had to be concerned with living a full life. The toll of this compounded trauma on a young couple was monumental, even as we were unable to fully appreciate the impact of the event, and the stress and pressure that was created at the time. We were just trying to survive. We were eventually able to bring her home and she recovered successfully. I certainly have an appreciation for any parent that has to watch their child suffer as a result of going through these experiences. The trauma of such an experience can create parents who are unwilling to allow their children to be in any situation that could in any way threaten their health. This and other natural reactions are understandable even as we can recognize that they may limit the progression of the child. For us, we were blessed and fortunate that ultimately both children came out healthy and continue to thrive to this day. But those moments in time left an indelible impression on me and I'm sure their mother, as challenges for a young couple attempting to figure things out.

    As a couple, we continued to clash over a number of different things including parenting, finances, and work responsibilities, all of which could have been resolved if I had a better understanding and control of my ego. As I mentioned, my wife had the capability of having an argument and being able to let it go. I did not, and after an argument, it would take me days to get over the argument. I was a master grudge holder, and this is something that I learned well from my mother. My not speaking which I thought was not engaging in conflict was actually a manipulative attempt at controlling the situation and, in fact, punishing her by withdrawing, leading to an unhealthy situation. We remained stuck in this cycle that did not seem to have an endpoint. Additionally, I was still struggling with making peace with her infidelity and found myself wanting to engage with someone else yet again, the justification now being that she had engaged in her own affair, so it made it ok for me to do the same. I know this does not logically make sense, particularly given my string of infidelities that she, at that point, still did not know about, but I'm sharing where I honestly was at that time. Of course, the energy that I was contributing to the relationship in terms of my dishonesty had to have an impact on our relationship and the conflict that ensued. Unfortunately, I did not possess the wherewithal to really appreciate this at that time. Arrogance/ego is a hell of a drug, I tell you. Ultimately, we reached a place where we decided yet again to separate, this time with me moving out, a serious step that we had not engaged in any of our previous breakups.

The time of this separation ended up being a pivotal point in my life where I finally began to actually do the work to align my actions and values. I started on a path to working on myself and creating a better person, not the fake person that could talk to and help people with values that I was in no way adhering to. I remember saying things to people in therapy sessions and thinking to myself, "wow, you should do that yourself," before continuing to be who I was. Now, life had enough of my shenanigans and required that I begin to find a space of humility and work to be what I talk about and walk in a space of accountability. I had no plan for this process, but as I was alone in my apartment on the days that I did not have the children, I had plenty of time to think. I developed a cycle of reading, meditating, and writing, and it seemed that the books that I needed for my progression showed up miraculously. One night I was reading a book where the main character discussed the impact of a vegan diet and I decided that the next day I too would change my diet for the next 90 days, eliminating all meat and sugar. I only intended to do this for the 90-day period, but after 60 days I realized that I no longer had a desire for the things that I had eliminated. This was particularly significant for the sugar as I was previously an addict when it came to candy and sugar. I knew every kind of candy there was and Willy Wonka and the Chocolate Factory was a favorite movie of mine. I even created an M&M commercial that I filmed in one of my classes in middle school. I loved candy! But this sugar was not good for me and as I continued to examine and understand the impact of diet on my overall health, I remained committed to maintaining these standards. I did not realize that I was laying a foundation of discipline for change while simultaneously improving my overall health. This discipline would prove necessary for me to correct the patterns of behavior that did not serve me and kept me from being my best self.

As I continued to do my own work after moving out, reading and meditating daily, I realized that a large part of this accountability was going to involve the fact that I needed to come clean about my prior indiscretions. The work that I was doing on myself necessitated this as the messages in the book The Four Agreements resonated with my spirit, and one of those agreements was being impeccable with my word. I had given her hell for her one indiscretion while holding on to knowledge that I had engaged in several. This was not fair to her and something I'm sure contributed to her own trauma. I knew that coming clean in this manner meant that we might not be getting back together and even though that's what I wanted more than anything in the world at the time, I knew that I could not continue to hide my dishonesty from her. So I told her about my indiscretions and predictably she was quite upset about this. No, actually she was monumentally pissed. Actually, I cannot really describe her level of anger adequately. All communication between us broke down and she stayed committed to the process of divorce. No one could blame her for this and I understood that I had brought this on myself through my actions that no one made me engage in. I needed to be accountable for me.

Eventually, a few months later, she made a decision that created another level of trauma for me in moving with the children back to her hometown nearly 1000 miles away. She did this in a way that made it that much more painful in that she initially stated that she was only going to go for the Christmas holidays to visit her family. It was only when she had been there for a few weeks that she informed me that she had decided that she was not going to come back. Yet as I went back to the house it was clear from the way she had packed everything up and the state of the house that she had no intentions of coming back when she left. I do not know the reason we could not discuss this. I surmised that maybe it was karmic retribution for my actions, although I did not believe the children needed to be impacted by the loss of either of us. After all the trauma we had been through as a very young couple, we were creating even more. When I was able to visit, it clearly impacted the children when I would initially see them and when I would have to leave them. I wish parents truly understood the impact our choices have on those that we profess to love the most. I've watched many other families undergo similar situations with their children, and each parent, just as we did, thinks that their position is THE correct position. We do horrible things to each other in these situations despite the fact that we once pledged an undying love for each other. We should spend more time thinking about this as a society. I did not press the issue with the children, and as we did not have a custody agreement in place, either of us could legally be entitled to the children if they were in our possession. I thought about just keeping the children but also considered that this would cause more terror and trauma for my young children. I think for most people in this situation, all types of thoughts naturally come into our minds as our egos tell us we are being disrespected or taken advantage of. So in these situations, we may choose to "fight back," but at what cost? My wife remained away for approximately one year before moving back, and during this time I had to fly out to see my children on several occasions and otherwise attempt to talk to them on the phone, difficult to do with young children, one not even capable of talking. This was quite a difficult time for me as the best thing I do is parenting and I had never planned to be a father that was not an active participant in their upbringing. I found it traumatic to be a father without his children as I had never considered this a possibility for me. To manage my feelings and the impact of this trauma, my resolve to continue healing myself increased and I stayed committed to what had become my healing regimen. I devoured book after book on improving myself and creating a healthier way of being. I continued to enhance my meditation and begin to see the results of this work. I committed to a process of being accountable for my actions no matter what, moving away from the negative rationalizing behavior I had previously engaged. These decisions required a lot of work to maintain, and I constantly had to remind myself of my values and focus so that I would keep my actions appropriately aligned. This does not mean that I did this without fail, and even now have moments where I have to work to remind myself of who I want to be. However, it has gotten easier with time, and I attribute this to a dedication to the process of creating true healing for myself and moving to a happier space.

After my wife moved back we proceeded with our divorce and determining custody arrangements. Parents who are separating and have decided not to continue their relationship often find that working together to try to decide what is best for their children is an area that comes with a lot of challenges. There are exceptions and certain situations where people are able to place their egos to the side and truly focus on the best interests of the children. In fact, I have been able, in my work, to facilitate this happening for many separating couples. Unfortunately, this was not something that we were ever able to achieve in our relationship in a consistently healthy manner. The dynamics that occur when you have two parents who fully believe that their thoughts and approach are correct and yet they are diametrically opposed to each other produces an energy of inherent conflict. In matters of custody most legal systems require parents to attend some form of mediation where they try to find a reasonable middle ground. This often does not work despite pleas from the mediator to find a middle ground. It has been my experience that the biggest challenge to finding a middle ground is ego.

When a breakup occurs, everyone is impacted by the trauma of the situation. No one "wins" in a custody battle. The children are often put in an untenable position of having to choose between parents and feeling as though they have to protect the feelings of one parent versus another. A young child who is still developing and does not have the emotional intelligence to adequately assess or understand the situation will be impacted by this trauma. Parents who often feel that they would do "anything" for their children, including giving their life, often do not consider that the harder thing to do is refusing to engage in any behavior that raises this stress level for their children. Indeed, if they would do "anything," then making the choice that has them push down their ego and not engage in conflict that would be certain to harm their children would have to be a part of the "anything." Yet when parents are faced with this outlook, anything quickly is seen to have exceptions, which underscores that when parents make this statement, they should actually state that they will do "almost" anything or they will do "some" things and not others. When it is clear that they will not do anything and a stalemate ensues, this will then lead to additional conflict which ultimately means more trauma inflicted on all involved. It is one thing to understand this concept cognitively, but yet another to put this thinking into practical practice.

This was the frame for what occurred in our custody situation. We initially negotiated an agreement that although I did not feel was fair was tenable. Of course, fair is relative again because if ego is taken out of the equation, fair becomes attached to the well-being of the children. But then who decides what is in the best interest of the children? These are the questions that percolated for us as they do for most couples endeavoring to manage the issue of custody and co-parenting. After an argument about the particulars of the schedule, we ended up heading to court to get an official order put into place. This ended up being stressful emotionally as well as financially. We were eventually granted equal custody with alternating weeks. Again no one wins in these situations and our children were left having to negotiate two households with drastically different perspectives and parents who were unable to communicate in a positive manner.

I had made it through this traumatic situation and having done some work on myself settled in for a smooth transition into being a single parent and a hope that we would one day be able to at least co-parent and communicate in a way that was healthy. At the time I was unable to perceive the impact that this situation had on me because I was immersed in it, and it has only been through reflection and a deeper analysis of my life that I have been able to appreciate the strain that this situation caused everyone involved including our extended families. This illustrates that the impact of trauma is not always noticeable, and it is not only the more forceful experiences like an automobile accident or death of a loved one that we can easily recognize as trauma but there are many more covert experiences that also impact us just as deeply. Additionally, some of the trauma may be self-imposed based on our choices and lessons we must learn in life, while others are beyond our control and imposed on us. Either way, we will ultimately have to do the work to create a different reality if we want to live a life full of happiness.

ACT II

I remained single for approximately four years after the end of my first marriage. My second marriage was one that moved quickly, too quickly and if there was a theme that defined it, it would be fighting and struggle for control. My first marriage had difficulties in it that I would say are normal and to be expected for a young couple. The second marriage exponentially increased the stakes and issues that we faced and brought into it a host of other external issues as well. There was so much conflict in this relationship, and I had not fully paid attention to the flags that were evident in the brief time that we dated. I saw them, but really did not want to see them, and as can be the case with a new relationship believed that things would eventually smooth themselves out. So many times I found myself after yet another bout of conflict, asking myself what just happened and how did I get here. Things would pop off out of nowhere often with potentially damaging results. There were many opportunities for my life work and license to be threatened based on exaggerations in some cases and factually inaccurate circumstances in others. I was fortunate in going through these situations that I never lost my psychology license as there were situations where this was very much in play. I will highlight just a few that proved to be the most traumatic for me.

We met in August at a conference for the Association of Black Psychologists. We talked and exchanged numbers and I called her a week later. She lived in the DC/Maryland area at the time and after talking on the phone for several weeks I surprised her with a visit. It went well and we continued talking and planning for a relationship. It is difficult for people to be honest about their pasts and who they are, and what they have been through when first meeting. I talk to people now about various questions to ask to get a better sense of this, but people can also choose not to be honest in their responses for fear of alienating the relationship. Ultimately, I think that if we are grounded in ourselves individually and are in the process of doing our own transformational work, it becomes easier to recognize the discrepancies that may exist. But even with the most diligence that one can muster, sometimes there are just lessons to be learned, children to be born, experiences to be had that are a part of our path.

So our first major argument occurred in early November a few weeks before our engagement party. We were having a conversation about the symbolism of wedding rings and what would we do in regards to getting her ring. She believed, as do many people that I should spend two times my monthly salary for a ring. As a critical thinker and one who questions everything, I wanted to have a conversation about where this rule came from and should we abide by this rule given other expenses that we needed to focus on with the wedding and getting her moved. Ultimately, I would go along with what she wanted but wanted to just engage the philosophical conversation about this matter. A large part of our relationship to that point had revolved around these types of intellectual conversations that I have always enjoyed having. This particular conversation she did not like and in the middle of the conversation, as we sat in the parking lot of Whole Foods, she became so upset that she got out of the car, slammed the door, and proceeded to walk back to her apartment. It happened so quickly that I took a minute to process what happened, then got out and asked her to come back and not walk as it was dark out. She did not respond and kept going. I drove back to the apartment and she eventually let me in after she calmed down. I agreed to just get her what she wanted to keep the peace and avoided bringing up the conversation again. In retrospect had I really analyzed this situation, looking at how easy it was for it to devolve, I would have at the least slowed down the process and taken more time. But we had planned the engagement party and had already started the process for an island wedding in the Bahamas. So not wanting to disrupt the plans, I ignored the flags and instead just prayed for the best, hoping that once we were together things would work themselves out. After all, I was a psychologist, and she was in the final stages of becoming one, so we should be able to figure this out. I would later learn that there were reasons for the behavior that was being displayed, and I could not be responsible for fixing those reasons. However, had I taken more time to allow the relationship to develop and get to know her better, things might have evolved differently. This might also be the case for her as well, as at that point in my life I was still not fully available emotionally and was not even aware that this was the case. My lack of emotional availability was certainly an issue in this relationship as it had been in the first relationship, even though I had vastly improved in other areas. Nevertheless, we tell ourselves what we need to in order to keep in check that rational or intuitive part of us that is telling us to make a different decision. That inner voice is often overruled, especially when we have not done the necessary work on ourselves to appreciate the wisdom that comes from taking a step back and slowing things down. After all, who wants to endure the supposed shame and embarrassment of calling a wedding off. Once again, ego comes into play and causes us to make decisions that do not necessarily serve us. The lesson of pushing down the ego is quite important and one I continue to focus on as important to complete healing.

Our next major issue came when she moved a week after our engagement to my home in Durham North Carolina. We got moved in fine and a few weeks later had a huge argument about a friend of mine that I previously dated who had a phone line on my account. I had previously had no reason to have this as an issue, the woman paid the bill and there was no problem. We had this arrangement in place for years. When she asked me about it, I was honest about the arrangement. She did not like the arrangement and suggested that I needed to end it. I agreed that I would but felt that I should give the woman reasonable time to make arrangements and not just end the arrangement suddenly. This turned into a heated discussion where she was so loud that others at my office could hear. I did not see why this had to be such a contentious issue but furthermore why it required such a high level of anger and yelling. Now I had real concerns but not only was she now moved in with me and planning for our wedding in a few weeks, but she was now also pregnant. The doubts of moving too fast were certainly present now but what could I do, we had moved so much around then I could not back out now. We patched things together and begin our marriage in a space of constant turmoil. For someone that really does not like conflict, I found myself back in another situation where conflict was constant, and this time it was not only constant but potentially volatile. Whereas I never felt that my first wife had any real intentions to bring harm to me, this became the case this time around.

    We were able to pull off the wedding without any difficulties and returned to settle into a pattern of living and engaging life as a young couple amidst intermittent conflict. We eventually had our child and moved into focusing on raising our family. We made it through several months and although things were not the greatest, they were not the worst either. Then began the start of a pattern of trauma that has impacted me immensely. The first time she called the police was the first time she decided to leave. I had no idea that she was feeling this way and had made plans to leave. We had not discussed ending the relationship in any formal sense although neither of us was really enjoying the marriage during that time. We had different ideas about a lot of things and clashed about these things and subsequently who would be in control. On the day she called the police, I had some cancellations in my evening schedule at work which allowed me to come home earlier than what she expected. I arrived at the house to see her and her mother loading a truck with her belongings. I walked up quite amazed at what was going on and still not understanding what was happening. She said something to the extent that she was moving and did not want to be in this relationship anymore. I picked up my daughter and walked into the house still trying to make sense of what was happening. I went up to our bedroom and locked the door as she tried to talk to me. She eventually decided to call the police to get me out of the room and get our daughter under the auspices that I was going to hurt myself and my daughter. Because her mother was involved and had a pattern of this type of behavior, it was easy for her to turn to this choice despite that there is no substance to this line of thinking. She made a choice to involve the police with no one in jeopardy merely to gain control of the situation and my daughter. The police came and negotiated the situation, ultimately telling me that I needed to go to court to try to arrange for a custody agreement. He noted that neither one of us had custody at the moment but given that our child was so young I should let her go with her mother. I relented and they soon left. She had also unbeknownst to me contacted social services to file a complaint against me at the same time she was calling the police, alleging to them that I was transporting our daughter without an adequate car seat, something that was not an issue for the months prior to her leaving, and which we had agreed would be the case. She created an issue where there was not one. I remember calling her father, who had performed our wedding and imploring him to talk with her about the things that she was doing as her impulsivity was threatening my livelihood and ability to provide for us all. He agreed to talk to her but his own alienation from her as a child left him with little power to sway her behavior. As it turned out, many of the similar types of issues he had dealt with were now repeating themselves with me and would continue throughout the course of the marriage. This situation was not only traumatic for me but for our young daughter as well who was now having the first of many encounters with the police and social services. Approximately a week after the incident she was apologetic about what had occurred and admitted that she did not think things through adequately. Eventually, we made up and began the process of working to repair the damage. "Why?" You might ask. Again I have asked myself these questions incessantly over the years. One factor that I considered was that my two older children were impacted by this situation as well, and not wanting them to have to go through another breakup and not wanting to have another "failed" marriage, I worked hard to try and move us to a better space. We went to marital therapy to help with this and saw some progress which allowed us to move back to a baseline space of coexisting, ultimately moving back in together. However, as the issues began to be more intensely analyzed, the pressure of facing this became too much and therapy was discontinued. This was unfortunate as had we continued to do the work and follow the prescriptions given, we might have had a different outcome. At the same time, I recognize that there has to be an internal willingness to fully engage the process, and without this commitment, lasting improvement and change will not likely happen.

We continued to traverse through disagreements in the relationship which centered around issues of control. Here

Individual Trauma

were two highly intelligent people who both believed that their way of understanding the world and doing things was the correct way. This is something that I notice as a theme with many couples, and the inability to manage that ego again continues to cause significant problems. And it does not have to be anything complex that causes the problem and sets off an explosion.

We were celebrating our anniversary that December 28th. Things were fine between us at that point, nothing out of the ordinary. We had traveled to Orlando to visit with family and our children were visiting with their godparents. We had a night to ourselves to enjoy the anniversary evening. Nowhere in my mind could I have thought up the events that would soon take place. Years later, I still shake my head thinking about how quickly my life could have been permanently altered.

After dropping off our children we were on our way to get takeout from Red Lobster and head back to our hotel. My wife was approximately 2 months pregnant at the time and we were planning a low-key evening relaxing and enjoying our time alone. After dropping off the children and on the way to pick up the food, we engaged in a conversation which quickly escalated into a disagreement. She suggested that if I did not want to listen to her I could turn up the music. Earth Wind and Fire are one of my favorite groups, so I gladly did as she suggested to which she then turned the music down. This, by now, was a familiar pattern, when I attempted to remove myself from a disagreement, she would instigate it even more. I turned the music back up she turned it back down. This was the way many of our disagreements went. I say one thing she says the opposite. She says one thing I say the opposite. Always difficulty finding a common ground, often about the most minuscule things that in retrospect really did not matter. We were driving down a busy stretch of three-lane traffic in Kissimmee and she grabbed the steering wheel causing us to drift out of the lane. Why she did this I have no idea as this could have potentially killed us both and others. I hit her arm to keep her from causing an accident and this stopped the tussle momentarily. I could not believe that she would practically cause an accident due to her impulsivity. We arrived at the restaurant within the next two minutes and as soon as I parked she threw a bottle at me and jumped out of the truck. The bottle hit the window and shattered in the driver's side seat narrowly missing me, and I got out to get her to calm down. She was extremely animated at this time, yelling and creating an immediate scene, screaming about me hitting a woman. People came from everywhere as I tried to get her to calm down and not make a scene. Two men threatened to fight me. As I realized that talking would not make matters any better, I instead got quiet. The police had been called and I got back in my truck. After they parked and came over to me, they put handcuffs on me and placed me in the back of a police car. I was in total shock at this time, my mind struggling to make sense of what just happened. Soon, I began hyperventilating as I considered my life flashing before me. Several squad cars pulled up and a big scene was created. They ended up putting her in handcuffs as well as they were able to see the shattered glass from the bottle that she threw at me in the car. We were both in danger of being arrested and processed and who knows what else. For some reason, the African American officer who took my statement found a soft spot in her heart after I explained to her that we were both psychologists and had a lot to lose behind this. I explained to her that it was our anniversary, and we were supposed to be having an enjoyable evening and I did not know how we go to this. The officer ultimately negotiated for me to leave on foot with my wallet and my backpack which I was more than happy to do. She stated that we needed to have no contact with each other that evening and again, I happily agreed, not wanting to have any further consequences. We ended up back together the next day as we picked up the children and continued our trip to Miami to visit my parents. Having both had some time to reflect on the situation and realizing how close we both were to negative consequences caused a drop in ego and we eventually squashed the situation and proceeded to move on without much discussion about what caused the situation to begin with. We just moved on. In retrospect, I think we often stay stuck in situations afraid to move on, afraid to be uncomfortable, afraid to disrupt the unhealthy status quo. Instead, we deal with the trauma, not knowing or willing to explore another way. For me, the trauma of being put in handcuffs at the mercy of the police and fearing for my life and livelihood was a challenge that impacted me immensely. I was fortunate that I was dealing with an African American woman who brought a degree of empathy and sensitivity to the situation that I do not know would have happened otherwise. Well, I'll just say I don't believe it would have happened, otherwise based on what I have witnessed in my life. There was also the trauma of violence that had erupted between the two of us. This was not something I was accustomed to, and in all of my relationships to that point, had not had anything escalate to this level. She had conveyed to me the reality of the presence of these agencies in her life previously and I believe that this shaped her willingness to engage with them when she felt she was being threatened.

The conflict in our marriage eventually reached a point of no return after the birth of our second daughter in July. We had somehow made it through approximately four years together, and the unhappiness and perpetual conflict had taken its toll. My wife decided that she did not want to be in a relationship anymore and proceeded to begin making arrangements to move out. Although I did not agree that we should end the relationship at that moment, especially with a newborn, I had in previous times also suggested that we should end the relationship. We began negotiating the terms of how we would manage the children as I was adamant that I did not want to return to a court situation again. We came to an agreement which I did not think was fair, but to avoid the previous outcome and any more court time agreed to, and she moved out in November. I really did not want to fight anymore. Then by January, her behavior became so erratic to the point that I feared that my children were in danger and was thus, forced to engage the courts for their protection. This was not a decision that I took lightly, and I only proceeded after being advised that this was the most prudent course of action by my attorney. To her, this likely appeared that I was retreating from our agreement and thus only infuriated her, which now created a hostile situation. The courts created a temporary custody order and I settled into a pattern advised by my attorney of communicating with her only through writing so as to have documentation. Nothing could go wrong this way, or so I thought.

It was just a simple visit to the doctor. As I had the girls that weekend, and we were scheduled to transition them, the drop-off instead of school would be the doctor's office. It was a cold January morning, in the 20s and we made it to the doctor's office and met their mother. The older daughter, perceptive as she was, seemed to intuitively sense the gulf that existed between her mother and I, and as a result, took advantage of this parental disconnect. This is something most children are aware of and will manipulate the situation to their advantage if their parents are not on the same page or send conflicting messages. Being clear about my limits regarding her behavior, she attempted to go beyond these boundaries now being in the presence of her mother. The appointment was for the younger daughter related to her having RSV. They called us back into the exam room and, at this point, her mother held her and the older daughter attempted to play on the exam table. I admonished her not to do this and she looked to her mother and continued to do so. I then picked her up and held her on my lap. She struggled to get down and her mother said that I needed to put her down. I ignored her not wanting to engage in any conversation and certainly not an argument. She told my daughter she would go tell the nurse who would make me let her go. At this point I decided to just take my daughter and wait in the car while she finished the appointment. I felt that she was intentionally disrespecting my authority in front of my daughter and rather than argue with her I would just remove myself. Her mother followed me down the hall and out of the door. Once we got to the door, I put my daughter down to put her coat on and then proceeded to walk to the car. Her mother blocked me and tried to push me back, all while holding our infant who did not have a coat or hat on in the 20-degree weather. I avoided her and walked in the opposite direction. She began following me, yelling and cursing. I kept saying to her you need to take our child back in the office and not have our already sick child out in this cold. She followed me around the building and across a very busy street a walk that took at least five minutes, time that our sick 6-month-old daughter was exposed to this extremely cold weather with no hat or coat. When I approached a wooded area, she went into an office and had them call the police claiming that I was abducting our daughter. I walked around the building, recrossed the busy street and went to my car where I called my attorney and explained what had occurred. She advised me to just wait for the police to come, tell what happened and then to take steps to get a protective order put in place so that I would not have to deal with her anymore in this manner. I waited for the police to arrive in my car outside the office and eventually three police cars showed up. When they arrived, her mother came out screaming and yelling about what had occurred. They made her calm down and asked for both of us to give our side of the story. Of course, there was a huge scene outside of the doctor's office, in addition to our daughter being in the middle of this catastrophe. The officers ultimately decided that since the custody was switching over, I should let her finish the appointment alone and I should leave. I should note that they did not find any reason for anyone to be arrested at this time. I had not touched her or said much to her other than suggesting that she take our younger daughter out of the cold. She had pushed me while holding our daughter trying to prevent me from going to my car. This detail would prove to be an important point in the next few months.

 I proceeded from there to the downtown courthouse to fill out the paperwork for the DVPO as instructed by my attorney. It took a few weeks before the case was heard, and I had to represent myself as I could not afford any more attorney's fees. She was represented by her attorney, so the predictable result occurred, and my case was dismissed as I could not effectively make my case. What I did not know was that she was going to once again involve the police in a way I did not even realize was possible. I lived this and still find it unbelievable. Here is what happened next.

 At the same time that this process with my second wife was going on, I was also in negotiation with the mother of my older children to restore our prior custody arrangement which I had willingly amended 9 months earlier due to yet another issue with social services. I must detour momentarily to explain what occurred with this traumatic episode of social services interaction. On this occasion, my second wife had accused my older two children of molesting our daughter, the first child that we had together. I should say that I deliberated discussing this aspect because of the sensitivity of the accusations. I do not take this situation lightly and have undergone extensive training to be a certified evaluator of child sexual abuse for victims and perpetrators. I ultimately decided to address it because this is an area that is often suppressed for a variety of reasons, and yet it is an area that produces a significant degree of trauma in our community and needs to have more recognition rather than being pushed under the rug. Vulnerable children are being harmed every day and there are pedophiles who take advantage of children. One need only watch the popular To Catch a Predator show to think about the numbers of people in the world who engage in this type of behavior. In one episode of this show over one weekend they may catch at least 30 people, typically men who are coming to a home to take advantage of a minor. These are people from all walks of life with many levels of notoriety, doctors, priests, teachers, etc. If they can catch this many predators in one small town in one weekend we can extrapolate this across the nation and see that there is indeed a large problem that we need to be cognizant of and address appropriately. Much more can be said about the trauma that exists in the arena of sexual abuse. But the situation with my children was nowhere near abuse and the subsequent investigations and evaluations stated as such. All three of the children had to deal with the trauma of this situation. In this situation, my wife was once again utilizing social services as a tool to fight but not considering the detrimental impact this would have on all involved. Eventually, the extensive evaluation found no evidence of any abuse, but the damage had been done. Ultimately, she did not stop her with this pattern of behavior in the future and, in fact, it only intensified.

The long-term impact that this situation would have on the other young children was of no concern to her and she was focused on what she thought was protecting "her" child. This despite the fact that we had entered the relationship with the clear mandate that all of the children were "our" children and not to be singled out, an important concern that often causes difficulties in blended families. The husband of my ex personified the ability to completely be a father, and he and his family have truly accepted my children as their children in an authentic manner. Despite any difficulties or dislike for our respective approaches that we may have had over the years, this did not prevent him from putting the focus on loving the children who did not ask to be in this situation. Unfortunately, this same level of acceptance did not occur in my relationship. On the other hand, my ex was understandably livid at our children being dragged into this madness. To stem the anger and protect our children from any further attacks, I agreed to allow the children to live with her, altering the schedule. I assumed that my first wife would never have reason to ever talk with my second wife because of this traumatic event, but common enemies can make for strange bedfellows.

So now returning to the situation with my ex-wife, this previously mentioned desire to resume a regular custody schedule was prompted in large part by my daughter doing poorly on her report card and my conversation with her teacher about the reasons for this. I believed I needed to reengage at a higher level to ensure that my daughter was completing and understanding her work at an appropriate level, and since the reason for the change in the first place was now out of the picture everything lined up. I was able to meet with my ex and her husband in my office and we were able to have a healthy conversation about the situation and they agreed we would each come back with possibilities that we could consider. After the meeting, I remember being exhausted and feeling that I always have to take the high road and not really express what was on my mind in order to keep things from deteriorating. My goal was to avoid blame and focus on solutions, as it seemed they had assumed it would be adversarial. I worked to make it clear that I was not interested in fighting, just finding a solution that would be amenable to everyone. I further stressed that it would be good for our children to see that we were able to work together in a positive manner. When we next talked, I was questioned by my ex about not feeding the children, something my son had apparently told his mother. As stated previously, the children recognized the conflict that was occurring, and as children are prone to do set about to manipulate the situation to their favor because clearly, I would not starve my children. As an aside, I do think that couples forget the person that they married and pledged undying love and to whom they pledged to live their life with forever. If we would remember the goodness that exists in the people that we chose to spend our lives and have children with, many of these ego-based situations would go away. Of course sometimes people just change for the worse, and that is a different story. I think that most people at their core in relationship have qualities that we find appropriate enough to have children with, and in this regard unless shown something drastically different, we should trust that the love that we have for our children is paralleled by the other parent. I asked their mother if we could sit down and discuss this and she agreed so I drove over to her classroom. After expressing our respective viewpoints, the conversation took a negative turn, and she became extremely angry and asked me to leave. I respected her wishes and did so immediately. I later sent her a message stating that since we could not reach an agreement, we could just go back to the order that was in place.

As we had the temporary agreement in place where I would have my two older children for dinner on Tuesdays and Thursdays, when the following Tuesday came, I followed with the order, visitation and planned to have the children for the week. The children and I proceeded with our nightly schedule as we typically would, and the children went to sleep. Their mom and her husband came to my house and called the police. When the police arrived, they listened to both of us and looked at the order before coming in to check on the safety of the children. They were satisfied that the children were safe and let them know that I was within my rights and they would need to leave. The next night was her night for dinner with the children and when I went to pick them up she would not allow them to come out. So I called the police and when they came her husband came out and suggested to the officer that they should check my license. The officer asked him if he were an immediate parent and when he replied no, he told him to go back inside and he would talk to the parents. I thought this was an odd statement to make and would come back to it later. The officer looked at the order and made the same decision as the previous night, whoever was in custody at the time had the upper hand and we needed to go back to court to get this resolved. I left and while driving was reviewing what had just happened in my head. That statement about checking my license kept resounding in my mind, so I called a friend of mine who was a police officer and described what had occurred. She suggested that there may be a warrant on my account, to which I said that's impossible I have not done anything. She agreed to check and said she would let me know the next day. When she called me back she said that indeed there was a warrant out for my arrest for assaulting a woman. I was dazed, shocked, in a state of utter disbelief. I knew things were contentious between us, but I never thought that their mom would make up something so serious and put me in jeopardy like this. Yes, she had gotten upset at our conversation in her classroom but I was not near her at all and left as soon as she asked me to. Why would she

Individual Trauma

lie like this? I contacted my attorney who informed me that this was a criminal case and I would need to get a criminal attorney. I guess I was just naïve about things like this as it had not even entered my mind the possibility of facing criminal charges.

I had completed a practicum in the state prison during my doctoral program. From there, I decided to do my year internship for the completion of my doctorate at a federal prison. Though I had worked in these settings I never got into any trouble that would find myself actually detained behind bars. Being accused of assault was the first time in my life I had been accused of anything of this magnitude. I remember feeling as if the world was closing in on me and had to pull over in the parking lot of a bookstore. I walked into the bookstore to clear my mind and came upon a book being prominently featured, Left To Tell[25], about a woman's survival of the Rwandan massacre. I read a few pages and decided to purchase it as focusing on her much more serious adversities allowed me to put my adversities in perspective as well as take my mind off of the turmoil momentarily. What taking an hour to delve into this book taught me at that moment was there is always someone with a more difficult situation and we should keep that in context. It was quite by accident but on purpose that I came across this book. To ensure that I got the message being delivered to me, as I walked into the parking lot after purchasing the book and prepared to back out I looked in my rearview mirror and noticed that the car immediately behind me had a personalized license plate with the word PRAY on it. I could not believe this was happening. It was as if I was receiving messages reminding me of what I committed to and to trust the process.

---

25 Ilibagiza, I., & Erwin, S. (2006). Left to tell: Discovering God amidst the Rwandan holocaust. Carlsbad, Calif: Hay House, Inc.

I got in touch with a criminal attorney that I knew and he agreed to help me. We planned to go to the court on Tuesday afternoon initially but as that was my day with the children I asked if we could go the next morning. The timing of this ended up being so important because had we gone down Tuesday I would have been arrested and had to stay overnight. We went on Wednesday morning and we were both thinking we would get things cleared up and I would be on my way. I had absolutely no idea I would actually be arrested. Even after we met the sheriff at the courthouse, who had actually gone to my practice to deliver the warrant that morning, and my attorney started explaining to me that he would try to get me on the court docket right away, it still did not register for me what was happening. Not until we were right in front of the gate did it finally dawn on me that I was actually being arrested. A wave of emotions came over me and I had to make myself push it down. After all, one cannot go into jail crying. I remember being looked at as if I were a criminal and at least feeling that to be the case. I was thinking I did not do anything. But the people processing you do not care, everyone says they did not do anything was what their looks communicated to me. I was processed and put in that wonderful prison orange and placed in a cell alone. I thought about how, back in November for my 40th birthday, I had gotten this idea to invite my friends and family to join me for 90 days of prayer, which would include everyone taking a minute at 12 noon eastern to engage in focused prayer for peace and positivity. I don't know where this idea came from, but it was successful and inspirational to those who participated. I had no idea that I was preparing myself to have tools to use in the time of trauma. Still, in my 90 days of prayer, I decided to engage in the process and release any anger. I sat in the jail cell and thought of Lauryn Hills song, "Forgive Them Father," and worked to keep my mind in a positive and forgiving place. After a few minutes I was placed in the ankle and wrist shackles that have caused so much trauma for my African people since the inception of this country, and walked to the courtroom where my attorney was able to get me released on my own recognizance. Upon arriving at the hearing, the details of the charge became clear. It was actually my second wife who had accused me of assaulting her, claiming that this happened at the doctor's office in the previously discussed episode, and not my first wife as I had thought. However, it was clear that they had begun communicating with each other and she had shared this information, making them aware of the warrant that she had taken out on me. So my first wife was now apparently working with the woman who had accused her children of molestation. I could not believe this was happening on so many levels. First of all, my second ex-wife had made this accusation a month after it supposedly occurred and after I had tried to get a domestic violence protection order against her with no success. Second, my first wife was so upset with the second one for what that episode of accusation put our children through that I could not believe she would even engage in a conversation with her. Third, what the hell is happening here!!! I was thinking, my mind racing, trying to keep up with the utter unbelievability of my life. In all, I was in jail for approximately 2 hours, which if you have to get arrested is probably the least intrusive way especially given that had we come the day before as we had initially planned, I would have been in jail overnight. And yet 2 hours is 2 hours to many, and the trauma of this incident would stay with me for some time. I was now the victim of a made falsified accusation, something many African American men and women in this country have been victims of, often to the detriment of their lives. Lonely, frightened, anxious, overwhelmed, violated, victimized, ashamed and embarrassed do not adequately describe what I was going through at this time. If I was feeling all this and more, what about the thousands who have lost their lives after a false accusation? Though my life was not in danger, my livelihood once again was, along with the ignominy of having a record. Ultimately, all I could do was rely on something greater than me, and remember the signs that reminded me of who I am. I needed to trust the process.

A few weeks following this incident, I was watching the news and a clip of someone being arrested and wearing the orange and shackles came on the screen and I began to panic. Like depression, I had never had an anxiety or panic attack before. I could not stop myself from feeling what I was feeling. I realized I needed to go to therapy myself to deal with this situation and it took me several months to get attain some degree of healing from this incident. Compounding my anxiety was the impending trial about the matter, which was delayed several times over the next few months, during which the prosecutor attempted to get me to take a plea, which I vehemently refused as I had not done anything. The prosecutor stated that if I would just agree to take anger management classes that they could come to an agreement and avoid the trial. I refused because again I did nothing wrong and was not going to admit to something that I did not do even if it would put an end to this situation and my by now heightened anxiety.

At the trial which finally took place in August, 6 months after the arrest, my ex continued to embellish the lie she had already told. Again, in my naivete, I did not think people actually lied so blatantly on the stand. I was incredulous listening to a total remake of what had occurred playing out. My attorney just whispered to me to be calm and not worry. That was easy for him to say as he was not the one on trial, I thought. It turned out that he knew what he was talking about and I should have just let him do his job. However, as an African American man, the justice system is not one that I take lightly at all, especially given what I had now personally witnessed. When he had his opportunity to cross-examine her, he asked several questions that caught her in the midst of her misrepresentations. When it was my turn to take the stand, her attorney attempted to ask me questions that had absolutely nothing to do with the trial at hand, such as had I ever been arrested for dealing drugs before. I found this to be very frustrating and even though I was later informed that that was just a tactic she was using, I thought it disgusting that she would use a tactic to try to disarm me when I am literally fighting for my livelihood. Later the police officer who wrote the report was called to the stand and my attorney made the case for my innocence a foregone conclusion in a few simple questions. He asked the officer what he should do if he came across any evidence of domestic violence during the course of his interactions with people. The officer responded that he would arrest them, and they would have to be in jail for two days as a result of the domestic violence laws in North Carolina. He then asked him if he had arrested me to which the officer had to reply no. My attorney asked him why he had not arrested me, and he replied that he did not see any evidence of domestic violence and that never came up in all of the statements that were taken. My attorney in his closing was then able to reiterate that the only reason this case was being brought was because she was upset that I had attempted to get a domestic violence order against her previously and she was retaliating after the fact by claiming that she had been assaulted on that day. The judge agreed and threw it out without giving it much thought. I was happy to be exonerated, yet I had to spend thousands of dollars to prove my innocence for something that never occurred. I was also arrested and my picture was placed in the Slammer periodical. Several of my clients noticed my picture and had questions about what was going on and if they should remain in my practice. Once again my livelihood was being impacted by something I did not do, on an impulsive action by my ex-wife. Seeing me in The Slammer caused people to question my validity as a psychologist, rightfully so. Unfortunately, they have not created the periodical Slammer Retraction for when they get it wrong and a person is exonerated. It is easy to tarnish a person's reputation and less attention is paid when this turns out to be false. C'est la vie, I suppose.

In retrospect, I could have avoided all of this by just leaving the doctor's office back in January. The incident was about ego and control. She wanted her way to be right and I wanted my way to be right. Either of us could have stood down. But these are the confrontations that happen when couples are not able to push down the ego and do what is truly best for the children. Or in any adversarial situation. Life is about balance and there are indeed times where we must stand up for ourselves and fight. There are other times though that we fight when it would be better to run. My martial arts teacher, late Master Fogg, taught that as a first rule, if you can avoid a fight, by all means, do so. On the other hand, in that moment I thought I was avoiding the fight by leaving with my daughter. I could have taken it another step and just left by myself and let her manage the appointment. But I wanted some say so, I did not want to be beholden to her dictating everything. My ego did not like that. And ultimately my children were in the middle of two out-of-control adults experiencing their own trauma. I was out of line and out of accord with my values. My actions did not line up. Of course, it is always easy to retrospectively apprise a situation. It happened as it did. My hope is that you are able to see how something so simple can become major and look at situations where you can go a step further and prevent a negative situation from occurring.

So what we have happening is the convergence of two generational trauma sets. This meeting of two family traumas then clashes to produce its own set of issues. This process gets played out on numerous occasions in our communities repeatedly, and we do not always recognize the impact of this convergence. What is amazing is that many of us have been able to be successful in creating any semblance of a healthy relationship. On its face, if we really analyze what has happened in our communities this system was not designed for us to be healthy and to be thriving. In fact, it is amazing that any of us in the African American community has been able to achieve any modicum of success given that our cultural system historically is not set up for our success. That we can survive and thrive in spite of these inequities is a testament to the ability inherent within to overcome. When we are able to understand the impact of the various traumas and do the work to heal from them we will truly be able to manifest that genius that resides in all of us and create our true reality, one that allows us to achieve at an optimal level. My generational trauma contributed to my cold detached behavior and aloofness which did not allow for a true intimate connection. Her generational trauma in my eyes was such that she played out in her reality the same thing that was imposed upon her with intense anger and constant interaction with social services and the police.

An important takeaway here is to recognize our own individual familial patterns and traumas that are evident in our actions in the way that we go about doing things. Being able to have these discussions prior to getting married and working through these things in a positive way will put us in a position where we can more readily ensure that we will have a healthy happy marriage. When we are not aware of these difficulties or ignore them, it is to our own peril and has the potential to result in our being in relationships that are not fulfilling. We have the power to change the trajectory of the negativity and the impact of the trauma if we are willing to engage in the process of doing the healing work necessary to overcome this multi-generational trauma. We do have the power to change and although it is not an easy path it is one that is attainable once we understand the dynamics that are at play. The things that were "done" to me were not really about me and I had to learn not to take them personal. She was dealing with her own trauma history and this caused her to act on so many different occasions in a manner that was not healthy for anyone involved.

 The last bit of trauma with this marriage was indeed the worst, the effects of which are still ongoing. I have spent a lot of time thinking about the worst things that can happen to a man, and I think that being accused of molesting your daughter has to be, if not at the top of the list, a close second. In March, one year after the arrest, I received a call from a social worker telling me that she had to meet with me today and it was an emergency. We were still in the midst of the custody trial, which had been delayed several times at this point, with many more to come. She offered to come by my house that evening and I agreed. By this time, I had begun dating my third wife and she was there visiting. The social worker suggested that we might want to meet alone but I said to her that I had nothing to hide so she could stay and listen. The social worker then shared with me the details of my having been accused by my daughter of molesting her. My daughter was just 3 years old at the time. Even the most precocious child at that age would be hard-pressed to report something like this in the way that it was described. I showed the social worker journals that were left that described the same thing has happened to her mother and implored him to recognize that she was doing this out of anger and to gain an upper hand in our ongoing custody battle. They noted that indeed that might be the case, but because of the seriousness of this issue, they would have to remove me from any interaction with the children until I and her could be evaluated. Even though she had previously accused my children of this, it still never dawned on me that she would find a way to pull this stunt with me as well. Complicating matters was the fact that I did these very evaluations for years and there was a small community of psychologists that do this type of evaluation and we all knew each other. As a result, they had to find someone from a city over 100 miles away to ensure no bias. The distance and the unique circumstances of the situation added time to their ability to find someone and get the evaluation set up and during this time, I was not allowed any contact my daughters. Three months following the accusation, they finally found an evaluator and a time for the evaluation, which normally takes several weeks and multiple meetings with the psychologist for both myself and the child. However, this psychologist met with me one time and met with my daughter one time before coming to his conclusions and submitting the report exonerating me of any of the atrocious claims levied against me. Once again, my livelihood was being threatened by someone who did not care and was willing to cause emotional damage to our child, putting her yet again through another evaluative situation with social services as well as potentially jeopardizing her own financial wherewithal given the child support that was being contributed to her for my children all in an effort to "win."

As before, I really do not have the words to describe the pain, frustration and anger that I felt having to go through yet another unjust situation. The trauma of this accusation was unbelievably stressful as now I was not only being separated from my children but again and in an even more serious manner, my professional identity and reputation were put on trial as well. I spent time pondering the possibility of winding up without my children or my profession. What would be the purpose of being here if these things were taken away for something that did not occur. I have to reiterate that I really cannot describe the agony and feeling of helplessness that results from being accused of something that you did not do but seemingly have no avenue to defend yourself. This trauma boils inside and produces frustration that causes one to want to lash out. Just last year, I watched the movie Just Mercy about Walter McMillian's wrongful conviction and death sentence in Alabama. This movie brought these feelings up again for me as the main character was clearly being violated by a system that debased and traumatized him because it could. Even in the face of clear evidence, Mr. McMillian was still made to jump through ridiculous hoops to be exonerated.

Were it not for the perseverance of his African American attorney, who himself was humiliated and traumatized for trying to do his job; he likely would have been put to death. How many times have situations like this occurred in the African American community? How many people in similar situations have taken their life or turned to drugs or alcohol to escape a living hell? How many people have turned to violence, unleashing those feelings of unfairness and lashing out at whoever is around? Although not healthy options, I understand what it is like to feel these things when you are experiencing things that are vastly unjust. After watching that movie, I felt a rage that reminded me of when I was in similar positions and even though I did not have my freedom taken away to that extent, I felt his pain and trauma as if I had. I remember walking through the grocery store after the movie wanting to knock everything over in rage. Of course, I did not do this, not wanting to end up on the news, but the feeling was there viscerally. This pain was familiar even if I did not recognize it having worked to a place of healing and peace regarding the incidents that happened to me. But it helped me to understand the need for vigilance in our healing process as things can trigger those old feelings and resurface traumas that haunted us previously. It took me months of reflection after watching the movie before I was able to make this connection to my own trauma. There was a part of me that still remembered that unfairness that I suffered, and even if I was not consciously aware in the moment, my body, brain, emotional makeup remembered. This helps me appreciate the need for healing to be an ongoing process, not a destination at which to arrive.

On a macro level, we watch this same type of trauma play out in our country at the beginning of 2021, with state governments working to alter voting laws to keep communities of color from exercising what is supposed to be a right of all citizens to vote. This action being taken after record numbers voted in the prior election. Despite the facts of the situation, in an effort to retain power, Republicans are changing the rules to disenfranchise voters, this time in more insidious ways. For those old enough to have lived through the era of blatant disenfranchisement, this is a recall of the trauma of old, and those not old enough to have lived through these times get to feel newly victimized. We must not allow ourselves to be consumed by the unfairness of situations where we do not feel capable of getting justice. I cannot presume to know the reasons why bad things happen to good people and people who seem to have such hatred in their hearts continue to thrive. This type of philosophical question has been pondered for centuries and likely will continue to be. In order to create a sense of peace and healing, I find it necessary to be clear about what I can control and let go of the things that I cannot control, trusting that my Creator has a plan for everything. I do not mean this in the sense of waiting for my piece of heaven, but rather from a position of trusting that as I keep planting seeds of goodness while simultaneously fighting for true freedom and justice, I can inspire change for myself, my family, my community and ultimately the world.

After being exonerated of the abuse of my daughter, I continued my path of trusting the process while working to stay in a positive space of forgiveness. Because I had now been separated from my young children for 6 months, again at no fault of mine, the court decided that it should remain this way until we finished the custody case scheduled for the following month. I could do nothing and had no recourse except to wait. Unfortunately, the court case was quite involved and subsequently took almost a year and a half to complete as there were delays and more time needed to get to all of the information. It seemed that every obstacle that could happen did and things would have to be rescheduled, which meant going for another 2 or 3 months later to fit everyone's schedule. Again during this time, I was not allowed to see my younger two children and no one seemed remotely concerned about this.

Throughout my court sagas, my lawyer wanted to be more aggressive in her representation of me. I was reticent to do this because there were things I was not willing to engage to "fight" in court. The court system by nature is adversarial and people fighting for custody tend to pull out all stops, going for the jugular to get the "win." I refused to allow my attorney to engage in this manner as although I and my ex-wives disagreed and they had done some things that were not in my best interest, from my vantage point, they were still the mothers of my children and I did not want anything but fairness and equal treatment. But not by any means, as this did not fit my value system, and although I wanted to "win" my ethics would not allow me to engage in a hostile manner. Everyone has to determine what that level is for them and stick to what they believe. Ultimately, the values we believe and the actions we engage have to be aligned.

I spent much of the time at our trials attempting to portray a positive attitude and at one point, my lawyer received feedback that I needed to appear more angry and emotional at the misrepresentations that were taking place. I understood the rationale behind this thinking, but in my mind, this belies the concept of justice, as I should not have to perform to achieve results. After a year and a half of various controversial testimony, my ex was granted custody and as it had been at this point almost two years since I saw my children, I was required to undergo an additional psychological evaluation in order to be reunited with my daughters. I spent over $30,000 fighting these battles at this point. I also simultaneously had the case with my older children scheduled to start immediately after this one with the same judge, and I was going to have to put my son on the stand to refute some of the lies that had been told. This was the moment I had to decide whether I was going to cut the baby in half. There is a parable in the Bible where two women claim to be the mother of a child and king Solomon must determine who is the actual mother. He suggests that he would cut the child in half so that they both can have a part of the child and one woman agrees. The other says no and relinquishes her claim so that the child can live. The king recognized that this was the true mother who would sacrifice her need to have the child so that the child could live. I was faced with asking myself did I love my children enough to let them go and remain whole or would I allow my ego to rip them apart. I pride myself on doing a lot of things well, but the best thing I do is parent, and with this decision, I was not going to be able to do what I love. It would take me many years before I could appreciate that by not pressing the issue and putting my children in more stressful situations, I actually was being the great father that I believe myself to be. My two older children were old enough that I could give them a choice about seeing me when they were so inclined. We had a conversation, and I explained the situation and let them know that whenever they wanted to interact with me, I would be there. With my two younger children, I was not going to compromise myself with this evaluation, yet again trying to prove to someone that I was innocent and deserved to be able to parent my children, who never should have been taken away from me to begin with. Additionally, there was nothing put into place that could prevent more explosive situations from happening with their mother and I no longer had the energy or desire to bring any more pain to anyone. So I gave up the fight and began the process of waiting. It took four years before my older two children came back into my life, and that has ultimately evolved into an incredibly wonderful story. As an example of how coincidental or not life is, at one point during that four year period where I did not see or talk to them, one Saturday afternoon I had a friend in town visiting and we decided to go to a movie quite spontaneously. We quickly scanned the movie theaters to see which place we would go for the movie that we wanted to see. When we found the theater, we realized that we would have to hurry to get there in time before the movie started. We rushed to the theater, paid for our tickets, entered to look for seating and the movie was completely packed. We had to walk all the way to the top of the theater where there seemed to be the last three seats. As I sat down, who would be sitting right next to me but my son on a date with his friend and her mom. Awkward. I could not believe that this was happening as the timing had to be completely impeccable for this to happen. And yet, it was not surprising as things like this have occurred often over the course of my life. I've come to think of these events, particularly during difficult times, as God's way of throwing me a life preserve and letting me know that everything is in order and to continue being patient and walking my path.

Another such incident occurred with my second daughter who had been used by my second wife to bring about the fabricated sexual abuse charges. It was July 26, 2015, my daughter's birthday. I will always remember this day for so many reasons. I was attending my annual conference with the Association of Black Psychologists, which this particular year was in Las Vegas, Nevada. I was rooming with my colleague from Graduate School and received a call that morning from a number that I did not recognize. The area code was a number from a friend who had left some things in our room the night before and I thought that she might have been calling to come and retrieve them. However, as I answered and the voice began talking, I soon realized that it was my ex-wife. She informed me that it was my daughter's birthday which I knew, and she felt that since she was now 10 years old, that she was now mature enough to have a conversation with me. I was also shocked because if I were the person that believed that someone had sexually abused my child, I would never want them to talk to him/her, certainly not at that age. She gave me a brief update on how well my daughter had been doing and then said she would put her on the phone. As I spoke with my daughter and she overcame her brief shock that it was actually me on the phone, she began telling me about her life. I was so caught off guard that I was really in a state of shock. I did not know how to respond or what to say as I had no preparation and no sense that this would even be happening. It had been over seven years at this point and I had resigned myself to not hearing from them until they were adults. We finished the conversation so that she could get ready for her party and I asked her to call me anytime as I would love to continue talking to her. Unfortunately, there have not been any other times that I have been able to talk to her since that time, but I remain hopeful that just like my older children, the younger two will return to my life at some point. Although this can be perceived as a sad situation and was once quite traumatic for me, I share this story so that we can appreciate the depths of experiences that we might have that make us who we are. Often when I share this story with others, the initial response is one that elicits sorrow or pity for my disconnect from my children. However, when I hear this, I immediately respond affirmatively from my current healthy position and I do not allow anyone to interact with me from the standpoint of pity. I believe that my experiences, our experiences, are purposeful. Although I do not fully understand the purpose, I embrace and accept the traumatic situations that have become a part of my reality. And the reality is that I have been able to help many people manage their emotions and make decisions in situations regarding custody or being separated from their children, and others have been able to have a better, healthier outcome because of what I have had to experience. The reach of my experience extends even beyond me as one of my friends shared with me some time ago how watching me go through my experiences and seeing the manner in which I have handled them has allowed her to help people that she knows with their similar experiences. For me, that means that there is a greater purpose for some of the things that happen to us in life, and it is important that as traumatic as these situations have been for me, I needed to do the work to heal from them and turn them into a strength rather than allowing these experiences to be something that keeps me constantly debilitated.

In February 2016, I received the strangest phone call, seemingly out of the blue. The cousin of my second ex-wife called my psychology practice in an attempt to find me. My mother was visiting from Miami and answered the call as she was at the desk in my practice. She gave me the message and

Individual Trauma

I ignored it initially as I had no idea why she would be calling me. She called again the next day and left another message stating that it was urgent, so I decided to call her back, thinking something had possibly happened to my daughters. When we finally spoke, she relayed to me her concern for my daughters and the erratic behavior of her cousin. I listened to what she had to tell me and could not believe that this was actually happening. She validated many of the concerns that I had that pushed me to engage in the custody battle to begin with. I wondered where she was during the trial. The trauma that I had already been working to heal that had resurfaced back in July was coming back again. Recognizing the pattern and focusing on what I could control, I just listened and responded that I could not do anything about the situation. And what I could control was not reengaging trauma and making a decision to keep myself healthy, lessons it had taken me years to incorporate into the fabric of my life. But lessons that I still needed to refine as evidenced by my next chapter in life.

ACT III

The end of my second relationship brought about the need to do another level of intensive work on myself. To really evolve and heal myself of the various traumas that I had encountered up to this point. In an interesting twist, my ex suggested a book to me on her way out of the relationship, Emotional Wellness[26] that proved to be instrumental in my next growth spurt to healing. I reengaged the process of doing the intense work in the manner that I had done this previously, following the dissolution of my first marriage, and began seeing results in a similar trajectory. The interesting thing that I was observing about myself is that I was finally able to begin really tapping into the emotional components of who I am and also understanding how I came to be this way. Adding to this growth in awareness was a conversation that I had with my mother as our family gathered for the Thanksgiving holiday in Florida. I had all four of my children that holiday, my youngest being four months at the time, and we made the trip to Florida to be with family. My mood was not the best as I contemplated the next phase of our lives. During this time, noticing my mood, my mother decided to share with me the story of my birth and the circumstances surrounding what was happening with her during that time. I found this story to be fascinating and could not believe that I had not heard this information before, information that shined a bright light on my understanding of myself. As it was, she had endured her own traumas, which impacted the woman she became and the manner in which she lived her life.

---

26   Osho 2007 Emotional Wellness Harmony Books

Individual Trauma

My mother gave birth to me at the age of 17. She described herself as a shy teen at that time, finally reaching a point where she was coming into her own and beginning to branch out in high school, having just made the majorette squad. She grew up the oldest of seven and was the de facto mother in the household as her mother and grandmother, the providers of the family, were out working. Like many teenagers in African American households during that time, she became responsible for managing the household at a very young age. My father was in the military and as he likes to say took my mother away from another knucklehead in the neighborhood while home visiting. I was the result of their "interactions" and there was a lot of trepidation about bringing me into the world at such a young age. They eventually got married a few months before my birth and my father continued his deployment in California. After I was born, my mother describes her life as being extremely difficult as her mother and grandmother were quite hard on her, and at every opportunity, they point out to her the need to be responsible because her "mistake." Approximately six months after my birth, she describes being put on a plane from Miami to California to join her husband. This was her first trip anywhere and what could have been an exciting time was one filled with a lot of trepidation. What she described next really got my attention. She stated that as she got off the plane and met my dad, she practically threw me to him and from that point, did not utter a word for approximately two months. She noted that she would do all of the things that were necessary to care for me but just did not have anything to say. Of course, I recognized immediately that she was suffering from depression but of course, in 1970, Black women were not allowed to be depressed. She had to suck it up and keep moving as if everything were fine and normal. But it really made me think about the impact that her depression had on me as a growing toddler moving around and trying to engage with the world. What impact does her mental wellness have on an infant who is not being nurtured emotionally? We learn culturally to just deal with it, suck it up, and there is no room for "weakness." She was a teenager, suddenly on the other side of the country 3000 miles away from everything she ever knew. She was a young parent and a young wife trying to figure out her rapidly changed life. As I reflected on this, in addition to looking at the disciplined manner in which my parents engaged the process of raising their children, I wondered how this impacted my own emotional development and ability to tap into my feelings. My mother was not the most nurturing and touchy-feely person, but what had she experienced that produced these circumstances in her? Processing this was not an act of blame but rather an effort to better understand how I became the person I am and subsequently understanding the impact this eventually had on my own interpersonal relationships. I finally felt like I had a window of clarity about the person that I had come to be. This was an incredible gift that my mother knowing or unknowingly offered me and one I wish more parents were able to do. I think parents resist having their children know any of their traumas and hardships in an effort to shield them from the negative and as a means of protecting themselves from looking weak or stupid or (insert several words here). But the reality is that none of these things is true. In fact, what parents do is present a patently false image of themselves that their children will ultimately be able to see through anyway. This lack of emotional honesty does not allow for healing for the child or the parents, instead of leading to continued episodic repeating of negative behaviors.

The information my mother shared clearly helped me understand myself better and connect to some of the attributes that I possess that have been challenging for me in relationships. It also shined a light on the concept of generational trauma, as I could also infer from the manner in which my grandmother and great grandmother lived their lives that they dealt with traumatic situations that impacted them, and some of this energy was passed to each respective generation. I would eventually recognize that my growth process, though productive and very necessary, took me from one extreme to the other, causing a different set of challenges and in retrospect, opportunities for learning and growth. Where I had previously been a master grudge holder who could likely outlast anyone in this regard, I was now moving to do the work to move to a place of getting over things quickly in an effort to fully engage life. I was now better in tune with my emotions and willing to truly be vulnerable in a relationship, letting down the walls of protection that I had built to protect my insecurities.

One of the things that helped my process involved a book on forgiveness that I began working with that helped me process and allow myself to let go of the residual pain and anger I had been storing over the years[27]. The feelings that result from the unfairness of the way some of the aspects of my life had turned out needed to be released. I could not keep crying about life not being nice to me. Instead of why me, I began to accept why not me. In essence, I stopped fighting the wave and instead chose to ride the wave, which eventually took me to happiness. The process of engaging this deep level of work assisted me in letting a lot of my negative emotions go and moving more to a deeper place of self-love, another area that needed healing. It was at this point that my heart yearned for love and the opportunity to engage in a healthy relationship. So life obliged me.

Like the beginning of this country, this third marriage was started on a foundation of lies. From the initial

---

27   Paul Ferrini, 2012, The Twelve Steps of Forgiveness: A Practical manual For Moving from fear to love.

conversation through the ending of the relationship, lies and misdirection ran rampant. It would later be revealed to me in ways mysterious and yet not so mysterious, happenstance and then by design, each lie would unravel and leave her striking out rather than admitting her wrongs. Much like those early heartless founders of this country, she doubled down in her justifications, refusing to be held accountable for the atrocities that she caused. Unlike my first two wives, who were not initially out to cause me any harm, this woman was conniving and saw me as a means to an end. The saying "believe people when they tell you or show you who they are" applies in this case. It is important to point out what may be obvious to some that we cannot change people. It is important to listen closely to what is shared and listen for what is not shared as well. To observe and pay attention to what the actions mean. Things I did not do this time.

We met online through the Black People Meet website, which I happened upon one lonely Friday night. Bored, I decided to make a profile for myself, signing up for one month of services to see what would happen. After two weeks, I decided I had enough and it was not for me, so I had planned to let the rest of the month lapse. I then got an email from this woman requesting to connect. She was from Georgia and I had set my limits locally, so I wondered why I would have a long-distance connection. After looking at her profile, it seemed promising, so we began writing back and forth and she spoke my language of healing and transformation. I sent her the words to a poem from the book The Invitation and she was able to converse with me about this in a manner that made me want to talk with her. Our first conversation lasted for hours and was quite lively. Two important points from that conversation. One, she asked me how long I had been on the website and I told her what I stated previously. She then replied that she had just gotten onto the website herself the prior week and she was so technologically challenged that her sister had to create her profile. More on this later. Two, she asked me if I drank alcohol and when I stated that I had never had any alcohol, she stated that she had not either. I found this odd as I tend to stand out in this regard and had met few people that had abstained from alcohol their entire life. However, I had no reason to doubt the veracity of her statement so I kept it moving. I would later find out in very unassuming ways that both of these statements were fabrications. The puzzling part to me was why she would make these assertions to begin with. Who cares how long you have been on the website? Even if you were trying to impress me, it was so nominal as to not matter. Two, most adults drink and my friends and former spouses did. I have always been able to be around people who drink and smoke and not feel any pressure to engage myself. I have no judgement about what others choose to do. I just made a choice for myself that I did not want to indulge in these things, so why make a big deal about it? A person interested in manipulation would engage in this way.

Have you ever been in a rollercoaster relationship? A relationship that is back and forth, up and down. A relationship that when it is good, it is very good and when it is bad, it is very bad. A make up to break up relationship. Cue the Stylistics. This is what this relationship was about, one that went from one extreme to the other. The relationship progressed at a rapid pace and we quickly moved into a pattern of talking daily. Our conversations were always lively and entertaining. She had been through a lot of adversity, as had I and we discussed these things and our approaches to moving through them. I was looking for the red flags throughout, though, particularly given the previous situations. I promise you I was looking for the red flags. I thought I had finally found one a few weeks in when she said to me that I was the most important thing in her life. I was immediately wary of this statement as to how could I be the most important person in your life and we just met and you have four daughters whom I would think are much important than me. I did not bring this up at the moment but thought about it for a couple of days, considering how I would frame the question. When I asked her about it a few days later, she promptly responded that I had to be the most important thing because she recognized that her daughters needed a man in their lives for completion and to model a healthy relationship given that their respective fathers were not present. She alluded to other things along this line of thinking, and not yet appreciating her gift and charisma for verbal charming and the manipulative qualities she had developed, I relaxed and accepted her explanation. Ultimately, I could also refer back to myself being in what I thought was a good place as I had done so much work on myself from the first two marriages that I simultaneously refused to believe that I was doing anything wrong. I was in the process of constant self-reflection, and also questioned myself tirelessly. I was allowing myself to be vulnerable and trusting the process.

The relationship moved forward and we eventually got engaged. When we got engaged, she called her mother to share the news. Her mother was less than enthused about this and this struck me as odd. She explained that her family did not support her and often looked down on her thinking as she would go against the grain and engage in thinking outside the box. In fact, I would later learn that it was more that they had witnessed the shenanigans many times before and were unwilling to cosign her inappropriate behaviors. Eventually, I would receive support from members of her family that ultimately saved my life—not being hyperbolic here at all.

Nearly a year later, we got married and ended up moving her and her daughters to North Carolina. We had talked extensively about our lives and I had told her extensively what had happened to me in my previous relationships. She was particularly enamored by my 90 days of prayer and decided that it would be a great idea to have as a theme for our wedding 90 days of forgiveness. We would ask those who came to support the wedding in lieu of gifts to embark upon a process of 90 days of forgiveness with us. The concept in and of itself was a noble one. I having had the prior experience, recognized that creating this type of energy produced a dynamic that would likely bring situations that we would have to employ the very thing we were talking about. I warned her about this, but she persisted and this still ended up as our theme. Although many people were inspired by the concept and discussed the inspiration they took from engaging the process, I remained wary of what was to come. Surely things could not get any more outlandish than what I had already experienced. My life was full of these unbelievable events, things that I would find difficult to believe if I were not living them, but I had to have reached an apex right? After all, I did a lot of serious work to get to a healthier place. The sun smiled at my naivete.

Initially, things were good as we attempted to parent and find a workable flow. When they lived in Georgia, her best friend had served as her nanny and she wanted to bring her to North Carolina. I was quite hesitant about this arrangement and did not feel that we had a need for a nanny, particularly given the ages of the children. Yet as I often did in this relationship, I ultimately relented to avoid any conflict. The nanny moved in with us as we moved to a new home and our first major conflict occurred within months.

At the time, my older two children were visiting several evenings for dinner. This particular evening I was working with all the children, my older two and her younger two, on their homework and the nanny asked me when we would be finished as she had a schedule she wanted to adhere to for having the 6 year old ready for bed by 7pm. We had done fine without this previously and as I was working with her on her homework indicated to her that it would be when the homework was finished. A few minutes later, she returned and stated that she needed to take her now. I said no, I am working with her and she should wait until we get finished. She came down the stairs and attempted to push me out of the way to grab the child. This caused the child to start crying loudly and the other children to be alarmed. She squared up as if she were going to fight me and my ex had to come out to diffuse the situation. I could not believe that this woman, who was the nanny, was challenging me in my house about my children. What kind of craziness was this? My wife tried to remain neutral about this incident, even as I reminded her of my prior hesitations. We somehow got through the situation with the nanny apologizing and assuring us that this would not happen again. But we had caused trauma for everyone involved as a simple disagreement mushroomed into something much larger. This was only the beginning.

In our next major incident, we had travelled to her hometown in Georgia for the weekend where we were going to meet with her friend who she had done business with before. We were considering opening a practice in Georgia, and this woman would be able to help us with getting it started. I had never met her before, and we decided to meet for dinner. My wife's sister also joined us. As we sat at dinner, her friend began reminiscing and telling old stories. She asked my wife if she remembered when they had gotten so drunk that my wife could not stand up straight and ended up having a hangover the next day with an intense headache. This was a curious statement to me as I remembered that she had told me that she never drank before. I made a mental note as of course, I was not going to say anything there and eventually got up to use the bathroom. My wife followed me outside and began to vehemently deny what the woman had stated and provided me with numerous reasons why she was lying. I could not understand why we were having this conversation at that point and also why this woman would make something up with no motivation for doing so. After an extended time of trying to convince me to no avail, we went back inside to finish dinner. Later that evening after, we arrived home, she attempted to continue the conversation. I would not accept her explanations as truth and she became frustrated being caught in a lie. Her frustration caused her to lash out and assault me physically several times. I did not respond and chose to just leave the room and go to another area to sleep. Reflecting back on this later, I realized that although I still found myself in a situation full of conflict, I did not respond in a manner that would have escalated it and potentially could have caused even more problems as had occurred with my previous relationship. There was a protective measure in place in that her cousin was also staying at the house that night and was there in the next room. She later told me that she heard the altercation, and this behavior was reminiscent of previous behavior she had witnessed her cousin engage in her prior marriages. The next day, I attempted to talk with my wife's grandmother to get an impartial voice of reason to help her get over her anger. This seemed to be helpful as we were able to smooth things over and move the pendulum of the relationship back to the happy side. But more altercations were to come, and I was not yet able to fully appreciate the impact these violent situations were having on me and everyone involved, wanting to focus instead on those times that were good.

One of the skills that this wife possessed was an ability to think about and manage finances in a creative manner that allowed for growth. This was good for me as the business side of things was not my strength as I preferred to focus on doing the work. The downside of her skills in this area is that she was consumed with money and was willing to step on others to acquire what she wanted. This was couched under a veil of giving where she used her charisma to be convincing to others. After the next incident, her sister shared with me that her sister would interact with people she was in a relationship with in superficial ways that made it seem as if she were all about them. She liked the books and concepts that I championed and spent a lot of time reading them and discussing the concepts. The application of the concepts was the issue, though as she was able to point out all the flaws of others without looking at herself. Anyone who tried to raise the mirror for her was not received well. As I think about it, this was probably the core issue for most of our disagreements as I could not unsee what I observed and would point these discrepancies out. I had committed to doing the work of being accountable and positioned myself to recognize the alignment of actions and values, and in this case, the actions and values were not aligned.

We had saved a significant amount of money that we kept in the home, and the rule was that this money was not to be utilized except for emergencies. However, this particular day she was violating this rule to do something to curry favor with her eldest adult daughter and I did not agree with this as it was nothing necessary and not what the money should be utilized for based on the rules she had been instrumental in establishing. Later that night, I went to look in the portable safe to see what had been taken out and she did not want me to go into the safe. She attempted to take it out of my hands and yelled upstairs for her nanny to come help her. The nanny and the girls came and began attacking me and trying to take the safe from me. The nanny took a broom handle and was prepared to wrap it around my head from behind and choke me while the daughters and my wife pummeled me relentlessly, scratching me and hitting me with no retaliation from me. Finally, the sister of my wife, who had recently moved up from Georgia and was living with us, came downstairs and threatened to call the police. They let me go at the command of my wife and I left the house with the safe. I called a friend to pick me up and spent the night at his house. The next day I got an apartment and moved out and my wife's mother talked to me and told me to take her other daughter with me as she could not believe they had done this to me. My wife's sister and I both moved out the next day into an apartment. That same weekend, another cousin and her husband were coming to town to attend a Jay Z concert the same evening that I moved out. I had secured tickets for us all to go previously. I assumed it would just be the three of us after this major confrontation, but my ex hopped in the car as we were leaving and invited herself along. This was unbelievable that she would have the gall to go along after such a huge confrontation, but this is what happened. Why did I stay in such a horrific situation? I have asked this question on loop for years and ultimately, through many therapy sessions and self-reflection determined that I was operating from a lack of self-love. You see, anyone that fully loves and respects themselves would never allow themselves to be treated in a manner that is riddled with disrespect. I had gone from one extreme to another in doing the work to tap into my emotions and this left me in a space where I would allow myself to be taken advantage of. Eventually, I would have to figure out the need for balance and make this one of the foundational cornerstones for how I live my life. But it would be a while yet before this happened.

My wife and I had made arrangement to travel to Senegal and Ghana three weeks from the time of the incident. Not wanting to miss this trip, she apologized to me and had her daughters and nanny apologize as well and agreed to have the nanny move out of the house and into the apartment I had rented. Yet again, we were making up to break up. At the time, I thought this to be a breakthrough as she had relented on something she previously would not, having the nanny leave as I had made it clear I would not have her in my home anymore. But ultimately, this was another part of the manipulation that would play out in the next few months. It did not take long as even while we were in Senegal, we encountered problems as she accused me of sleeping with her sister, who had moved into the apartment with me. It seemed to be lost on her that her mother was the one who suggested this to begin with after their attack on me and she was now unwilling to take responsibility for her actions. While in Senegal, we met a young man from the states who was there doing a writing workshop with the author we were visiting, and we became friends with him. At one point during our time there, he noticed the tension and my wife always eager to talk and attempt to get people on her side shared her story with him about our difficulties. Although he was younger than us, he was quite astute and after listening to some of her comments, made her stop and reflect on the things that she was saying and the problems laced in her positions. He was the first person that I can remember not falling for her charismatic attempts at manipulation and calling her out on this in a way that she could not avoid. This produced a lot of emotion from her and again, I thought we had made some progress.

When we returned from Ghana and having seen some positivity, we decided to try going to therapy. I was not convinced that this would work given what I had observed about her love for talking about concepts rather than engaging in them, and I honestly did not believe that she was being sincere, but I agreed to give it a try. The therapist was quite good and asked that we trust the process, so I did. One of the first things he had me do, to which I thought he was out of his mind, was to instruct me to have a conversation with the daughters and in this conversation, I was to listen and not respond at all. They would have an opportunity to express themselves and any frustrations they had and I could not explain or react in any way. This was a challenging task, but I completed it, despite feeling that there were many inaccuracies in what they shared that I could not address. Each session, he would give us homework that she seemed eager about in the discussion of therapy but would always have a reason why she did not complete it. Because the attention was placed on me initially, this seemed to appease her and allowed her to believe that the major issue was with me. However, as I trusted the therapist and the process, he eventually moved to challenge her on her stuff. This was not what she expected and having been caught in an area that she was accustomed to working around, she decided she did not want to be in the relationship anymore. That was fine with me as I did not think she was really willing to do the work and I was tired of the hypocrisy.

She began making plans to move back to Georgia and I resigned myself to yet another failed marriage. In the process of deciding what she was going to take back with her, she began parceling off the things that she was going to take, some of which were mine prior to her even meeting me. This was not surprising but again, I did not want to fight in a breakup and figured that I could always build myself up again. I think this theme of lessening myself or making myself small is something that I've had to struggle with throughout my life. There are some things that just are not important to me and I work to put a lot of effort into walking with humility to keep ego out of the equation, or at the very least minimizing ego. Again though, balance is an important lesson for me, and this last relationship was ultimately about finding and understanding balance and then maintaining balance. Because I was not looking out for myself in this regard, I think that God, my ancestors, and all the benevolent energies that surround me decided that they would intervene and give me a push in the direction of moving back towards balance. No one is meant to be a doormat walked on and treated recklessly. But we have to demand respect for ourselves or no one will give it to us. Similarly, we have to love ourselves fully or no one can truly love us. When we walk with an uncompromising love for ourselves, then by definition, it is impossible for anyone to maintain a place in your life when they are disrespecting you. The two cannot occupy the same space. This was a lesson that I was in the process of learning and one that has proved most valuable.

My wife had a truck that was in her mothers' name, an SUV that was hers. I had recently purchased an SUV myself after having my SUV repossessed in a judgment that was placed against me—another long story beyond this book that is equally unbelievable and unfair. Because I had this outstanding judgment we decided to put the SUV in her name so that that car could not have a lien placed against it and potentially suffer a similar fate as my previous truck. I paid for the car in cash, and we initially considered putting both of our names on the title, but she convinced me that it would be better to just put her name on the title. In retrospect, I realize she was already planning for her leaving the relationship. I ignored that nagging twitch in the back of my mind warning me not to do this and agreed with her despite at this point having observed the way that she had operated when it came to a number of other things that were not fair. We were at a good spot at that time, and I did not want to do anything to rock the boat. How many times do we stay or ignore the bad for a temporary reprieve of good that gives us a false sense of hope that things are improving? In addition to all of the things she was going to take, she somehow came to the conclusion that she should be able to take both of the vehicles because her nanny would need the other vehicle to transport her children while she used her vehicle to do whatever it was she was going to be doing. I could not for the life of me believe the logic of thinking that it would be fine for me to be without a vehicle and she has two vehicles, particularly since I paid cash for the vehicle and it was mine, purchased for me, and only in her name because of the aforementioned reasons. This was the height of her selfishness, and although I had been willing to allow her to have everything else, this selfishness proved to be the proverbial straw that broke the camel's back.

The morning of the final incident, I got ready for work and when I went out to the car with her cousin, who had just moved up to live with us, she raced out to jump in the car as well. Yes, we had a lot of different people living with us at various times and it was not a big deal to me as our house was more than large enough to accommodate everyone comfortably. Reflecting on it later though, I realized it was just too many energies in one space and although trying to help others, it may have been a detriment. At any rate, as I was driving the vehicle, my wife came to my office to have another conversation about taking the vehicle. I maintained my position that this made no sense and I would not be giving her the vehicle. When we arrived at my office, she eventually called the police to come out to my practice and they informed her that as we were married, we both had rights to the vehicle and there was nothing that they could do to make me turn the vehicle over to her. A colleague and friend who was quite aware of all of the drama that had been going on in the relationship attempted to reason with her about the matter and get her to see where she was being unreasonable. He talked to her for over an hour about this and she refused to budge her position. Her cousin who incidentally was the one who had previously witnessed her physical attack on me told me that she had seen this behavior before, and knew that my wife was not going to let it go. My wife soon decided to contact a tow company to have the car towed to the dealer to get a new key made for the car so that she could take it that way.

It was an extremely hot summer day and she had called her nanny and daughters to come to the practice so they could sit with her in her truck while waiting for the person to come make the key. I did not realize this at the time and at some point, I went out to go have lunch. When I got in the car, she opened the passenger side door and refused to move. Her nanny and daughters were parked right next to the car and I asked her to close the door so I could go and get lunch. She refused to move and continued arguing with me about the need for her to have control of the car. I began to slowly back up to get her to move and she started screaming that I was attempting to run her over. Her daughters jumped into the back seat and grabbed me by the neck while the nanny came to my driver side window, punching me and attempting to pull me out of the car. I was being attacked by four people again and could not fight back. My wife managed to get the key during all of this and they left me alone after she had achieved this. They had broken my glasses, having knocked them off my face, in addition to scratching up my neck and face. Camel's back broken. Enraged that I could do nothing to fight back, I broke the gear shaft of the SUV in anger and frustration. I had been pushed to the limit of abuse that I could take and was tired of taking the high road and receiving the short end of the stick. As I got out of the car and started walking back to my office, her eldest daughter had gone into her car and pulled out a 2 by 4 piece of wood and came over and hit me on the back with it twice. I did not respond. My wife's cousin had come out of the office and observed the entire episode and fortunately for me, she was there because

Individual Trauma

otherwise, I would have been lied on once again and likely arrested. The cops arrived on the scene, one of which was the same one from that morning, and her nanny had driven off with her daughters. My wife attempted to control the situation and talk to the police officers first and begin telling a distorted version of the story. I was amazingly calm during this time and waited for her to finish and for the officer to then come talk to me. I explained to the officer my side of the story and told him he could ask her cousin what happened. I said to the police officer yet again as I had in the altercation with my second wife, I am a psychologist and we are in the parking lot of my practice. I help people sort out their issues and here I am out here totally exposed with my own serious issues. I had clients that I had to cancel that day due to the hours it took to resolve the drama. I had to explain why I had all these police officers in my office and several people were getting arrested.

Her cousin had said to me that she was not going to allow them to railroad me and lie about what had occurred. She had been in the next room the previous time that I was attacked physically. With the cousin of my wife giving the correct version of the story, in addition to her nanny having fled the scene with her daughters, in addition to me having scratches from then attacking me, a scenario was created where it became obvious who the perpetrators were and who the victim was in this situation. The police officer arrested my ex, her nanny and daughters, who by then had returned to the scene after the officers went to pick them up.

An unintended consequence of this incident was that I was now given complete control of the house, and as I had an order in place now, she could not return until the court matters were resolved. She was only allowed to get her clothes, and then accompanied by a sheriff. So in a matter of hours, she went from taking everything in the household to not being able to access anything to move back to Georgia. I was not even concerned about the material possessions in the house and now I had complete control of everything. Despite this, she still managed to have her people break into the house several weeks later while we were at court and take some things, but she did not get all that she wanted. When talking about this incident, I refer to it as my "Braveheart" moment. I was trying to peacefully leave the situation, again not wanting to have a disastrous end to another relationship. I ended up being pushed out of my complacency and finally truly standing up for myself. I pressed charges on all of them except for the youngest daughter, as I still managed to have compassion as she was only 16. She ended up assisting the people who her mother had come to break into the house while we were in court for this matter several weeks later. She was that bold and audacious that she would think up a way to violate the court order and have the house broken into and load up a truck to take what they could back to Georgia. My wife and her nanny had followed me from the court house that day, and I did not understand why, but soon realized as I happened to go to the house that they were engaged in this scheme. The sheriff came to investigate and it was clear to them who broke in as the neighbor saw the daughter and they also took the dogs and placed the inoperable car on a dolly to be transported. Because it was clear to the sheriff what had occurred, he never took any fingerprints. They were able to go to court and lie about any involvement or knowledge of the matter and never received any consequences for this violation.

 Even with all the trauma that I suffered through in this relationship, I was fortunate that for the major events that could have jeopardized my career or even my life, a family member of my wife was there to witness what occurred and thus served as a protective barrier to anything worse happening. Had they not been there, the situations certainly would have had a disastrous outcome for me. For this reason, I have to believe that these incidents were purposeful and indeed, as I have shared them with people who have been able to help others in their various situations.

An important lesson for me from this final incident was one of balance. I had done a lot of work to stay humble and stay in a place of forgiveness, thinking that this was the best way to be. Indeed these are qualities that one should aspire to. One must also recognize that the world operates on a universal law of balance. Extremes on any continuum are generally not good. Furthermore, we could not understand a concept without the understanding of its opposite. What is good if there is no bad? What is love if there is no hate? What is aggression if there is not passivity? We may have strengths in one domain that serve us in a given situation but there are other times where the strength can become a weakness if we do not understand how to mute it when necessary. I was operating at an extreme that allowed me to be taken advantage of and hurt. I have to emphasize that no one did this to me. I made choices that led to me being disrespected and taken advantage of and a first important step for healing was for me to be accountable to that. Indeed there are situations where things can happen beyond our control, such as the previously mentioned example of being falsely and improperly arrested. But in dealing with the things that we control, we have to own up to our choices that create the situations that impact us in unhealthy ways. It was up to me to learn the lesson of balance and respect for myself that would not allow mistreatment. Furthermore, sometimes fighting and defending oneself is quite necessary and in our best interest. I had to accept that I allowed myself to be disrespected and again, I would submit that any person that truly loves and values themselves would never allow another to disrespect them or treat them in a manner that is anything less than positive. Period. There is never an excuse or reason to explain it away. You cannot love someone else more than you love yourself. The legacies of trauma are what create this unhealthy pattern of thinking, and we see this dynamic unfold in all types of abusive situations.

In this convergence of trauma, my older two children were witness to the first altercation that occurred over homework along with her four children. In the other altercations, her four children were witness to the domestic violence. This does not include the many instances of verbal arguments and obvious tension between us that the children witnessed. How were they impacted by what they observed? Do they carry these remembrances forward and will they present issues in their own relationships? What could I have done differently to prevent any of this trauma and why did I not make those choices? Some of these questions, which I have turned over in my mind repeatedly and engaged in the process of therapy have been answered and others have found some degree of answering. It is these and more questions that we as parents should consider as we provide a model that will impact and influence the behavior of our children and undoes the legacy of multigenerational trauma. I must say that each of my wives has had an impact on the man I am today, and despite the trauma and the drama, I embrace all of the experiences and the lessons that come from them. I can no more eliminate those aspects of my life than a tree could not eliminate its trunk. These experiences are a part of me and my growth; this is true, but they do not define who I am and who I will continue to become. We are all engaging in the behaviors we engage in for reasons related to how we have been socialized and trained to understand the world. If we are to move to a place of healing, it will involve eliminating the old negative and traumatic patterns and replacing them with newer, healthier modes of being. This most important aspect of the book will be the focus of part three of the book.

CHAPTER 12

SOCIETAL TRAUMA

In 1991 George Holiday on the balcony of his apartment used his camcorder to make a video of police traffic stop that he had observed. He could not have imagined that this video of Rodney King being beaten by police officers would become a seminal moment in history. This video would change and impact race relations and our understanding of police. The historical impact of the treatment of the African American community by the police would have a monumental impact on the direction of this country. Up until that time, people in the African American community knew and understood that violence by the police happened regularly. At the same time, most white people had no sense of the violence, and in fact, thought that much of what they might hear regarding police violence was absurd. This video was irrefutable evidence that these things did take place. Despite this video evidence, the officers were ultimately acquitted, which resulted in days of uprisings and millions of dollars of damages as a result. But the can had been opened, the veil had been lifted and we would not as a country be able to go back to pretending that nothing was happening. I do not believe it would be an exaggeration to suggest that this video clip has been watched millions of times since it was first aired. It was the lead story at a time when the news was not as prevalent and instantaneous as it is now. It was all anyone could talk about for quite some time. Of course, there was a lot of outrage amongst many people in the African American community and a lot of protesting and discussion about the inappropriateness of the actions was taking place. Lost amidst all of this was the impact that continued observation of this traumatic experience was having on the psyches of many members of the African American community. For myself, each one of those blows could be felt personally as if I were the one receiving the blows of the batons. As if I were the one that was teased and kicked. Watching this trauma play out only continued to cause difficulty for my overall mental health, even as I was not fully aware of it at the time.

Since that time, there have been a proliferation of videotaped incidents of people from the African American community being harassed, abused and murdered by police. This has included young children. Janelle Monet, an artist, fed up with the lack of concern and respect for those in our community created a song emphasizing the names of some of those that were taken away as a result of the callous indifference of a police force that did not see them as human. Many of these individuals would not have been able to have any semblance of justice without the eyewitness account provided by video. We know the names and say them in an attempt to keep their spirits alive and continue the fight for justice. Yet even as we say the names, we are also reminded of the trauma associated with why we have to say the names. Sandra Bland, Trayvon Martin, Freddie Gray Jr., Alton Sterling, Atatiana Jefferson, Laquan McDonald, Tamir Rice, Botham Jean, Oscar Grant, Terrence Crutcher, Michael Brown, Philando Castile, Walter Scott,

Societal Trauma

George Floyd, Breonna Taylor, and Daunte Wright are just a few of the many.

The proliferation of eyewitness videos have evolved in large part with the evolution of cell phones. I consider these instruments to be a blessing and a curse. A blessing in that anyone can document injustice at a moment's notice, and there have been a plethora of such videos documenting injustice. A curse in that there are many videos out there showing these injustices, serving as visual reminders that these types of incidents are subject to occur to any one of us at any moment. Watching these videos sends a message to our subconscious, conveying the status of things and the unlikeliness that they will be changing. The videos send a subliminal message of inferiority and unfairness that become default mental chatter, reminding us to keep our hands in our pockets while walking through stores, speak in a way that is non-threatening to diffuse situations or be overly polite and non-threatening (whatever that means) when in an interaction with the police. The videos are so prevalent in our current culture that perpetrators have been given names like Karen and this has come to be understood as someone who is being nosy know it all and intervening in an area they should stay away from, as their assumptions are often incorrect.

In 2015, I was on my way to Chicago, incidentally after attending a Black Alumni reunion at the University of Notre Dame. There was a house music party I wanted to attend with several friends and one of the more renowned Chicago DJs would be playing the set. I left a bit later from South Bend than I intended to, and as such, was driving above the speed limit in an attempt to get to Chicago to catch the party. Of course, I was not paying attention and drove past a police officer who crossed the median and pulled me over. As he prepared to approach my car, several thoughts went through my brain. Get your paperwork out of the glove compartment.

Then no don't do that because he might think you are trying to get a gun. Well, you already bent over, so he still might be suspicious. Ok put your hands on the steering wheel. No put your hands outside the window so that he can see them. This is what I ended up doing. As he approached the car, he looked in with a quizzical look on his face as if to question why I had my hands outside the window. I shrugged as if to say, "I don't know man, I just want to live." He appeared embarrassed by this and collected my paperwork and went back to his car. When he checked everything out and came back up, he informed me that even though I was speeding, he was only going to give me a warning. I don't know this for sure, but based on the interaction and the manner in which he handled it, I think he was embarrassed that I would feel the need to put my hands outside my window to ensure that I do not die. This is the unfortunate reality of being an African American man in this country. The actions I engaged in are the result of internalized trauma. Watching so many people who look like me being gunned down when clearly a white person in the same situation would not have suffered the same fate. This is not debatable at this point, despite the efforts of some to do so. Whenever I have occasion to talk with white people about my encounters with the police, they find it so unbelievable, and yet they have to believe it because they are having the conversation with me and trust what I am saying. Because they know that I am a psychologist, this allows me to have credibility and they have to accept what I say as truth. But why do I need to have a degree to be validated? It is a given for most African Americans that harassment by the police is a part of life. I have observed people curtail what are normal human behaviors out of fear that something could happen to them. This trauma has people unwilling to jog in their own neighborhoods or having a high level of fear at the sight of a police officer.

Societal Trauma

The collective trauma compounded over the years creates a sense of survival that pushes this response to avoid situations that could potentially cause problems. Furthermore, many in the African American community experience this often unconscious push to prove who we are, to be seen as good. Even as I have worked to not do this and have it define me, to be unabashedly myself and not give a damn, there are still times that I find that need to fit in and be "received well" turning on and taking a life of its own. I believe it has been fomented by the trauma that we have experienced.

This trauma can also appear in things that symbolically remind us of traumatic events through print or visual media. There are some authors that are amazing at creating works that allow you to feel what it might have been like in certain situations in time. Through their writing, they place you there where you can viscerally feel with all your senses what happened in the situations described. Ta-Nehisi Coates is one such author, and I was reading his novel The Water Dancer last year, which discusses aspects of the trauma of American slavery that make you feel as if it's happening to you. For me, this meant that I had to read the novel slowly and in pieces because I did not want to overheat and have my anger consume me. At certain points, I questioned whether I would finish the book because I could feel the anger rising at the injustices portrayed. However, I can never leave a book unfinished so I just read it much slower than I normally would. This matter was further complicated when the movie Just Mercy came out and I went to see it soon after opening to support the work. I left the movie so angry; I don't know if I have ever been that angry after a movie. The fact that it is a true story likely impacted my level of anger. The injustices that were perpetrated to the main character framed for a crime he did not commit and spending years on death row as a result was infuriating. The trauma this caused each member of the family and their community just because someone could do it and get away with it defies the logic of justice for all. Furthermore, the indecency and humiliation subjugated to the lawyer who dared to take on the case and violate the racial-hierarchal system was unbelievable to any person who considers themselves to be a fair thinking and positive person. The themes in the movie resurfaced the pain and frustration from the microaggressions that I and my community have had to deal with constantly with very little relief. I was livid leaving the theatre, so much so that walking through the grocery store afterwards; I had the strong urge to knock everything off the shelves. This is how deep the pain and frustration resonated for me. If I as a trained psychologist, discussing positivity and remaining calm with clients every day, can find myself in this emotional state, what about those who do not have the benefit of such introspection to control themselves. The rage and frustration caused by this societal trauma had an effect not only in the moment but in other ways as well, such as health. Experiencing negative effects of high blood pressure or having an aneurysm due to stress is a real consideration for those impacted by this trauma. Holding it in day after day, year after year, without a release valve is potentially dangerous to the ability to live. The challenge of letting these emotions out in a positive way is certainly something that would be beneficial to the health and well being of our families. It took me six months before I could get back to The Water Dancer, and it proved to be an excellent read. But I had to honor my need to have space from the feelings that it elicited in me and come back to it at a time that I could fully appreciate all that the book provides.

There are other elements of our society that continue to manifest ways to create traumatic situations under the guise of fairness. I am not one to worry much at this point in my life, having done work to appreciate the flows that life brings.

However, I have found that recently there has been a heightened sense of concern in the midst of this current environment of reckless "patriots" feeling emboldened to make unilateral decisions about their need to administer justice. My worry in this case, is for my children, hoping that they will not be the unwitting victims of some vigilante that has decided to act out on pent up misguided emotions of unfairness.

There has been another departure point here recently with the murder of George Floyd and the subsequent reaction to that murder. The level of disdain that was present in the officers' negligence in committing this murder was present for the entire world to witness. There is a groundswell that hopefully can be a maintained tipping point to justice that may finally move the needle forward in a positive way. The sacrifice of Mr. Floyd has had worldwide implications and his name has served as a rallying cry for true change and justice. We are currently waiting to see if the evidence that is abundantly clear will lead to justice or if we will suffer the trauma of yet another situation where justice is denied. Even as I bring the writing of this book to a close, awaiting the outcome of the trial that has many affixed to the process that may bring justice, yet another incident is in the headlines involving an African American man, a lieutenant in the Army being traumatized by the police. The impunity enjoyed by these officers allows them to treat this lieutenant and speak to him in such an atrocious manner, even as they have their own cameras on documenting the behavior, which again defies logical thinking. Additionally, at a time when tensions are heightened as it relates to police and the inequities during the time of this trial, one would think that more effort would be made to at least give the appearance of trying to do the right thing. This man did the same thing I described that I did when I was stopped by the police, putting my hands outside the window. He was afraid for his life and did not want to remove his seat belt for fear they would use that as an excuse to shoot him, even with his uniform on. He was mocked by the officer stating that he should be scared. This public servant had the audacity to speak in that manner to someone who is fighting for his country. One can only conclude that these officers do not care about how they come across and they will likely not suffer any consequences from those in charge of them, continuing the reprehensible legacy of policing in this country. Once more, these things will not change until those in charge do more than provide yet another task force to study the situation, thereby effectively maintaining the status quo.

As an aside, there is a parallel issue of trauma that impacts the white community. We can draw a line between those people who would have a celebration of lynching a man and those who would celebrate the murder of George Floyd by engaging in a George Floyd challenge where they reenact the murder on video as a means of making fun of the tragedy. Most sane people would question how could someone be so callous to even consider doing something such as this. In my mind, the same way trauma is passed down generationally, lack of caring and heinousness is also passed down and there should be studies conducted to better understand and correct the internal psychological disease that would yield such behavior. Of course, that is beyond the scope of this book and frankly, my own interests as I could spend the rest of my life trying to develop prescriptions for the healing of African American people and still not have enough time.

Another current societal trauma that recently happened occurred on January 6th, 2021, at the sacred United States Capitol. We were all watching as the capital of the United States was breached and overrun by insurrectionists with the intent of taking the capital and undoing the election. They were willing to kill and take hostage members of Congress who did not vote in the way that they wanted. For African Americans, watching this play out was a prescient image that we have observed many times over the years. Seeing a mob of unbridled white people spewing hatred and anger brings back memories of vicious assaults on our community that have taken place since the beginning of our time in this country. This trauma was reinforced in the admonitions from those in our community by family members, friends and others to make sure we stay safe and keep our eyes open. Since the election of 2020, these warnings have increased, creating a need to stay hypervigilant and in a constant state of awareness. This creates unnecessary stress that reinforces and emphasizes the traumas that have been perpetuated for far too long. It is not hard to imagine the anxiety, depression or physical health complications that can arise from this constantly being in this hyper-aroused state.

This trauma is further exacerbated by the manner in which the repercussions of the actions of the people who stormed the capital are being currently debated. There is actually an ongoing conversation about whether or not those who perpetrated these crimes should be held accountable. One of the reasons for not holding them accountable that has been suggested to justify this position is that prosecuting all of these people will clog up the court system. For people of color this is an insult and an affront to our sensibilities. Because of course, we know and what has been widely stated recently, is that if African Americans were to act in a similar manner, the reaction would be swift and potentially life-threatening. This double standard is triggering and also causes a degree of sadness at the concept of white privilege. And again, this incendiary position by those who perpetuate this privilege of whiteness is condescending in its approach to negating the valid concerns that are raised by those who have been impacted by the actions of those operating within this privilege.

Having watched so many incidents, I could not subject my psyche to any more of these situations and have refused to watch them anymore. I do not need to watch as I feel the pain, frustration and energy just knowing about it. Watching heightens this and takes it over the top.

Ultimately we are dealing with the trauma of the Great American lie. This lie manifests in the differences in policing that we watch where a white terrorist can be arrested without incident repeatedly but an innocent African American is murdered. This lie manifests in the disparate school systems that exist in different communities. The lie manifests in the inequity in the way African American students are treated versus other students, including disproportionate use of suspension as a corrective measure. This lie manifests in the variation in the sentencing for crack cocaine versus powder cocaine. This lie manifests in the treatment of the opioid addiction crisis versus the crack cocaine crisis. This lie manifests in the disparate sentencing and criminalization of the African American community. This lie manifests in the lip service paid to diversity in the workplace. This lie manifests in the sporting arena where supposedly Christian coaches who love their players can support a president and policies that would literally kill that player and their families. This lie manifests when there can be outrage about Michelle Obama showing her arms but no outrage exists about Melania Trump having completely naked pictures available for anyone to see. This lie manifests when people can be outraged about a simple, peaceful protest of kneeling while they simultaneously vandalize, kill and blaspheme the sacred halls of the capitol, hurling invectives and fighting those very police that they supposedly support. I could do this for a while but I'm sure you get the picture. We have a fundamental problem in this country in that what we say we value is all too frequently misaligned with the actions that we actually engage, and it is these actions that truly reflect our values. More discussion of this concept will follow in a subsequent chapter, but suffice to say that every instance of these lies occurring adds another level of societal trauma that impacts all involved. In the African American community, when we see justice being meted out differently, we frequently and continually say if this person was black, this would not be happening this way. Regarding the most recent president, we have said if President Obama had acted this way, there would have been an uproar. When this dialogue occurs, we know that we are being traumatized yet again. Because what is not being said is that despite the fact that this is wrong and problematic, very little if anything is being done to correct the matter, and in fact people are carrying on as if it is business as usual. There are very few repercussions happening for those that are engaging in the disparate treatment of black people. If senators can make up their mind about how they will vote on innocence or guilt in an impeachment trial prior to even hearing the evidence, let alone their own internal knowledge about what is right, then we as Black people are being traumatized. This traumatization does not lie with one political party exclusively as both engage in some form of political hypocrisy. One party is just more likely to at least pretend to care and do things to that effect.

One final thing I will say about societal trauma centers around the gaslighting that often occurs around issues that shine a light on the inequities of our society. Those who do not like to be held accountable for their actions will attempt to find a way to place the blame on those who are being impacted. Statements such as "If you do not have anything to hide, there should be no problem," or "You are not really in pain and do not need any medication for this" speak to an implicit bias and distrust that those making these statements choose to ignore. Rather than take ownership, the effort is instead to misdirect attention and responsibility on those that are being marginalized. We see this with the blatant lying that occurs in the political arena, even with lives at stake. We see this in the attempt to make those protesting injustice and inequity feel that they are wrong for the manner in which they are protesting. Acquiring video evidence has been a key in combating some of the deceptive impacts of those that engage in gaslighting and as awareness increases about the nature of gaslighting, accountability for those who would engage in this manipulative practice will be paramount.

PART III

Walking the Labyrinth of Healing

"He who knows others is wise. He who knows himself is enlightened."

LAO TZU

CHAPTER 13

FINDING A PLACE OF PEACE, BALANCE AND ACCEPTANCE

Now that we have explored the etiology of trauma and the various methods that have allowed them to manifest and considered how our own personal stories of trauma have evolved, we must now move to what do we do with the things that we have unearthed. In this healing process, we are going to move from being a passive receptor to an active participant in the process of healing. We are going to be Co-creators in crafting our very own healing prescription. As previously mentioned, we as a society can become focused on the trauma far more than the aspect of healing from the trauma. This is the thing that gets the most clicks and eyeballs, the promoting of the negative. Much less attention is given to those things that free us and allow movement towards our optimal selves. We say we want to be free and yet our behaviors are often contradictory to this. That is why it is important to begin the process of healing by focusing first on the mental aspects of our lives.

Before we dive into this though, I must state unequivocally that healing is not a quick fix. This bears repeating. Healing is not a quick fix. It requires a commitment to do the work that can be draining at times, which can seem as if it lacks progress at others. And yet, as with anything, what we put in will be reflected in the outcome. We have the ability to do this work and make things better for ourselves. True contentment and happiness are the rewards that come when we see this process through. I should also add that this is not a process that one completes. As long as we are breathing, there are things to learn. We are evolving and transforming and hopefully getting better as we move through life. Employing a willingness to ask more and better questions, to refine our thoughts and our behaviors, to ultimately exist in the space of love and a connection to the Creator within, no longer driven by outside distractions and petty standards are goals that would be appropriate for anyone on the path to healing. Embrace and enjoy the process. Smile and laugh at yourself. Allow yourself to be human and embrace every aspect of that humanness. This is what we are striving for. It is also important to note that there is not a singular prescription for trauma. There are so many variables that come into play and the same trauma suffered by ten individuals might require ten separate completely different approaches to bringing about healing. Unlike the science of how to heal cancer or sickle cell anemia, the science of healing trauma requires an approach open to knowing and understanding the various aspects of an individual and the manner in which life experiences have impacted the individual to produce the trauma effects. I am endeavoring to give you some things to think about to help facilitate your healing. This is not an exhaustive list and can be tweaked to your benefit. We have to begin conceptualizing a new reality for ourselves, which centers us and ensures that we are providing love and nurturing for ourselves and our loved ones. It is in this manner that we will be able to create lasting change.

Having been to numerous conferences and workgroups where theories about problems have been discussed ad nauseam it occurred to me that we need more emphasis on solving the problems we face in our communities. The practical application of how we overcome the problems and create healthier models of being is of the highest necessity. Ayi Kweh Armah, in his work The Eloquence of the Scribes, notes that much of the time and discourse among intellectual communities is spent on deliberating problems and raising consciousness about issues rather than developing the much-needed solutions to these problems[28]. Furthermore, it is his contention that the academe trains people to regurgitate information and remain in a perpetual state of status quo as opposed to tapping into our natural talent and intellect to develop solutions and newer, better methods for living on various levels. It is clear to me in the work that I have done to deal with my own trauma that we have everything that we need within us to solve our problems and create a space of optimal health. We may need guidance to help gain clarity and insight about these tools, but we are all equipped with an internal guidance system for how to live our lives. My hope is to provide a symbolic understanding of the traumas that may plague us while also developing methods for solving these traumas moving forward. As such, I will elaborate on particular traumas that I have had to deal with and discuss techniques utilized to overcome these issues. Ultimately, I am interested in the process of healing, first on an individual basis and then on a more collective level.

    We have three choices as I see it in response to trauma. We can allow the trauma to continue to reside within us, keeping us unsettled and unable to thrive to our highest capacity and in a perpetual state of sadness and anxiety. We

---

28 Ayi Kweh Armah 2006 The Eloquence of the Scribes, Per Ankh, Popenguine, Senegal.

can do the work to bring about healing such that the trauma has less and less power over us, ultimately freeing ourselves to engage with life at our most optimal level. Or we can maintain the status quo, recognizing that we are impacted but being unwilling to do the necessary healing work to get ourselves unstuck. There is not a correct answer and we should have loving patience with ourselves and others as we manage our response to trauma in whatever way we see fit. Everyone moves as spirit and their life inspires them to move. It is easy to look at someone from the outside and suggest that they just get over it. But healing ourselves from something like trauma that has been present in such an insidious way, often for very long times, is not that simple. We all will move when our spirit inspires us to do so, and we should have compassion and patience for wherever one is on their respective path. One might have given up on Malcolm X at several points in his life where he did not appear to be doing things that were positive. In doing so, the germination of the seeds planted in him would have been missed and the greatness that he offered to humanity not realized. It is for this reason that I encourage you to have grace and compassion with yourself and others, even as you may be frustrated from what you see as a lack of progress.

If we decide that we are going to choose healing, we must first come to an understanding of what healing is. What does it mean to heal? How does one heal? How long does it take to be healed? These questions are often asked of me and I often found myself replying that you have to do the work to bring about healing and the completion of this will vary depending on the person. "But what is the work?" I would be asked. This would force me to get specific about the various things that comprise the work, many of which I had done in my life to facilitate my own healing, bringing me to a space of peace and acceptance. We will spend time detailing aspects of the work that you can consider adding to your personal healing kit, modifying things as you see fit to help you reach your ultimate goal. First, we must reframe our minds so that we are approaching this task from a perspective that will allow us to optimize our work.

One of the foundational components of healing for me involves a restoration of balance, symbolized by the Chinese symbol of yin and yang. This concept embodies the idea that everything has an opposite pole, which complements the meaning and allows for an understanding of the continuum. Passive-Aggressive, Work-Play, Soft-Hard are examples that illustrate this. Too much of any side causes an imbalance and work towards the balancing of the two entities signifies the importance of yin and yang. When we are first conceived as the sperm meets the egg, those two things coming together create the beginning forms of life in perfect balance. It takes both of those two things coming together to create one positive life. As we grow in the womb, there is a symmetry that occurs if we are growing in a healthy environment where our bodies evolve in a balanced way. There is also an evolution occurring internally as our minds and hearts begin to grow and develop. There is a balance that exists between these two entities as well. Our cognitive knowledge and our heart knowledge are both important in understanding and being who we are, and ideally, we should strive to find a balance between the two. As we are developing in the womb, if our mother is stressed, angry or frustrated, the energy of her disposition can be communicated to the embryo throwing off the natural order and balance. As a child is born into the world and has to learn to navigate their place in the world, disturbing or unsettling incidents or emotions can impact the child's balanced aura and introduce imbalance. There are a continuum of things that can impact the child, some seemingly very simple and having a small impact, and others more obviously multifarious and horrific, causing a tragic unsettling requiring advanced treatment. A three-year-old yelled at by a parent who is distracted and frustrated and has a momentary lapse in self-control that does not normally occur might be a small impact. On the other hand, a three-year-old who is molested repeatedly by an adult who is supposed to be providing a loving and nurturing environment would be quite catastrophic and have an impact that lasts into adulthood. The balance of the individual, in either case, is thrown off, slightly in the prior case and more intensely in the latter case. Healing would involve returning the body to its natural state, not allowing the imbalance to continue to dictate the path of the individual's life. Cognitively, we have to think positively about ourselves with no allowance for negative self-talk, and emotionally, we have to love ourselves fully and completely with no exceptions. Trauma upsets this natural balance and creates unsettled problems that leave us in a state of flux. If you think about the stories presented thus far in this book or maybe even your own personal stories that have involved dramatic situations, you can see the dynamic of imbalance in each situation. If there were a healthy person from the start, adversity would not have caused an imbalance to the point where the person would respond to the adversity in an unhealthy manner.

We next need to understand what it is that we need to heal, what caused the imbalance in the first place. This can be a very direct recognition of the particular trauma e.g. police violence, or it could be something that's more complex and subtle, such as the gaslighting that often takes place in corporate America. Everything is the result of something that happened prior to that thing occurring. Or simply put, everything has an origin story. So we must understand the past so that we can have clarity about how we came to be in the present. To be clear, when we look to understand the past, we are not wallowing in the past and staying in a place of apathy. Instead, we are looking at the things that have occurred simply for an understanding of how those things have evolved us to the place that we are currently. From there, we can then look to whatever we need to do to change the negative patterns that created the imbalance introducing newer, better, healthier ways of interacting that allow us to create the best version of ourselves moving forward. It is important to emphasize the necessity to not remain mired in the past as there is nothing that we can do to change the things that have already happened. This is about understanding ourselves without condemnation. Ultimately, we want to know how did we become the person that we are today.

This is not an indictment. You were paying attention to the story of my life right. This story was presented precisely for this reason. We all have areas that can be improved; it is an integral part of the process of life. If we did not have something to work on, life would actually be rather boring. Ponder this. Have you ever enjoyed reading a book or watching a movie where the main character lived a perfect life and had everything go perfectly throughout the course of the story? This would actually be a pretty boring book or movie. We expect to see adversity and the ability to overcome this adversity. The hero has to have downfalls, has to overcome some things. This resonates within our spirit and causes us to feel the successful conquering of the adversities presented. This same concept applies to life.

There are several components involved in shoring up our mental attitude. Sojourner Truth offers an exhortation in her sentiment "it is the mind that makes the body". As such, we must first start with what the ancient Egyptians referred to as knowing thyself. We all have to explore the inner workings of who we are to understand our own specific and particular purpose here in this lifetime. I do not believe that anyone can tell you what your purpose is specifically. We can and should receive guidance and feedback from others about how we present in the world. Ultimately though, we have to tap into the core being of ourselves, that space that we go to when we are feeling a certain way, that space where the Creator resides, and allow that sense of knowing to guide our thoughts and subsequently our actions. To help think about the process of healing, we are going to embark upon a progression of crafting a healing space. We will begin by thinking comprehensively about what and how we ultimately want to be at our best, creating a blueprint of how we want to see ourselves.

A second important component is love. We hear the concept of love bandied about in a number of different perspectives. In this context, we are encouraging you to think about self-love and what this encompasses. When we truly love ourselves, we are in a space of happiness and satisfaction with ourselves. Outside opinions are useful but do not define us and we do not allow these opinions to impact our mood and belief in ourselves. Additionally, there are certain things that we will not allow to happen in our lives, particularly those that bring discomfort or sadness to our lives. We will not make decisions that do not affirm us or allow us to be our best. We will not put our well-being below that of others, recognizing that we have to take care of ourselves first if in fact, we are going to be in service to others. We will not allow ourselves to be disrespected or treated in a manner that is below the standards we have determined are necessary for us. Ideally, this mindset is groomed by our parents, who provide a mirror that reflects the specialness that we all embody. This reflection should be a positive picture that focuses on viewing ourselves as having everything that we need within us and sends constant reaffirming messages that we are perfect embodiments of the Creator even as we strive for perfection.

Absent of receiving this nurturing in childhood, we will have to create this framework for ourselves as adults. Although more challenging, it is quite possible to create and necessary to disrupt the pattern of negativity imposed by trauma. As we embark on the healing process, we will continue to emphasize the necessity of this self-love as a fundamental aspect of healing.

In short, self-knowledge and self-love are two cornerstone concepts that are necessary for the building towards a space of healing. Ensuring that these two things are engaged in our lives is critical for ensuring happiness.

Walking the labyrinth of healing

I took a trip to Australia once, and in the home that I was staying, there was a labyrinth in the backyard. I have always enjoyed the intricacies of a labyrinth and found them to be quite enchanting, but had never seen one so large in person. I decided to walk the labyrinth for fun and was not expecting to get out of the process of what ultimately happened. Walking this labyrinth allowed me to center myself and pay attention to being in the moment. I could listen to the sounds that nature and my surroundings were providing. I was able to find a space of peace that I did not know I needed. I became fascinated with what I got out of walking this labyrinth, and over the two weeks that I was there made a decision to walk the labyrinth each morning. It was quite an exhilarating uplifting. And insightful experience and I have since tried to recreate this energy. I managed to find a small metal labyrinth that I can trace with a pointer when I am feeling worried, angry or frustrated, and this process can bring me back to my center, helping me to put things in context, remembering what is really important, working to not focus on those things that I cannot control. It is important to have things that help us remain aware of the truly important things in life.

The many twists and turns that it takes to find your way to the center of a labyrinth, not in a rush, but taking time to reach the core, allows for focused introspection. The process of healing is much like embarking upon moving through a labyrinth with many twists and turns, working to get to the center, or in this regard the soul. As long as we keep going forward, we will ultimately reach that center point. Everyone that walks a labyrinth arrives at the center at a different time and finds different things along the way. A person that walks a labyrinth repeatedly will find that they learn something new with each trip. Our healing process is much like walking a labyrinth in that each person will find a different path and learn things particular to them as they embark upon this journey. The symbolic representation of the labyrinth is a good visual to hold as you think about your own path. Walking a labyrinth does not allow us to cut any corners or take any shortcuts to arrive at the middle. If we attempted to do this, we could assure that problems will arise later on that we may have to expend more energy and resources to correct as opposed to doing it correctly the first time. One can consider the example of building a house correctly with a solid foundation and quality materials such that it will last and not need major repairs at some point. We should ultimately want to build our body, our personal temple, in such a way that we are strong physically, spiritually and mentally.

This process focuses on the internal evolution, and I should point out the inclination in the tendency to put more emphasis on the physical aspect because that is what we see initially and is the thing that drives us. Our society is replete with images of "beauty" that have us chasing an often unattainable goal. These images of beauty often come from a place of trauma for those in the African American community who have been programmed to try and achieve what are unachievable standards. For us as African Americans, this is exponentially problematic as can be seen with just one example of skin bleaching to attempt to attain the "lighter" skin which society has deemed better. This thinking is not only out of balance; it is also unhealthy, and similar to a home that is built with faulty materials, it will cause problems emotionally for those that engage this line of thinking. The resulting colorism issues that plague our community are an example of this harmful disease and keeps us away from the more important focus of healing and forward movement. The trauma of this and similar situations can be hindrances in the building of your house.

A comparable issue can be seen in regards to hair and hair texture. Our society has engaged in an assault on the images of African American hair and this again is traumatic. For a most recent and clear example of the insidious manner in which this trauma can manifest when least expected, consider the teenage wrestler in New Jersey who mid-match was forced with an unthinkable choice. Cut his locks or forfeit his match, potentially costing his team the title. He was given 90 seconds to make a decision. With tears in his eyes and the pressure of a gym full of observers, he decided to allow his locks to be cut by his coach. He ended up winning the match but was clearly despondent afterwards. The resulting national attention brought tremendous pressure for the racist referee to be removed. This is one example of an infinite number of incidents that occur daily that shows how one person can inflict trauma and a lifelong imprint on a single unsuspecting soul. This young man likely woke up that morning with dreams of winning his match and celebrating the victory with his family and never envisioned that his life would be turned upside down with him becoming an unwilling national figure in the process. It is not hard to believe that he had to manage the symptoms of depression, anger and anxiety as a result of this and likely will have to continue working to keep these emotions in check.

In another incident, a young student in Texas in 2019 was forced to have the part in his head, which he had gotten during a recent haircut, colored in with the black sharpie after his administrators decided that this part was outside of the school dress code. This student had never been in any trouble before and he was a member of the track team. He was given the option of being suspended if he would not comply with having his part colored in with the sharpie, which would have gone on his record and removed him from the track team. His parents were not called and three administrators proceeded to engage in this action. None of these administrators considered the trauma that they were inflicting upon this young student who had to go back to class with this aberration amidst his peers. Self-esteem being very critical to teenagers, this was a difficult situation for him to deal with. The resulting anguish and turmoil that this student felt again likely produced symptoms of trauma that he will be managing for some time. As these administrators will have gone on with their life, this incident will be something that this student will likely think of every day. It is not unreasonable to think that he will have poor associations with sharpies or magic markers moving forward, and every time he sees a sharpie may have a reaction suggestive of this. This is trauma. There are other parallel issues that are beyond the scope of this book but indeed contribute to the traumatic historical conception of self within the African American community.

Moving towards solutions, we will conceptualize the process of healing from trauma as similar to building a house in that we should create a mind, body and soul that is strong and will withstand the inevitable challenges and adversities that arise in life. To begin this process, I encourage you to acquire a journal and begin to write down your thoughts as it relates to the interventions we will be discussing. This will help you to craft your own personal manual for healing, which is important because the process of healing will not be the same for everyone. We will be asking many questions to help you critically center yourself and really consider how you have become the person that you are and what needs to change to become the person you want to be. Writing and seeing things in black and white helps to hold you accountable to the change process. I have observed that people often like to skip this step of writing, sometimes due to not wanting to engage the effort and others in an attempt to avoid the accountability that comes along with seeing it in writing. I use the analogy of someone wanting to get into shape using a personal trainer to assist with this. The trainer essentially holds you accountable and does not allow you to give up or take shortcuts. If you really want to see the progress, you follow the instructions the trainer provides. If not, you stop going. There is no right answer; you just get out of it what you put into it. In this regard, I encourage you to eliminate any potential barriers that could serve as limitations to you creating your best life and engage the process fully. So as you embark upon your own process of healing, whether it is an extremely complex situation or one that is relatively simple, it all starts with self and being willing to walk that path to understand and tap into our center, our soul, the very essence of who we are.

CHAPTER 14

INSPIRATION

Creating Our Personal Blueprint

"The present is where we get lost—if we forget our past and have no vision of the future"

AYI KWEH ARMAH

We must begin the process of self-building by creating a blueprint for what it is that we want our life to be. Central to this is a question pondered by a man likely since the beginning of time. What is our purpose? Why are you here in this moment at this time? Why are you reading this right now at whatever time it is currently on whatever day of the week it is? How did you arrive at this precise moment in life? What do you hope to accomplish in your time on earth? Are you merely watching the days go by, hoping that something will come along and bring you excitement? Are you hoping to win the lottery or come into a windfall from someone that will suddenly make your life better? Do you know who you are and what your gift to the world is? Everyone and everything has a purpose; what is yours?

If we were to envision our lives fully healed of any trauma that has impacted us, what would we see? This is a time to close your eyes and imagine yourself being your absolute best. Think about if you were doing and living your life in exactly the way that you would like to live; what would this look like. Where would you live, what would your relationship consist of, what type of hobbies would you engage in? What would your career be? Would you work for someone or have your own business? What would your work day look like, how would you spend your weekends and spare time, and what would your family dynamics include? How would your spiritual life manifest and what types of actions would you engage as you walk your spiritual path? How much money would you make, how much saving and investing would you do, what would you do to build wealth for your family and your community? These are some of the questions that can begin to get you started on creating your own personal blueprint, and they presume that an absence of the impact of trauma would be a fundamental aspect of this life. This blueprint should be extremely extensive and cannot be specific enough. The amount of time you spend working on your blueprint will yield a direct correlation to the ability to create the life you want to achieve from that blueprint. It is important to allow yourself to dream bigger than you have ever imagined as you are creating this blueprint. Even though it may not seem possible in your mind right now, this is the beginning step in creating a new reality, and as we continue building out these steps, the interventions necessary to bring into fruition this belief will begin to take shape. So allow yourself to admit to that dream that you have kept buried inside you, that you have never told anyone, and that you may have been told at some point is impossible for you. Because as we build, we will be clearing away all of the trauma that has been programmed into our minds and replacing that negativity with possibility and attainability. Of course, we have to balance our goals with a degree of realism as well. At 5 foot 8, I really would like to be able to do a 360-degree windmill slam dunk that would shame Lebron James. I also would love to sing with the harmonious blends

Inspiration

of John Legend. However, I have just not been blessed with these wonderful talents that these brothers have. As a result, I must temper what I would like with what is realistically possible with the body and the natural skills that I possess. You have within you the courage to take the first step and begin healing; you just have to allow it to come out by committing to this process. Little by little, the change will occur.

As you embark upon the process of creating this blueprint, a critical component that I believe is necessary for healing but also the continued advancement of ourselves once we are at a balanced space is stillness and meditation. The aspects of blueprint development are able to evolve from the quiet spaces where our minds can work effectively to create the template for the new reality that we will build. And yet, our present society really does not foster the intuitive practice of being still and quiet that would allow for this information to come forward. We are constantly assailed with information and stimulation. For instance, we cannot even pump gas without having commercials blaring from the pump in that short time. Someone bombarding your mind with influential advertisements in an attempt to get you to do something or buy this item. This constant stimulation keeps our brains overactive and focusing on things that are not providing healthy sustenance. We have to be willing to make choices that pull us away from these distractors, allowing us to get in touch with the creative energies that reside within us all.

The ability to be still and allow the creative elements of the universe to speak to us, to guide us, to refine the intuitive wisdom that resides in us all is vitally important. Think of all those times you have had an inclination to do something, to turn the corner and go a different way to pick up a certain book in the library. These and more are aspects of our intuition, guiding us along, nurturing our movement along our path. If we pay attention to the signs and nudges that life brings, we more easily move in the flow of life. It is in this quiet space that the answers come. It is in this quiet space that we solve problems. It is in this quiet space that life reveals itself to us and allows us to engage with it in a process that is collaborative and lovely. In short, I can fight the current of life in the space of noise and distractions, or I can join the current of life in my place of solitude and understanding. Consider the rushing waves of a river and the concept of swimming against the current. It takes much more energy to swim against the current. If instead, I chose to swim with the current of the river, I can now move with strength and cover ground very quickly. Choose to engage your strengths facilitated by the practice of being still. Do not encumber yourself with rules about meditation. Just start small and sit alone in quiet for 5 minutes in the morning and 5 minutes in the evening. You are worth 10 minutes to begin creating your healing from trauma. Commit to doing this for 90 days. Take some time and begin your work before moving on, as this will help you get centered and think clearly about being the director of your healing process.

The next aspect of creating the blueprint involves considering the ingredients necessary to get from where we are currently to whatever we have defined as our ultimate goal. Incidentally, although we are discussing this in relation to the aspect of healing, it also applies across areas and so can be used in a number of different contexts. When we think of the vision of what our life would look like operating at our best and highest state, we can take these images and plan out what it will take to achieve these things. We will process in detail how to think through the necessary steps of specifying what we need to successfully bring our vision into fruition.

Let us take for example, one specific part of my vision as living a healthy life free of medication and break down the thought process that goes into what needs to happen if I want to make this an actual aspect of a goal that I want to achieve. On the surface, this sounds like a reasonable goal but what are the various components that are involved in achieving this goal. First of all, I would have to consider my diet and whether or not I consume too much fast food or processed foods. If I were really serious about this goal, that might mean I could no longer eat at my favorite fast food restaurant for lunch. I would need to find a healthy place to eat or plan to bring my lunch. Thus I would have to choose what is not necessarily a convenient choice and have the discipline necessary to avoid what was previously a guilty pleasure. I would need to be honest with myself about whether or not I was willing to make the necessary sacrifice for the rest of my life to truly attain this goal. No one would be forcing me to make this choice as I have developed my life vision independently. I am now faced with aligning my values and actions to accomplish the goal that I have set. We have only touched on one component thus far, but this line of reasoning and acceptance would correspond to all aspects of making change. Continuing with this example, I would next need to consider my sugar intake and the need to decrease this so that there is not a possibility of diabetes. I might need to decrease eating my favorite breakfast food of eggs to avoid any potential issues with cholesterol. Can I forgo the eggs to achieve my goal or will my love for eggs prove more important than reaching my goal of living a healthy life free of medication? Other areas of diet would need to be considered on an individual basis as there are things unique to certain people that impact diet that may not affect another. Next, we would also consider the impact of smoking and alcohol use. Would I engage this in moderation, or am I using these substances too much to the extent that they would be problematic for me? We would next contemplate looking at the physical aspect of health and what we would need to do to maintain our health physically. How often and what type of exercise would we be willing to consistently engage on a daily or weekly basis. Again this is an individual choice, but for instance, I might decide to run 3 miles three times a week for cardio and lift weights for 30 minutes 3 days a week for muscle tone. I also might engage in yoga or Thai Chi to enhance my flexibility and mental acuity. If I find that doing something consistently is problematic, I have to return to the beginning question and ask am I willing to do the work necessary to achieve my goal. The amount of effort and work necessary to ensure that each goal can adequately be met will vary, but no matter what, consistency will be key. Ultimately what I am doing is considering all aspects of things that could prevent me from attaining my goal and ensuring that I am doing the work necessary to attain what I have determined I want to achieve.

Once we have a substantial vision of what we want to create developed, we can then consider the potential pitfalls that can get in the way of our development. I have identified a few of these as fear, guilt, addiction, and lack of motivation. Let's take a closer look at each and how they can get in the way of our forward progress.

FEAR

Fear is a huge impediment that dwells within the deep recesses of many of us. We are born with an instinctual sense of danger that gets developed more accurately as we age. The brains of infants are wired in such a way that information is being sorted and categorized at an extremely high speed. Ultimately, this information can be exacerbated by the training and the teaching that we get from the adults and society around us. For instance, consider a child that grew up in the Jim Crow south and how that child was taught which areas of town to avoid because of the color of their skin. The parents,

Inspiration

recognizing the power structure and the need to keep their child safe, taught their child the appropriate "rules" for their survival. This information was then passed on and encoded into the norms of the family and collective society.

One year I went to the State Fair and happened upon the animal exhibitions. As I was by myself, I decided to just sit and observe the proceedings. There were different categories of animals and there were different age groups of children who were managing the animals. At one point, a group of younger children came out and they were leading sheep to be judged on their appearance and ability to follow directions. I saw a young girl who the judge noted was four years old proudly walking with the sheep that was approximately 150 pounds. The discrepancy in their size was quite noticeable, but the young girl managed the sheep with no problems and had a level of confidence in what she was doing that was impressive to observe. It made me consider what it was that allowed her to engage with the animal in this manner. I also considered what it would be like if this sheep was bought to a group of young children in the city who had never been around the sheep before. It became clear to me that this young girl was raised on a farm where this was the norm in terms of her behavior and interaction with animals, and as such, fear was never introduced as an option. In another example, I was walking on a dock while visiting San Francisco and came across a man and his daughter who were fishing for crabs. They had a bucket full of crabs and many people who were walking around were observing the crabs. The daughter, who said she was six years old would pick up the crabs and show them to anyone that was interested in seeing them. Many adults were amazed that she was able to pick up the crab with no fear, as you could see that most of the adults around were themselves fearful of picking up the crab. She even offered for some to hold the crab, and most refused. What is it that allowed both of these young girls to interact in a way that seemed quite natural for them? I would suggest that they had never been introduced to the concept of fear, and in fact had been taught that this is how you deal with this situation and this is what we do as a result. So it became a norm for them to engage in this behavior, and there was never any reason introduced to them to fear what it was they were doing. It is easy to see how this also works in reverse as a father who is afraid of worms can very easily pass on his fear of worms to his children in what he says and how he reacts around snakes.

Most of us have had some level of fear introduced at some point in our lives in some capacity. If we spend time thinking about what it is that we are afraid of, we can likely trace the origin of that fear. Once we are clear about the origin, we can then do the work to eliminate the fear. Upon getting clear about the direction of this book, fear thrust itself into my thoughts. The questions of do I really want to put myself out there like this? And what will people think about me and my life? Managed to creep into my thinking. However, I ultimately decided that I am writing this book from a true space of humility, wanting to provide guidance about how people can systemically engage the process of healing, and so those questions cannot be a concern. The goal is to truly help others and I cannot do that to the highest level without the level of honesty I have chosen to employ. Any one of those questions or versions of those questions likely creeps into your mind at various times for different things that you might engage in your life. Many of us are worried about what others will think of us or how we would be perceived in this social media society. But there is something else that lies underneath these questions that I would suggest is a lack of self-confidence. When we are clear about who we are and what we are doing, the worry about what others think evaporates. If we go a step further and ask ourselves, what does it really matter what people think? This moves us along a line of truly freeing ourselves. If we honestly and objectively consider the nature of human beings, it is impossible to please everyone. For example, you cannot find a YouTube video that has ever received 100% positive likes. Even the most lovable child video will have some dislikes. Someone is always going to have something to say that takes away from where you are. Someone is always going to critically object or be the naysayer. Often these very people could stand to do their own work in their lives to manifest their own happiness. Because they are unable or unwilling to do this, they choose instead to focus on attacking other people with their negativity. We should not take these critical thoughts personally instead, focus on being true to ourselves, knowing that we are perfectly aligned and can be satisfied with what we achieve.

GUILT

The next area that we need to be aware of centers around guilt which can manifest in a number of different ways. Guilt occurs when we feel that we are not worthy of something. Often the reasons that we feel we are not worthy are centered around ways that we have been socialized and taught to believe, often the result of trauma in some manner. I have interacted with people who felt guilty because they were able to find some degree of success in their life and many of the friends that they grew up with did not find similar success. In addition, some may feel guilty because they think that others are more deserving or that they are not qualified enough. We can see this manifested for example, in what has been referred to as impostor syndrome, a belief that somebody will "find out" that we do not know what we are doing and do not really belong in this position. This feeling exists despite the fact that we have all of the degrees, all of the training and all of the experience commensurate with anyone else who would be in this job. Years of being marginalized and left out end up creating a self-doubt that is not consistent with reality.

ADDICTION

When we are faced with difficulties that we do not know how to solve, we often choose to find an easy way out, something that will temporarily take us out of our misery to a place of freedom. Things that offer this temporary escape serve merely as a phantasmic relief and can often be addictive in nature. We can look at the current opioid crisis that exists in our country and the continuing problems with crack cocaine as examples of what happens when attempts to find a pleasurable relief from life take on an addictive quality. One choice to avoid the trauma leads to worse trauma, and without the proper rehabilitation for this addiction, it can result in a significant decline in health and ultimately death. This addiction extends to alcohol abuse and other forms of drugs as well. Food and eating can also serve as addictive escapes from reality. Gambling and sex can be seen as outlets that are turned to in an attempt to relieve the pressure of life and the impact of trauma on that life. The temporary respite that addiction provides ultimately only serves to keep us from engaging in the process that will allow for true complete relief.

LACK OF MOTIVATION

When we feel trapped in the throes of trauma and have nowhere to turn, malaise and apathy can set in, often leading to depression. We can find ourselves trapped in the cycle of going through the motions of our days in a repetitive mindless manner. Each day during the week appears to be a carbon copy of the previous day with the hope that we can just make it to the weekend. Arriving at the weekend, we produce a carbon copy of the prior weekend and soon, we are back at the beginning of the week to continue the cycle. If we find ourselves in this position, we have to refer back to those questions that challenge us to explore why we are here. If we recognize that this lack of motivation can be one of the pitfalls, then we can do the things necessary to ensure that we create healthy alternatives that keep us inspired and away from lethargy.

Moving past these impediments allows the implementation of our blueprint that becomes our life vision, something that we can focus on at the beginning of our day to remind us of the way in which we want to live our lives. Containing all of the components of things that contribute to our happiness, this vision will be comprehensive and attainable, and as we continue to put forth positive energy into this vision, we will begin to see the specific aspects of this vision manifesting. Having a blueprint enables us to enact rituals and patterns of behavior that allow us to heal and achieve the goals the blueprint outlines. It will be important, to be honest with ourselves about the degree of commitment we have to create what we have outlined in the blueprint, and we will explore this more in our exploration of actions and values. In this section, we have completed the foundation of our healing process by creating this blueprint, taking into account some of the potential pitfalls and how they might impact us, and are now ready to move forward with the next step of the building process.

CHAPTER 15

TRANSFORMATION

The Process of Rewiring Our Brains—

"A mind attacked and conquered is guided easily away from its own soul"

AYI KWEH ARMAH

It is possible to reprogram our mind to undo the negative impact of trauma, replacing these limiting beliefs with beliefs that are instead affirming and allowing us to evolve and transform in an optimal manner. How do we do this? There are multiple methods and any one or a combination of methods may work. Before engaging in the methodology, though, one must decide mentally that they are willing to engage in the process of change. This means opening oneself up to reframing your mind and deciding to allow a different way of understanding and viewing the world to emerge. This can be a challenging and scary proposition for most of us who become comfortable in our present reality that has been crafted for us. Fear of the unknown keeps us locked into situations and patterns that we logically and intuitively know do not serve us. Our society does not look kindly upon those who would dare to go outside of the norm. Persecution and ridicule typically await those who dare to think outside of the box. However, when one decides that they can no longer live with the dissonance created when their minds and spirit are not in alignment with the actions that they engage in, fertile ground for planting new seeds of change is the result. From here, we can now begin to consider the possibilities of the various interventions that allow us to remap and heal our mind so that we begin to move away from the trauma and its negative impact. The body responds to the mind and what the mind tells it to do. This happens so very quickly with millions of decisions and actions that we engage every day. Although we do not think about it, every action that we engage starts with an impulse, a signal from our brains that goes to the various parts of our body and directs what it is that we do. Every step that we take, every breath that we inhale, when we tie our shoes, when we drive our car, our brain is processing information at an incredibly high rate. If we stop to think about it every single thing that we do in a day, our brain directs all of these actions, seemingly unbeknownst to us. When we can appreciate the power that our brains possess, we are then able to focus this power in a determined way and we can accomplish some really amazing things, not the least of which is our own healing.

One way of thinking about this is epigenetic programming, or simply put, rewiring our brains. Information is conveyed to our brain through various dimensions beginning with auditory and feeling, then visually, written and speaking and lastly, in our meditation or dream state. We want to change the way we think about the trauma so that we no longer think about it in a way that keeps us mired in pain and suffering. We want to shift the focus of the way we think about this situation that has occurred from one that is limiting, painful and paints us as a victim to one that is empowering and sees us as a victor able to overcome the negativity of the situation. Some of these situations that we will need to consider are historical in nature and in doing this, we will be remapping generations of thinking that may

Transformation

be embedded in our biological makeup. Other situations will be more immediate, actual things that have happened to us that we will begin to think about differently. I can choose how I want to think about a particular thing and we see examples of this all around us. We have the ability within us to overcome anything presented to us. We are manifestations of the Creator which means that we are imbued with the same energy of change and the ability to produce miracles. We just often do not treat ourselves with the love, respect and self-knowledge that will allow us to be our best selves.

    Consider Richie Parker, an engineer with the Hendrick Chevrolet racing team who was born with no arms. If you watch his motivational story, you see the elements of the ability to overcome working at its highest level. His parents instilled in him a mindset that he could accomplish anything. Tasks that others would look at and consider impossible for him to do, his family decided that they just needed to dig deeper and figure out a way to make it happen. How is it that a person can ride a bike or drive a car with no arms? If this were you, would you have settled for the impossibility of this situation and resigned yourself to never doing these things? One person doing it proves that it can be done. The choice then becomes do I want to engage the work necessary to overcome the difficulties of this particular situation. I'm sure Richie Parker fell down a few times when he was trying to learn to ride his bicycle, but he did not give up and ultimately was successful. Really his experience was no different than most people who learn to ride a bike and fall down many times before mastering the activity of riding a bicycle. This element of perseverance is essentially the progenitor of innovation and we only need to consider all of the various inventions that were created because someone challenged themselves to think beyond the realm of possibility and create new realities. Someone was willing to go further when the vast majority were saying that this was an impossibility that could not be done and they needed to be satisfied with where they already were. How did his parents know to have this level of perseverance and equip him with the seeds that created an attitude that allowed him to overcome the trauma of not having any arms? They were able to flip a negative situation that could have found him wallowing as a victim and turned it into the positive story of him thriving and successfully living his life fully. Are we doing less with more? Ultimately this is not a contest of traumas. The point of this example is not to compare and try to put one situation above or below another. The most important takeaway is we have the capacity to determine how we will think about a situation and subsequently what we will do about that situation. We get to determine whether we will complain incessantly about the things that happened to us or if we will accept life happening and do what we can to continue moving forward, thinking outside the box and creating the life we want to see. There are countless examples of people all over the world overcoming the most traumatic situations one can imagine and there are also those stories of people who decided they could not overcome the situations. This is the human condition. But as you are here currently contemplating these points, you have an opportunity to choose your path.

You may still be saying, "but my trauma is different and there is no way I can heal from this". When my clients respond in this way, my response is simply to say in a very lovingly way ok. This communicates to them that I respect their decision to make choices and live their lives as they see fit. If they want to focus on taking the deeper, often painful dive of healing as we have outlined for them, that is fine, and if they are not ready just yet, that is fine as well. They may not be ready for another 5, 10, 20 years or never. It is important to allow people to be where they are and deal with the internal dialogue that will either push them forward or keep them stuck in the place that they are. So I say to you again, be loving with yourself and appreciate that you are ok where you are until you are ready to be someplace different.

Expanding this dialogue to a more collective position, it becomes clear that as adults, we can choose to engage in a process of change that will move us forward in a healthy manner that will then impact our community and eventually the world. Spirituality can play an important role in this process as for many people; this informs the values that we choose to abide by. In my study of religions and spiritual systems around the world, I have come to believe that the systems themselves are not the problem. In fact, most of the religions or spiritual systems at their core advocate similar things. It is the ego of man that comes in and distorts the essence of the teachings for its own internal gratification. If we all actually did the things we say we believe, much of what ails us as a society would cease to exist. Instead, we as a society make an implicit agreement to abide by an unspoken set of rules that we intuitively know are broken but choose to follow them anyway so as not to upset the status quo. This is not meant to be a blanket indictment, as there are certainly those out fighting for change and advocating for things to be different. However, I would suggest that there still remains an unwillingness to truly engage this process in a way that is totally freeing.

If we consider the United States and the concept of liberty and justice for all. It does not say liberty and justice for some or liberty and justice for those who can afford it. It does not say liberty and justice for men or liberty and justice for those who look a certain way. It says liberty and justice for all. Is anyone able to say that this statement happens for all? Is it that the power structure is so strong as to withstand any attempts at correction? Are we not able to hold people accountable in this system of "justice" or does this word not mean what we think it means? A system of justice that was created by the very people engaging in injustice seems to be the ultimate paradox. Essentially, the foundation of this entire system is built on a lie. How can it hold up when challenged with the truth of the actions of the system? If we had a house and continued to ignore the rotting foundation or made minor repairs to avoid the costly undertaking to truly fix it, any good inspector would tell you that you are only delaying the inevitable. This country has a rotting foundation, and we as a whole are ignoring it, hoping to patch things together rather than attacking the core of the problem and making systematic changes that will truly heal the problem. Some who think they are part of the solution are merely interested in repurposing methods that have not previously worked but will allow them to stay in the perches of their powerful positions without impacting their own bottom line. We must challenge and change this dynamic if we are to truly heal. The prior example with Richie Parker applies here in that we can simultaneously work on healing ourselves as we also bring corrective measures to the systems that cause some of the trauma. One person can make a change, and even more importantly, the power of a collective can induce change. The same thinking outside the box and considering a different reality is necessary for our society as a whole. Can we consider revamping the entire system or do we remain wedded to a system that we know causes damage because we do not want to upset the status quo? Similar to how we want to rewire our brains, the brains of our collective society also need to be remapped.

Ultimately, the systemic trauma is not in our direct control. We need to be cognizant of the impact of the systemic trauma but not allow our energy to be depleted, focusing on the enormity of effort that will eventually be required to produce change. We can control ourselves and the remapping of our brains and, through doing our work, hopefully inspire

Transformation

others to engage in the process of self-healing as well. The momentum of individuals changing, healing and growing now has the potential and critical mass to change the system.

Once we accept that we have the capacity to remap our brains, another important question to consider in the process of the remapping is are we willing to be vulnerable and honest with ourselves, calling those things that plague us for what they truly are as opposed to trying to cover them up to make us feel better about ourselves in the eyes of others? I could not ask this question and not be willing to engage the process myself, which led me to write about my personal trauma in the manner that I have. I believe in the power of change and the healing process and have found that those that I work with see it useful to have a vision of what this looks like in real time. Though you may not share your story with the world, it is there and you know the story and can choose to do the work to write the next chapters in your story in a way that centers you and creates your happiness.

Why do we have challenges and adversities? I have often wondered aloud why I have encountered many of the adversities that I have faced in my life. The various events that have occurred in my short time on this earth could fill volumes as I have probably only addressed 1/100 of the actual story. I have ultimately come to accept that each event in my life is purposeful, and in fact, allows me to have the wherewithal to write these words. You see, how does one know if healing works if one has never really been healed? I do not want to suggest that the concept of healing is ever complete. It is a process that is eternal and is more evolutionary in nature. Similar to working out, one has to continue to apply the actions and concepts in a consistent manner to ensure lasting change and healthiness.

One question that I have pondered centers around whether I would have worked as diligently at growing and refining my connection to God if I did not have the numerous challenges that I have had to face in my life? Would I have been able to avoid complacency or mediocrity without the gentle nudging or painful kick in the behind of life? Given the manner in which the adversity and my progress have been entwined, and looking at the times where I have been stagnant and entrenched in the routine of life, I would say that these adversities have certainly propelled me forward. As an example, I wrote this during one of the down times after an intense argument with my 3rd wife. In looking back at this, I am able to see the remapping taking place, allowing me to appreciate the dichotomies of life and the push that I receive from the various experiences. Let me be clear; these experiences were not enjoyable. Yet, these experiences were a part of my path. Looking back and doing a postmortem, of course, there are many things I would do differently. Life does not offer us a do over in that sense. I can point to the future and do things differently in the actions I choose to engage. There are elements and areas of my life that I will not repeat again. There are other lessons that still must be learned. Being honest with myself was an integral step along this healing journey.

Pain. Happiness. Pain. Happiness. Pain. Happiness. Do we really know which is which? What is it that we are here for in this flesh to do? What is the purpose of the many experiences that we have? Pain. Happiness. Pain. Happiness. Pain. Happiness.

I would like to believe that most of our existence should be about happiness. However, so many of us struggle to find just what happiness truly is. Our society has become so oversaturated with material things. Bigger houses, faster cars, designer clothes, expensive jewelry all accumulated in massive amounts. But still, we find hollow insides. Our souls call out for more, for true substance. But this calling is like a faint candle in the far away distance straining to stay lit in the midst of a massive hurricane. Fighting to keep burning, to gain strength and grow against overwhelming odds. Our souls are calling for healing, for nurturing, for substance, for growth and expansion. But where will this come from? The odds are overwhelmingly stacked against progress in a society that breeds conformity and places those who would dare to go against the norm in the box of outcasts. And still, there are souls that call out for healing, that want that nurturing, that want to be safe, secure, and at peace. Many of us have lost ourselves, have lost our souls, the essence of who we truly are. But we can reclaim this sense of self if we are willing to search long and deep in the very place where it begins, where the very source that sustains us in spite of ourselves exists—within.

One day I woke up to this realization. It's about me finding my soul. This shift had been trying to be birthed and it was finally here. Having four children did not matter. Being with another woman did not matter. My financial condition did not matter. My house and car did not matter. My work did not matter. What came to matter for me was being true to that authentic part of me, all of me actually that is God, and the essence of God. Living life fully as a result of being fully aligned with God and my purpose in this existence. Living and being the ancient Egyptian concept of Maat. Because God is everything and I am a part of everything. Limitations are not limitations when thought of as an aspect of God. Poverty is not poverty when thought of as an aspect of God.

For instance, an important part of the healing process involves reframing the manner in which one conceptualizes life events. In other words, "They did this to me" becomes "life presented me with the opportunity to find my soul and heal it." It is up to me to take on this task or choose to continue living in the abyss that is life in this capitalistic society. To live fully in the comfort and glow of the almighty or to continue being a slave to whatever the vice is that keeps our minds numb, even if partially, and thus unable to achieve our true destiny, our greatness.

As a person who has been charged with helping to bring about healing to our community, this question serves as the cornerstone for helping to fight through the myriad of problems we face on an individual, familial, community, national and ultimately global level. The atrocities waged on African people worldwide have been vastly documented, and the resulting trauma that produces unhealthy actions is clear. It is thus essential that we begin to move from discussion to clear, specific action. In other words, healer heal thyself. The healing process starts on the inside and moves outward. The specific actions the individual takes to engage and internalize this process will ultimately have long-term benefits for the outer circles of family, community, nation and world. The ancient Egyptians began their initiation into the mystery schools with this simple edict: Know Thy Self.

As I reflected on this writing to myself from years ago, I realized that I unknowingly had continued the process of healing and created something that would serve me and others many years later.

As we continue to think about the process of healing our personal traumas, I want to introduce the next exercise. Here I would like for you to think about your parents. I would like you to write a letter to each of them that will be in two parts. The first part will consist of all the reasons that you have been angry with them or that you are upset with them. This should be done over several days as you allow this question to marinate and remember things that you may still be angry about but you have not given any conscious attention to. After you have had some time to do this next write a letter of gratitude to your parents. This should include all of the things that you are grateful for them providing you that allow you to be at the place you are currently. Again time should be given to thinking of this in an exhaustive manner so that you are clear about what you were given and are thankful for. You are writing these letters not to give them to your parents but rather to allow you to purge thoughts and more critically think about the impact certain events have had in shaping the person you have become. If you find that intense themes come up that are troubling for you, it may be helpful to process this with a therapist. Next, I would like for you to think about yourself as a parent and how you would like to be in terms of providing the leadership and nurturing as a parent you would like to ideally provide. Be specific as you think about the things you would need to include that would allow your child to develop into the adult you would like for them to be, free of any negative impacts of trauma.

The purpose of this exercise is to begin to get at some of the root causes of the issues that you might be dealing with. Our parents are our first connective source. They are our initial nurturers and the people that we look to for sustenance as they are the ones who produced us. They give us our first set of values that teach us how to understand the world from their perspective. And in doing so they pass on all of their fears, worries, biases, and prejudices, often in an unconscious manner. Most parents do not have intentions to inflict us with these negative characteristics. Most parents would believe that they are doing their absolute best to create a good reality for their child. We just are often unaware of the complexities and the manner in which the things that we do come to affect other people. There is a paradox in this in that most people, when thinking about their own lives, recognize the manner in which they have been impacted by others. Once again, the ego comes into play as it keeps us from stepping outside of our bubble and considering our impact on others going the other way. A parallel example that might make this clearer is to consider the concept of hazing. Most people who go through a process where they are being treated in what may be a hostile and unfair manner say to themselves that they would not want to treat someone else in this manner. And yet, when they get through that difficult situation and become the ones doing the hazing, those feelings that were driving them previously are forgotten. Working in the medical profession allowed me to observe this phenomenon firsthand. I was in charge of working with first, second and third-year medical residents in a family medicine program. Additionally, I was on the faculty and so was privy to information from four different perspectives as my responsibilities required me to meet with each group individually. During this time, I got to see the progression of attitudes shift as the transition took place from the first year to third year. The first year resident who was frustrated with the way they were being harassed by the third year and faculty soon progressed to the third year and became the ones doing the harassing. Of course, this did not apply to everyone, but the general theme was quite evident in the program and other similar programs that I have observed. The residents were not inherently mean and most were generally nice people who thought that they were helping those below them to get the training necessary to advance in the program.

Our parents are no different in general. Again, I am not referring to those parents that engage in abusive behavior and who may be dealing with their own traumas and thus unable to parent effectively. Most parents want the best for their children and believe that their actions are in accord with providing a good upbringing. This exercise helps us to identify those things that were done to us and have become a part of our life that inadvertently keep us from living a fully healthy life. As we are able to identify these patterns, we can then recognize how to change those patterns and put newer healthier ones in their place. Simultaneously we can also consider what we need to do to not repeat the same mistakes and refine the lessons we are teaching our children moving forward. In this manner, we began to create a new paradigm for our generational legacy.

CHAPTER 16

POSITIVE THINKING TO CREATE A NEW REALITY

"If You Think You Can Or If You Think You Can't You're Right"

There has been much written about the power of affirmations and positive thinking. Many people appreciate the use of affirmations on a basic level. The engagement of the use of affirmations is necessary for undoing negative patterns of behavior that have been created from childhood and developing new patterns that serve to create a healthier self-outlook. A key element that needs to be highlighted here is to not just have the affirmations and repeat them, but to create the energy within which you believe what it is that you are saying. Even if you do not initially believe what you are saying, think about having the energy of saying it in a way that makes it real. The more you can do this and practice this concept in a practical way; you are communicating to your brain that this is so and undoing negative patterns replacing them with positive ones. Because of the oppressive nature of our environment and the negative behaviors that have been passed down through generations for reasons that we have discussed previously, it can be challenging to alter our patterns of thinking. It may feel awkward to speak in affirming ways as opposed to in self-deprecating or doubtful ways. This is especially true if you have been inundated with negative thoughts and considerations from your entire family and social circle. It can be a challenge to change the mindset from one that hears negativity to one that embraces positivity.

If you doubt the importance of affirmations and the power that they have in remapping the brain, consider the billions of dollars that are spent yearly by various companies in an attempt to persuade you to spend your money with them. Psychologists understand that powerful slogans can take root in the brain and cause a change in behavior and attitude. This is why billions of dollars are spent each year on advertising designed to convince us to buy this, do this, go here, and support that. Every inch of space in some places has been utilized to generate a connection of influence to the brain. For instance, watching an NBA game on television, one will notice that advertising has been placed on the top of the backboard with a camera showing the action from above. Why would they go through the trouble for a shot that will only last a few seconds? In that small amount of time, the brain recognizes the words or images and makes a connection to it that can drive your behavior to engage that particular thing at some point. If these advertisers recognize the power of influencing our brain and are willing to spend so much to take advantage of it, we should be more cognizant of what we are doing for our own influence.

Historically we can see important examples of brain remapping coming out of the Black Power movement where a simple song with the refrain "Say it Loud I'm Black and I'm Proud" sought to begin unravelling generations of self-hatred that had been foisted on the community by the images generated by mainstream society. "I am somebody" became the phrase used by Jesse Jackson as he attempted to continue this motivation and speak to the subconscious of youth, encouraging them to rise above mediocrity and find greatness. This has evolved to simply saying Black Lives Matter, a refrain that forces people to consider the humanity of those who have far too often been marginalized. We see a phrase that was initially given a tepid response suddenly picked up by the mainstream after the death of George Floyd and those that would speak this phrase are no longer outcasts but normalized. If we can remap our brains on a larger communal level, we can also do this on smaller individual level, which will then move us along the path towards healing from trauma.

Our brains are extremely powerful, and I think most people fail to appreciate the amount of power that our brains are able to generate. Our brain can simultaneously process millions of actions in a second, the overwhelming majority of which we are not consciously attending to. Similar to a computer hard drive, every experience that we have had in our life is stored in our brain. That means the positive and negative encounters that we have are all factored in to how we see our current reality. We can change the perspective with which we look at these experiences and that will then impact our response to how we live our lives. The positive experiences foster a sense of confidence that allows us to move through the world, knowing that we can accomplish whatever we put our minds to. Negative experiences keep us mired in mediocrity, afraid of extending ourselves for fear of being perceived in an unflattering fashion.

We use this powerful organ, our brain, to generate positive change for ourselves. Look around the room or the space that you are sitting in currently. Even if you are outside, allow yourself to ponder all the man-made objects that are in your visual field. If we think about every single thing that we can currently see that is not of nature, it is the case that each one of those things came out of the brain of some individual. Every single thing you see was first a thought, an idea in someone's brain. At some point, someone was inspired to create that particular object. Whether it is a couch, or television, or a picture, a stove, the very building that you are residing in, all of these things came first out of someone's head and imagination. Some of these inventions are so enormous as to defy logic, such as a satellite that allows our cell phones to enable us to talk to someone on the other side of the world. Or a huge skyscraper that spans over one hundred stories and allows for thousands to enter. Or a double-decker airplane that is able to rise up in the air carrying hundreds of passengers whisking them off to another part of the world. All of the little things that go into making the airplane, the seats, the bolts, the plastic that holds the luggage, the windows, the tires, the oxygen mask, the flotation devices, every single thing on the plane came out of somebody's brain. When we can appreciate the concept that every single thing we see came out of someone's brain, we can recognize the immense magnitude that is an indication of what our brains have the power to develop and how quickly this development can occur. Consider that just 10 years ago, larger smartphones were considered by many to be too unwieldy and unreasonable to carry around. They aren't practical was the consideration most people adapted to, and only a small percentage of people ignored this and began utilizing smartphones. Fast forward to the present day and in just ten years, practically everyone has a smartphone, including five-year-old children. In just 10 years, the trajectory of life on earth has been altered quite noticeably through the technological advances that have occurred with a smartphone.

 The same brainpower that can create these wonderful inventions can also change the course of our lives. My mother used to have a cartoon on her bedroom door that said, "If you think you can or if you think you can't, you're right." I looked at this practically every day and did not fully grasp the essence of the message and just how powerful of a concept this is. It was just a funny cartoon that I thought was contradictory. I don't even know if she fully grasped how powerful this sentiment was. Essentially what is being conveyed in this cartoon is the incredible power of the mind. I would suggest that this same sentiment would apply to the concept of using our minds for our own personal healing.

We have the power to heal ourselves because the energy of the Creator resides within us and allows us to tap into that genius to bring about change. The designs to create the things that you observe surrounding you were likely developed in a space of being patient, in a space of being still and allowing inspiration to come and produce creative juices that developed a given thing. We all have the ability to tap into this power, and in tapping into this source we can also create our healing.

The challenge in today's society is engaging this process in a consistent manner, given all the many distractions that we are faced with. We have to make ourselves stop and be still. Building from our previous intervention of being still, we can now add to the equation giving our subconscious a problem to solve. We can write down our particular challenge or thing that we want to be healed, along with what we have considered to be the ideal resolution. We can then spend some of our time being still contemplating the answer, communicating to our subconscious the need to come to a solution. Our subconscious is powerful enough to begin doing the work to develop solutions and put things into place to bring these solutions into fruition.

Now that we understand this, we need to chip away at the negative structures in our mindset that hold this back. We will do this in two parts. To illustrate how powerful our brains are and how our thinking impacts the actions we engage, I would suggest engaging the activity of charting any negative thought that enters your brain over a three-day period. Just write down the thought without any judgement as if you are just collecting data. The purpose of this is to help you to get a clear sense of just how many times you are speaking to yourself in a manner that is not healthy or affirming. After you complete this, now analyze the manner in which you talk about things and even talk about yourself. Most people who do this exercise are shocked at how poorly and disrespectfully they talk to themselves. Those internalized feelings, the result of years of training, automatically send messages to your brain and you are constantly inundated with thoughts reflecting this. You're not good enough; you suck, everybody is going to see how horrible you are, you're not pretty, you're overweight, you eat too much, your breath stinks, they're going to see you don't belong, no one really likes you, you are such a jerk, you big dummy, how could you be so stupid. These statements and more may play on a loop inside your brain daily. If these are the sentiments you are feeding your subconscious, what do you think will be the result? The internalized negativity creates turmoil internally, leading to those previously mentioned issues of depression, anxiety, frustration, low self-esteem, lack of confidence and more.

    Were there times that you called yourself a stupid idiot? Were there times that you complained about things that were outside of your control? Were there times you made assumptions about someone doing something that you did not like that you yourself have also done, for example, driving slow in the fast lane? Did you allow your rage to manifest in a way that caused you to call someone out of their name? Did you tell yourself that you were not smart enough, pretty enough, well off enough? If so, you have allowed yourself to take a peek inside the inner workings of your thought process and see what you need to do differently to think in a way that is healthier and affirming rather than destructive and negating. You would not allow anyone to talk to your child or family in this manner, so why do you accept it from yourself? Answering this question and deciding to act differently begins to move you out of the malaise of indifference into being a conscious and active creator of your reality.

Conversely, this exercise will also help us to appreciate how much work we have to do to truly love ourselves unconditionally. We will use the affirmations to generate a positive sense of self-love and confidence in who we are and what we are capable of doing. Eventually, we will radiate the energy from the work of doing this affirmative engagement to all of those around us and to our progeny moving forward. One ritual I like to suggest people work to include into their life flow involves using reminder alarms to keep them focused on what it is they are trying to change. This is important because we can often have the best intentions but be drawn back into unhealthy patterns by the slightest challenge. For example, I can decide that I want to have a ritual of engaging in prayer and meditation every morning when I wake up so that I can keep a healthy positive attitude throughout the day. This might be a challenge for me because others have identified that I complained quite often during the course of the day and in order to eliminate complaining and replace that with positive gratitude, I have to utilize a system of ritual to help me with this. Although awkward at first, the more we utilize these affirmations, the stronger we will get. One way I suggest people use affirmations in this capacity is to develop a set of positive affirmations that pertain to the particular thing that they want to heal. Then they can set an alarm on their phone that will go off every hour on the hour with the particular affirmation they want to reinforce. The intensity of this can be adjusted based on your comfort, for instance, moving it to every 30 minutes or every two hours. For me, every hour seems to be a sweet spot that allows continual reminders throughout the day doing the work to rewire the brain in a positive manner. This will replace the negative thoughts that linger from the traumas that we have suffered from a positive line of thinking. Because patterns of behavior are difficult to change and require the implementation of consistent alternate behavior methods for how we talk to ourselves, discipline with this process is extremely important.

Commit to this process and remember to be patient with yourself and the process. We do not have to solve all of our problems at once, and in fact, that is an unrealistic expectation. As a comparison, we can think about how long it takes a bruise to heal when we have fallen and suffered intense bruising to the skin on our arm. We know that the bruise will not heal in a few days. In a simple explanation, it will take time for the bleeding to stop as the blood cells gather together in a clump to slow the bleeding. This will eventually turn into a scab that hardens and protects the impacted area. Eventually, the scab will begin to fall away, leaving skin that is discolored. If we remove the scab too soon, we will find ourselves bleeding and a new scab will have to return, delaying the healing process. There will be discoloration in the area where the bruise is and over time, the discoloration will fade away and the natural color will return. The healing of this bruise is a process that takes several months, and with all of our technological advances, the healing process cannot be rushed. This is what happens to us physically and there is a parallel process that happens emotionally and spiritually. So if we consider the internal emotional wounds from the trauma that we have faced, we can recognize similarities in the process that it will take for our internal wounds to heal. The time necessary for healing will be impacted by the intensity of the wound caused by the trauma and the length of time that has elapsed since the trauma was suffered, plus the amount of effort placed into the healing process. In short, healing is a process that requires us to be patient with ourselves even as we work diligently to create a new paradigm for ourselves, and if we try to rush this process or peel the scab too soon, we will delay our healing. Having patience with our healing process is necessary to ensure that we are truly successful in breaking negative patterns and creating healthier positive ones.

CHAPTER 17

THE POWER OF CHANGE

Discipline Comes From Doing

"Your beliefs don't make you a better person your behavior does"

SUKRHAJ DHILON

Another component of healing involves understanding change and its impact on the healing process. Anyone embarking on the process of healing is dealing fundamentally with the concept of change. Change is not an easy concept to put into practice. First, let me provide a working definition of change. Websters defines change as to cause to be different; to give a completely different form or appearance to; to transform[29]. One of the major impediments to change is the inability to maintain a disciplined approach doing the work required to bring about change. Discipline comes from doing is a saying that I engaged to remind myself to be in the practice of applying the change process on a daily basis.

When we contemplate change and human behavior, one need only consider the ritual that takes place on January 1st every year. This is a time when many people utilize the passing of a new year to think about changes they want to

---

29 change. 2021. In Merriam-Webster.com.
    Retrieved March 28, 2021, from https://www.merriam-webster.com/dictionary/change

incorporate into their lives for the upcoming year. They embark upon these New Year's resolutions that rationally they want to incorporate into the fabric of who they are. However, what typically ends up happening for most is that they will maintain the behavior or changes for a short time, maybe two to three weeks, before resorting back to their baseline behavior. Why is this? Our bodies, minds and emotions are accustomed to responding and interacting in a typical learned way and attempt to undo this are met with resistance. I like to use the example of working out to illustrate this point further.

When one first begins the process of working out, the exertion of building muscle is very tedious and painful. In fact, for the first three to four weeks of the process, the muscles are responding to the process with a lot of pain and discomfort, which often deters people from the goal of building muscle. However, if the person were able to just maintain their discipline and get over the hump of the initial pain, their body would begin to acclimate. This may take approximately four weeks. The body has accepted that this is a new reality and then they would begin to see results of their efforts at about the 5-6 week period. By the 7-8 week mark, the body, mind and muscles are beginning to not only welcome the workout, but are completely accustomed to the new reality of working out. By the time one reaches 8-9 weeks, they are beginning to look forward to the process of working out. Finally, when one has reached 12 weeks working out has become a part of the nature of what one does and visible results of the hard work and dedication are embodied in greater muscle mass and strength. The goal from this point now shifts to maintenance and continuity. If one reaches this point and then stops, they will return to where they started prior to beginning to work out. The problem with this process is that most people do not allow themselves to get over the formidable hump

The Power of Change

of working through the pain. They tell themselves that this pain is too great and as a result, fall back to the previous patterns and behaviors that are "comfortable" to them. Our minds and bodies are comfortable doing what we have done for so many years. Change requires stepping outside of the confines of what is comfortable and stretching the muscles by doing something different. Stretching the muscles involves tearing the muscles down so that they can be built back up. Biologically this is the thing that is happening when a person is working out. The muscles are being torn apart and in the rest period, they are reforming and getting stronger, creating new muscle mass. The process of change undergoes a similar pattern, as old methods of being and doing are replaced with newer more appropriate methods for presently existing that over time get stronger.

Yet another factor to consider in the change process revolves around how motivated one is to change. In motivational interviewing a person is often asked to describe their level of motivation to change a given behavior on a scale of 1-10. The manner in which a person answers this question gives an indication of their level of commitment or resolve to do whatever is necessary to bring about change in this regard. For instance, a person who says their motivation level is at a three has little chance of seeing change actually manifest for them. Likewise, a person whose motivation level is at a 5 is on the fence and unsure if they are willing to do the work necessary to bring about change. They would like to change but do not necessarily want to engage in the work necessary to bring this change about. These people would prefer to have change magically occur without any dedication or hard work. It is also possible that they have not learned how to discipline themselves to do the work necessary to bring about the change. When asked this question about motivation, most people respond at a 7 or 8. It has been my experience in my psychology practice that most people that come in for therapy, outside of those mandated to come, really do want to manifest change in whatever area of life they are facing. However, just like those persons who make resolutions on January 1 every year, their level of dedication and discipline for doing the work necessary to bring about this change may not fully be there for a variety of reasons. Some of these reasons include the aforementioned patterns of behavior that have been evident since childhood.

So the goal for the person who comes in and answers a 7 or 8 on the motivational scale is to help them understand what it would take to move them to a 10. A person who responds at a 10 has essentially confirmed that they are willing to do whatever it takes to make the change or healing happen, or in other words, to make their goals manifest. This is really important because it helps to establish the urgency and commitment to which a person will be taking on the challenge of making the changes that they are faced with. So, for example, a person who comes in and wants to change their addiction to alcohol will be at a ten when their actions indicate that they are willing to take all of the suggestions given to them to overcome their addiction, without any excuses. These might include going to ninety meetings in ninety days, ensuring they have daily connections with their sponsor, working on changing their thought processes by doing an in-depth analysis of their history of alcohol use, and avoiding places where they have used previously.

If a person makes excuses and says, well my car broke down or I do not have transportation so I cannot get to 90 meetings, or they say I don't know the phone number to the treatment facility, this gives an indication that they really are not as committed to making the change happen as they are professing. In this instance, the refrain action speaks louder than words rings clear. Ultimately a person can say

The Power of Change

that they are at a 10 on a motivational level, but it is always their actions that will determine this. People who are at a 10 when it comes to making change happen do not allow any hindrances or roadblocks to deter them from their goal. When you consider successful people in our society, people at the top of their professions, their motivation to achieve that level of excellence is typically at a 10.

Take football star Jerry Rice as an example. He was not highly recruited out of high school and attended a Division II predominantly Black college where he did not get a lot of exposure. He worked to become a gifted wide receiver. When he was drafted into the NFL, his desire was to become the best wide receiver to ever play the game. His motivation level was at a 10. As such, during the off seasons, he would work diligently while other players may have been taking time off, relaxing and recuperating. He studied tapes and film of the best in the profession while simultaneously shaping his body and crafting a mindset that would take nothing less than being the best. The energy and passion behind his determination and dedication yielded results that created a player who ultimately achieved his goals, becoming the all-time leader in yards and touchdowns for a wide receiver. There are other receivers who might have been as or more gifted in terms of skills, but they were not willing to put in the effort that he put in and thus did not achieve as much.

So, as you think about healing yourself, ask yourself honestly about your level of commitment to action so that you can have a clear indication of where you are currently. It is more important to be honest about this so that you can deal with why you are only at a 7 or an 8 rather than trying to convince yourself that you are at a 10 when you are not. The person that attempts to convince themselves of this will likely not be successful and have to deal with further layers of self-doubt. A more appropriate approach would be to gain an understanding of why they are at a 7 or an 8 and then determine what it would take for them to move to a 10, ensuring a greater likelihood of success.

This same procedure of understanding commitment to action occurs when one begins to change any aspect of his/her life. We do not necessarily think of this level of commitment when we want to stop cursing, smoking, losing weight or any other various resolutions people make about changing their lives. But this is what happens. The mind and body are in the process of tearing down old behaviors and establishing new habits. These new behaviors and habits are often outside the scope of what we are accustomed to and so are often very painful and uncomfortable. However, the true healing and change that must occur require us to move through this pain and get to a space of peace and being comfortable. These are the things that shape the hard work that must be done as it relates to changing behavior. The formula is the same; the thing that changes is the particular behavior and thought patterns and the specific actions that need to take place to create new behaviors and thought patterns.

CHAPTER 18

EQUILIBRIUM

Understanding Family Dynamics and Undoing the Negative Traits

"Equilibrium is attained when the state of mind body and spirit become one"

SHARMILHA KARTHIKEYAN

Once we have established a baseline of actions for preparing our minds, bodies and spirit to be in a space of change, we are now prepared to deal with some of the more specific components of managing various trauma. We will begin by looking at the source of many of the difficulties that people face that being unhealthy familial patterns of behavior. Family should be our source of nurturing and comfort. The people that render us love, care and support, helping us to navigate our place in the world. However, as we have been able to observe in the examples that have been discussed throughout this book, there have been many occasions where inappropriate behaviors were engaged, which contributed to the inability to effectively be our best selves. It is important for us to explore and understand these familial patterns so that we can determine which ones serve us well and need to continue being utilized and which ones do a disservice to us and need to be eliminated.

Understanding the origins of who and why we are is a fundamental aspect to creating healing. We will build from the work that we did previously to understand ourselves. I will describe a detailed process for doing this moving forward. Because we are a combination of our unique personalities and the environment in which we have been shaped, it is clear that there are some things about us that we are in control of and others that we likely have no control. For instance, a person who is an introvert would likely have difficulty attempting to suddenly become an extroverted life of the party. This is because being an introvert is a fundamental aspect of that person's personality or an internally derived characteristic. On the other hand, an external characteristic such as a person that hoards food because food was always in scarce supply for their family has developed this pattern of behavior as a result of external forces. In other words, due to the fact that food was not available. The hoarding behavior could be altered by changing the environment and retraining the person's understanding that food is now in abundance and will always be available. Depending on how long the person engaged in this behavior, the elimination of this behavior can take some time. In some cases, what has been learned is so entrenched that the behavior is never eliminated.

A useful method for uncovering the information that helps understand the family influence involves creating a family chart that documents the positive and negative characteristics of the influential individuals that have impacted a persons' life. This would include great grandparents, parents, aunts, uncles, cousins, siblings, or friends of the family. In short, anyone who was overly present in your life and exacted some degree of influence on your actions and ability to think and conceptualize the world. After there has been an examination of the characteristics each person has, one is then able to look for themes that emerge. These themes are sometimes familial and other times, may be individual. The person can then look at the relationship that exists between the information gained and their current persona. This will likely open up a deeper understanding of why we engage in certain behaviors or think a certain way. In the social sciences, we call this type of chart a genogram and use it to get a basic understanding of family structures and the dynamics that are in play that we would not be able to recognize if we did not see it in black and white on the chart. Many of the people that I work with that have done this exercise have been amazed at the amount of information that they were able to unearth and the clarity that results from this organization of information. It is particularly useful when older members of the family are willing to engage dialogue about historical issues that have been prevalent and what they have been able to remember related to these issues. Genograms are also used in the science field to help trace diseases or chronic illness, and this could also be a useful benefit for understanding yourself depending on the impact of a particular medical condition.

For this exercise, it will be useful to have a large piece of cardboard to draw out the diagram so that you are able to clearly see the patterns that exist. As we start putting ourselves in the middle of the chart, any siblings that we have would go on the same level with us. Any children that we have, we would draw a line and they come below us. Similarly, any nephews or nieces from our siblings would also be on the level below us. On the level above us would be our parents. Then each of the parent's siblings would be on the line with them going out to the left or to the right. Underneath the parent's siblings would be their respective children. Going above the parents would be the grandparents. Similarly, the parents and grandparents' siblings would be on the line with them and below them would fall their children. And we could go further to the extent that you have the knowledge of your family that extends that far. Those with larger families will have a significant amount of data to analyze. Additionally, when blended families are involved, the possibilities of how these dynamics merge to provide a broad range of options to consider. This opens up many possibilities for the understanding of self and the many components that may have influenced the current state of self. As an aside, this graph can also be useful to have a visual representation of your family tree and the history of where your family came from.

Now that we have the structure of this chart, we can begin to put in the various characteristics that help us to understand our family and the dynamics that have been passed down through generations. For the purpose of working on healing, we will focus on those negative aspects that have been trauma-related and passed down that do not serve our families in a positive way. It is also possible to focus on the positive aspects of family that has been passed down and this is something that can be highlighted to show and teach our children the strengths of the family structure.

Here is an example chart that illustrates these points clearly.

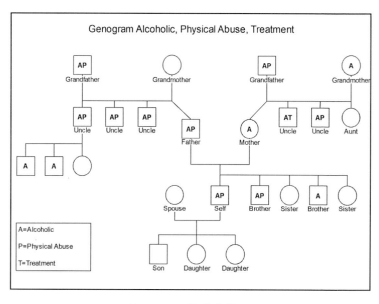

Genogram Alcohol Abuse

Equilibrium

We will focus on the patterns of alcohol abuse that are evident in both sides of the family. We can see that the men on the father's side all had issues with alcohol abuse and subsequently drunken behavior and physical abuse. Only one male on the father's side did not engage in physical abuse of their children. This illustrates the pattern of learning and incorporating what was done in the household and passing this on to those that we then parent. On the mother's side, we see two of the men having issues with alcohol and one having issues to the degree that it caused significant problems requiring intensive treatment. The main person in this chart is an alcoholic and had engaged in physical abuse, as is the case for his younger brother. The youngest brother, although an alcoholic, did not engage in physical abuse. The two sisters so despised the behavior that they witnessed from the alcoholic rages that they refused to drink at all and abstained from any substances that would alter their behavior. It becomes easy to now hypothesize about the possibilities for what might happen with the children of the parents if they are not aware of these patterns and make a conscious decision to do something different.

We will now look at the issue of anger that comes up in the family. We see that on both sides of the family, there is a lot of yelling and vehement expression of feelings. In several cases, this included physical interactions where police had to be called. We can see that the maternal grandmother had an issue with anger but chose to suppress it, especially when her husband was around as he was quite dominant and abusive. All their children had an issue with anger and the older two children engaged in a lot of yelling modeling what their parents did. Subsequently, in taking care of the younger siblings while the parents were gone, they engaged in yelling at their younger siblings. On the paternal side of the family, we can see that both

No More Trauma, No More Drama

the grandfather and grandmother engaged in anger and yelling, with several instances of police involvement for both. We can see that all the uncles engaged in anger and yelling, with three having police involvement due to an altercation. The cumulative effect is that the main individual in this chart engaged in anger and yelling. All of his siblings were angry and four became yellers, with only the youngest sibling choosing to do the opposite of this and become very passive, abhorring the yelling that she observed growing up. One brother had several instances of police involvement. Finally, all his children are seen to be angry and frequently yelling at each other

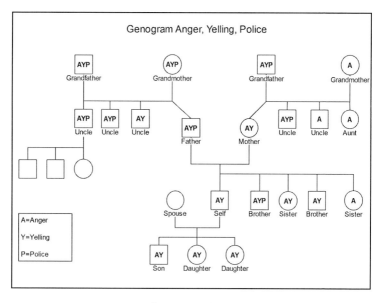

Genogram Anger

Creating your chart allows you to see the patterns that have manifested in your family that might not have been consciously considered before. You should think about themes or conditions in your life that you find challenging or difficult and think through how those themes may have been passed down to you. Most people that I completed this exercise with are amazed at the clarity that comes from seeing the visual depiction of patterns, positive and negative that exist in this format. Understanding the etiology of patterns in our life is quite effective and a necessary component of healing from the generational trauma present in our families.

CHAPTER 19

--- ALIGNMENT ---

Connecting Your Values and Actions

"When you are in alignment with the values of your heart things have a way of working out"

IYANLA VANZANT

An integral aspect to being able to heal from trauma is understanding your core values and where they come from. Everyone has values that guide and dictate how they live their life. Most people just do not think about in specific and critical detail what those values are and where they got them from. Most people engage the values that they do primarily because that is what their parents taught them. It is unfortunately rare that people really do a critical analysis or why they believe the things that they believe or support. It is my belief that you cannot fully understand yourself if you do not know what values you stand for and believe in.

It is easy to speak the words of a particular set of values. People do this very eloquently every day in a variety of ways. It is much more difficult to have our actions to be a reflection of the words we speak. We see this as a challenge across all aspects of life and in many different areas. Whatever it is we believe, it stands to reason that we should be able to put that belief into action. From this perspective, it then makes sense that whenever we are faced with a challenge, that challenge is only an opportunity for us to apply what we say we believe. Rather than focusing on the negative things that were "done" to me I can choose to appreciate that each of those experiences gave me an opportunity to employ the values of life that I believe in.

I'll give an example to clarify. I often ask people who identify themselves as Christian to think about what the dialogue will look like as they stand in judgment. Based on the values of Christianity, there are guidelines for how we should live life. Beyond the obvious ten commandments, there are standards for what is considered Christian values. Probably the most important standard is love. I may be working with a Christian couple and one of the presenting issues is that the husband often lambasts his wife, calling her out of her name and talking to her in a manner that is nasty and disrespectful. After ascertaining that they are not being forced to follow a Christian doctrine, the next question is for them to explain how these actions are in alignment with how God would want them to treat their wife. Would these actions be considered love? I ask how they believe that God will respond as they are standing in judgement. Will they be able to say, "well, I did everything right except for when my wife was getting on my nerves, then I did not follow the values of loving my wife". I think it stands to reason from God's perspective that this may have been the very challenge that was provided to see if in fact, you were going to stay consistent with what you believe and apply the lived example of the values you believe, or if you would falter from the path allowing your ego to dominate and engaging in negative and inappropriate behaviors inconsistent with the teachings of the Bible simply because your wife got on your nerves. Of course, I get that we are not perfect. However, we often make excuses for behaviors that are inconsistent with our values, and this does not serve us well. Ultimately, if the behavior is not in accordance with what you believe, more of an effort should be made to change the behavior so that it is in alignment with the values. On the other hand, one could change the values to be in alignment with the behavior. This is an individual decision between you and God that no one else can make for you, and as long as you are not hurting anyone, your choice is right for you. Just be accountable for whichever path you choose, and we must choose one or the other if we expect to have positive change occur.

This example provides a symbolic representation of the way we might choose to think about this issue, and the roots of the example apply across any belief system. It is important for us to have a check and balances that will help us to honestly assess whether or not the stated values that we profess and believe in wholeheartedly are in alignment with the actions that are the result of our everyday behaviors. Ultimately, we have to hold ourselves responsible for what happens on our path of destiny as we are Co-creators of the direction of our lives and the things that will manifest in our lives. There are some things that we can control and others that are outside of our control. Those that are outside of our control we have to let go. Those that we can control, we have to make sure that we are thinking and acting in ways that move us forward consistent with what we believe and what we want to accomplish. In my estimation, the lack of consistency between actions and values is the primary issue with many of the problems facing our country currently, and this is not a new phenomenon. This lack of alignment is in fact, built into those most sacred documents that are at the foundation of the United States. All men are created equal. Oh really now. What about that little 3/5ths thing? Why are people with melanin in their skin treated differently by the police and justice system? What about the term justice? We do not like to talk about these inequities, though, preferring instead to pretend that what was said was not really said. From my perspective, until we deal with that root cause, anything else is lip service and will continue the status quo, as has been illustrated in several of the examples discussed previously. Here is an interesting exercise if you happen to be a bit bored one day and have some extra time on your hands. Get a copy of the bill of rights and go through it, asking yourself if it actually works in a practical sense for all of the citizens of this country. I don't know about you but I would prefer for people to just be honest with me that it does not apply to everyone and then I can adjust from there. To tell me this is the case when my eyes, mind and common sense suggest differently is gaslighting and if I am not strong enough mentally can have a traumatic impact on my sense of reality.

Moving back to us as individuals, what if we realize that our actions and values are not aligned, what should we do? Smile. Yes, that's it smile. Appreciate the fact that you are human and it's ok to be human. But by acknowledging the lack of alignment, we can then be accountable, which moves us into action one way or the other. We can be gentle with ourselves and commit to beginning a practice of self-love rather than beating up on ourselves for not being good enough, not trying harder, not finishing that task. We can bask in our humanness and awareness that we did not hit the mark but we have another opportunity. We then can make a decision about what it is that we would like to change, our actions or our values so that the two are in alignment. It does not matter which you choose as it is your life and you get to decide how you live it. But something has to change, the action or the value, or we will remain in an unhealthy state of discomfort from the misalignment.

The following values will give you an opportunity to gain some clarity about what is really essential and important to you. Complete the exercise and we will elaborate further on the meaning of your results.

EXERCISE

Place each word into one of three categories: Very Essential (Must have) Important (Cool to have but can live without it) and Not Significant (Not necessary at all). After you have done this, rank order each category from most important to least important. As you are considering the various words, think about how you would define the word and why it would be important to you. These are examples of relative words that although we might be able to define but the way we conceptualize the practical application of each word differ depending on the person. It is often the case that as individuals in a relationship began to define the words for themselves, they recognize the problems that arise from their differing understanding of how they conceptualize a particular word. Having this awareness then allows for the bridging of a gap that moves people to the same page.

Tradition	Popularity	Attractiveness	Creativity
Intimacy	Romance	Flexibility	Skill
Sexuality	Influence	Money	Passion
Independence	Growth	Generosity	Risk
Being Loved	Simplicity	Excitement	Fitness
Achievement	Helpfulness	Commitment	Openness
Stability	Purpose	Responsibility	Self-Esteem
Challenge	Caring	Freedom	Loving
Fun	Inner Peace	Health	Forgiveness
Self-Control	Learning	Laughter	Hope
Self-Respect	Honesty	Fairness	Spirituality
Faithfulness	Safety	Acceptance	Family
Friendship	God's will	Loyalty	Courtesy
Joy	Surrender	Believe	Spontaneous
Focus	Discipline	Trust	Humility

Service	Vision	Peace	Material possessions
Compassion	Balance	Boundaries	Patience
Service	Authenticity	Appreciation	Order
Gratitude	Unconditional love	Cleanliness	Budgeting
Savings	Investments	Integrity	Confidence
Assertive	Variety	Work	Career
Education	Empowerment	Affection	Recognition
Control	Equality	Reliability	Excellence

Now that you have completed this exercise, we can look at the patterns that have emerged from what you have come up with. If you look at the top ten values that are most important for you, ask yourself if someone were watching a movie of your life, would they see these 10 values manifested in the actions you engage daily. Be honest with yourself when doing this so that we can get a clear picture of whether or not there are indeed discrepancies between your actions and your values. I will explain the importance of this shortly. For some people, there may be an unfortunate awareness that what they say they believe and what they actually engage in do not match up. This is ok as we are bringing this to awareness so that we can begin making the changes that will move us more in line with who we want to be.

The foundation of my work with people involves this concept of aligning actions and values. It does not matter what the issue is when we talk about healing and producing change; a central component of that change process has to be the alignment of one's actions with one's values. It has been my observation that often when people are experiencing difficulties, these two areas are misaligned. When actions and values are not in alignment, dissonance is created, which our subconscious is aware of but which we do not necessarily process consciously. There are a number of reasons why we may not be processing this, including not wanting to really change what it is that we are doing. However, we may ultimately reach a point where we are tired of the discomfort that comes from the misalignment and are at that point moved to do something different. I will give a couple of examples to illustrate.

A family comes in for counseling after their 15-year-old son has been suspended from school for the third time for being disruptive in the classroom. The parents express that they have tried everything to help their son to no avail. They note that they are well off financially and have given the report that he did not display any of these difficulties prior to entering high school, and these behaviors seem to have appeared out of nowhere. The family appears to be supportive, engaging and highly motivated to provide the help that their son needs. When I talk to the son individually, he states that he is often left in charge of his younger siblings as his parents both work highly demanding jobs that require a lot of overtime and late nights. He reports that even when his parents are home, they are often engaged with their laptops and phones responding to work-related matters. He gives a most recent example where they were out to dinner as a family and his parents both chose to take business calls that disrupted their time together. Overall, he reports that he would like more attention and interaction with his parents and does not care about the material possessions that their employer provides. I ask if he has expressed this to his parents and he states that he has but they do not listen to him. I convene the family together and ask for the son to share his feelings. As the session ends, I ask the parents to do the values exercise together so that we can discuss it the next time they come. When they return the next time and review their list, their top 5 are God's Will, Family, Peace,

Stability and Fun. Money falls at the bottom of the first category number 23. Career is in the 2nd category. I ask them to analyze the connection between their stated values and the current manner in which they live their lives. This is uncomfortable for them, but they have to admit that their actions indicate that career and money are more important than their stated values. The husband attempts to employ the rationale that their work allows them to provide for the family that is so important, giving them opportunities they would otherwise not have. I refer them back to the conversation from the son last week and what they heard him say that he would prefer. They are now faced with determining how they will proceed based on the information gained from this exercise. Will they change the behavior to match the values or will they change their values to be more in line with their behavior? This is their choice and there is no right answer to this question. Only an acceptance of whatever outcomes result from how the question is answered.

Another common example of things that occur and quite challenging to talk about is centered around the concept of sexuality and religion. There are a number of different circumstances where this might come up, such as a single person navigating the throes of dating or a young couple in the process of being engaged. As we discuss sexuality and their desire to engage in sexual intimacy, this must be placed against their value of being a Christian. As mentioned previously, most people who consider themselves to be Christians follow the tenets of the Bible and as such, we must discuss the concept of fornication and the process of engaging in sex prior to marriage. I think most people are aware of this contradiction and rather than deal with it, prefer to pretend that it's not there. This, on its face, appears easier than the more difficult option of choosing between abstaining, changing the actions to match the values, or engaging in sex, changing

Alignment

the values to match the actions. If one is truly going to honestly look at themselves, then a decision must be made about how they will proceed regarding this situation as opposed to ignoring it. These are just a few examples to highlight how lack of alignment between actions and values can ultimately cause a number of different issues for the person and it is in addressing this misalignment that true growth can occur.

When I talk to people about these concepts, I always make it clear that it is not my position to determine what a person's values or actions should be. That is an independent choice and something that has to be resolved for that person internally based on their connection with the Creator. We all have different ways of understanding the world and I do not believe that anyone can dictate this for anyone else. What I do instead is serve as a mirror, helping people to make an honest assessment of whether or not their actions and values are in alignment, and if they are not, helping them to think through which of the two they would like to change. Of course, there is a third option where they could change neither of these two and remain in a space where the dissonance dominates their life, but that means that they would have to acquiesce to the unpleasant feelings that brought them in for help to begin with. Sometimes this ends up being the default choice for people who are not willing to engage in the process of doing the work to bring about change in their life. Whatever we choose, I want people to come out of their comfort zone and be willing to challenge themselves to gain a more comprehensive understanding of who we are.

Lastly, I think it is important as one is considering what the alignment of actions and values means for themselves, that they block out the noise of society and the external expectation that we often place on ourselves. I find it to be a healthy exercise for us all to analyze why we believe what we believe, as that is inherently what makes us who we are.

Without doing this deeper level thinking, we can remain trapped in a space that is unknowingly limiting us. People often do not want to explore anything that is different than what they know, but this actually stifles growth. It has been my experience that when I ask people why they believe what they believe and we drill down in the conversation really looking for the answer to this question, we ultimately come to a point where the eventual reason is that this is what my parents believed. Based on this, we all believe and do what we believe and do primarily because this is what we were taught. So if we were born in a different culture or in a family that understood God differently, this way of being is what we would be doing as adults. This belies any critical analysis of our choices and a true understanding of are we doing things that are truly in our best interests.

The field of psychology has engaged in a lot of work centered around how to convince and manipulate people to do certain things. Marketing as an aspect of this is geared towards making things appear shiny and appealing so that we will engage those things and spend our money in an attempt to acquire them. In the book Brainwashed: Challenging the Myth of Black Inferiority, Tom Burrell makes a compelling case that goes in-depth in analyzing this very concept[30]. It is clear that social media outlets have been designed to shift our thinking and move our values in directions that benefit the manipulators at the top of the capitalistic society. The recent documentary Social Dilemma addresses this manipulation in more detail[31]. The point is that we have to be willing to question how we came to believe what we believe and analyze does this belief truly serves our best interests. This is

---

30 Tom Burrell 2010 Brainwashed: Challenging the Myth of Black Inferiority, Smiley Books, Carlsbad,CA

31 The Social Dilemma, Netflix, 2020

Alignment

a question that we must each grapple with and resolves for ourselves and not the interests of others.

Exploration can do one of two things; it can make us stronger in our resolve to continue believing what we believe, or it can help us to expand our view and incorporate potentially newer, stronger, better ideologies that can really increase our understanding of who we are. This moves our analysis away from a limited minute perspective to one that is broader and allows for the growth that comes with critical thinking. As I have traveled around the world studying different cultures and their value and spiritual systems, it becomes clear to me that there are some constants that can be applied across most cultures in the world. Basic tenets such as love for your neighbor, always doing your best, not killing, and not stealing to name a few, seem to be consistent no matter where you reside in the world. I think the problem comes in when the ego of man attempts to dictate for other people how they should be, which then makes it a judgmental type of interaction. This is why it is more important for me to pay attention to the actions of an individual as opposed to the words of an individual. Ultimately, the alignment of our actions and values will provide a healthy direction to our path as we continue undoing the negative impact of trauma.

CHAPTER 20

CREATING POSITIVE RITUALS

"A daily ritual is a way of saying, I'm voting for myself, I'm taking care of myself".

MARIEL HEMINGWAY

Rituals serve the purpose of helping us to integrate a way of being that we would like to adapt into our life. Every culture has a set of rituals that define the culture and how things are to be done. There are rituals regarding childbirth, marriage, and rites of passage into adulthood, to name a few. As it relates to healing from trauma, rituals can help establish new modes of thinking and being that replace outdated modes of thinking that no longer serve us. However, rituals also have a downside. There are some things that we have learned to do ritually that do not serve us and in fact, contribute to us holding on to unhealthy patterns of behavior. Sometimes the rituals that we engage were necessary as we attempted to survive the trauma that was inflicted upon us but they no longer serve us currently. Think about the rituals that exist in your life currently. What do you do in a consistent ritualistic manner that is important to you? Why are these things important to you? What happens if you fail to do them? How have you taught your children to engage in these rituals? What would your life look like if you eliminate these rituals? What are the positive rituals that your family has passed down? What are the unhealthy rituals that exist in your family?

In this context of creating healing from the trauma, we need rituals to provide the seal that keeps the healing inside of us and does not allow us to slip back into prior unhealthy ways of being. Rituals allow us to cement the work we are doing to create lasting change rather than momentary gains, similar to what often happens with fad diets or exercise programs. We are looking for a lifestyle change that reaches the inner core of who we are and becomes the standard for how we live our lives moving forward. Ultimately we must fortify our house so that we do not allow anything negative to penetrate our solitude. A very useful ritual in this regard is one that most people identify with in some capacity that being prayer and meditation. Unfortunately, we sometimes only engage in this process when things are bad or we are in some type of trouble. If we instead engage these actions in a ritualistic manner on a daily basis, this will enable us to build up our strength such that when the time comes that we find ourselves facing adversity or tribulations, we will have fortified ourselves such that we can withstand these moments in a healthy manner.

When we think about the way rituals are taught, we can see that we are guided by those who are in charge of us at a very young age to learn certain things that dictate and establish how we live life. Used in the proper context, rituals can be a very valuable way to pass down traditional information that allows the culture to continue thriving and evolving. On the other hand, the same process can also cause unhealthy behaviors to be passed down and continue to be practiced even though they may cause a significant amount of harm. In this section, as we are continuing to build our healthy self free of trauma, we want to consider those rituals that do not serve us that we engage in. We will have to think about the various

Creating Positive Rituals

things that we do in a ritualistic manner and really process what it would mean to engage differently. We will offer positive rituals that can be utilized and engaged in a consistent manner in the process of building this healthy self. Of course, these principles can be modified to fit your circumstances, the goal being to create a healthy life free of trauma.

Do you consider complaining to be a ritual? Do you know people who find something negative to say about most situations? Maybe it's a coworker that complains about the temperature of the office. Maybe it's a friend that complains about the weather being too hot or too cold and never just right. Maybe it's you complaining about the government or your employer or your neighbor. For many people complaining becomes a rite of passage. If you grew up in a household of complaining, it's likely that you yourself are now a complainer. Do you like being around people who complain constantly? Does the energy of these conversations lift your spirit and inspire you to want to be better and live your life in a grander way? We have to ask ourselves what does complaining accomplish. How is this moving our lives forward in a productive way?

I could not believe these people broke into my house and stole things after being told by the judge not to enter the home. To compound the situation, they then lied about what they had done in court. Who does that? I was ruminating about the ridiculousness and unfairness of the situation yet again. A friend said to me that if I wanted to free myself from the negativity surrounding this situation, I needed to stop talking about it. He suggested that I attempt to go 30 days without mentioning it at all. I was shocked that he wasn't "on my side." Are you listening to me? Did you hear what they did to me I wondered? However, when I got to my quiet space and contemplated his sentiments and considered his perspective, it occurred to me that he was tired of my complaining and simultaneously wanting to see me free myself from a situation that I could not control. I've tried many things to help me grow and evolve and so decided to adopt his suggestion. I would not talk about this situation for the next 30 days at all to anyone. After a week, I recognized that I was feeling better, although I had not yet attributed this to what I had committed to do in terms of not talking about it. My spirits continued to rise and by the end of the 30 days, I felt miraculously better and seemed to not even care anymore about what had occurred. The angst and anxiety I had been feeling was removed as I had shifted my energy and was more focused on the things that I needed to do to move forward in my life. It was as if the issue had miraculously disappeared. For me, this is an example of the concept that what we give our attention to grows and what we ignore fades away. I had unknowingly benefited from a lesson of controlling what I can control and letting go of those things that were out of my control. This has proved to be very valuable in how I live my life currently.

When we decide to stop giving the trauma energy, we eliminate the power supply of the trauma. A great symbolic example of this can be seen in the movie After Earth starring the father and son Will and Jaden Smith[32]. In the movie, his son must overcome his fear, in particular from alien creatures who thrive off of sensing the fear of others. This fear is their energy source. When they cannot sense fear, their powers are no longer effective. When his son is able to control his fear, he eliminates the power supply of the aliens and easily defeats them as they are no longer able to sense where he is. The symbolic lesson of this movie is again to focus on the things that are your source of energy and that move you forward in a positive way rather than those things that drain your energy and keep you trapped in

---

32 After Earth, Columbia pictures, 2013

Creating Positive Rituals

a space of lethargy, frustration and depression. The more we are able to create rituals that channel our energy properly in a healthy manner, the trauma of a particular event will no longer have power over us.

Interestingly, an antidote for complaining is gratitude, a ritual worthy of having in our lives. When we are able to focus on things that we are grateful for as opposed to complaining, this shifts the energy from one of stagnant negativity to one of dynamic happiness. Doing something as simple as writing reasons to be grateful on a large sticky note on your wall or in a special gratitude journal on a daily basis can do wonders for lifting your spirits and helping you heal from the negativity that may be present in your life.

One of the most important rituals we can engage in is a ritual of forgiveness. I refer to it as a ritual because it is not something that I think we can necessarily achieve by simply saying, "I forgive you." It is something that, at its core, requires continual work and reminders to stay in the place of forgiveness. This is why I believe it is one of the most important rituals that we can engage in on a recurrent basis. Forgiveness presents a conundrum in that the very people who inflicted trauma on us we are now being asked to seemingly forgive that person. How can I forgive someone who enslaved my ancestors? How can I forgive someone who raped me? How can I forgive you shot my son? These are legitimate and very important questions that we will have to each answer for ourselves. I would suggest that there is no one correct way of understanding and responding to these types of questions. Instead, I would challenge us to consider the alternatives of not forgiving and critically ask ourselves does our lack of forgiveness bring any harm to us or keep us from advancing along our destiny path. Put simply, does our lack of forgiveness cause us to suffer in any way? If your answer is that it does not cause you to suffer, then keep doing what you're doing. If it does cause you to suffer in some way again, keep doing what you're doing. You get to decide what is best for you. We can contemplate in meditation what our spirit communicates to us about whether our position moves us forward or keeps us stagnant. Does the bitterness and anger block your forward movement? Again there are no right answers and whatever you arrive at will dictate your actions moving forward.

Continuing this dialogue, I would suggest that forgiveness does not mean that we do not hold people accountable for their repulsive or inappropriate behavior. If someone has violated your space or perpetrated harm upon you or your family, they should be held accountable and steps can be taken to ensure that this happens. Instead, it means that we do not allow their actions to dominate and control our life. I am not the trauma that you inflicted on me. So I am not letting them off the hook, and in fact, will do everything in my power to ensure that justice is served. At the same time, I am letting me off the hook by not holding on to a situation that brings pain and frustration to me. When I am suffering from holding on to a given situation, the offender is likely not even thinking about me. Instead, it is me giving them the attention that I could be utilizing elsewhere in a positive manner.

Think about the worst thing that you have ever done in your life. How many people know about it? Have you forgiven yourself for it? Have those that you offended forgiven you? Do you feel that you deserve forgiveness? Why or why not? I consider myself to be a good person and yet there are so many things that I have done in my life that have been problematic or caused harm or hurt for other people. Most have been unintentional but some have been intentional. Human. I can be accountable for the times where I have fallen short of living according to the values that I believe, not explaining

Creating Positive Rituals

away the faults, but owning them and making a commitment to being better moving forward. This self-forgiveness is an important step in moving forward, healing ourselves from trauma and living our best lives.

The reason forgiveness needs to be a ritual is because it is easy to think of forgiveness in a philosophical and idealistic sense. I understand and appreciate the broader concept of forgiveness and would aspire to live my life in that space. Yet when I see another example of trauma inflicted upon my family or my community by someone who appears thoughtless and unconcerned with the harm that they have inflicted, my commitment to those values that I say I believe are challenged. At that moment, I don't want to forget. I want to be angry, I want revenge. Inevitably though, at some point, I move to my quiet space and the energy of the values that resonate with my spirit challenge me to see if I am aligning my actions and values. Am I doing things in a way that the energy is in my best interest and keeps me moving forward positively. I did not want to forgive my ex-wives for what they had "done" to me. I wanted for there to be retribution and I spent a lot of time pondering how this could happen. What would the Creator do to restore justice and right the wrongs that had been perpetrated on me, I wondered. Surely in a righteous world, there is something that will happen to restore order. Indeed it did not happen in this way. I learned one of my most valuable lessons of releasing the need to have "justice."

The essence of forgiveness is not about the other person but rather ourselves. Forgiveness is similar to balance in that it is something to be strived for rather than achieved. Just when we think we have it all figured out, we can be presented with yet another opportunity to practice forgiveness yet again. Without this constant awareness, it becomes easy for us to slide back into the realm of grudge holding and unforgiveness. I would suggest another way of thinking about this. When we engage in the process of forgiveness, we are really freeing ourselves. I can happily say that in the course of working on myself, I reached a point where I no longer remember the details of any arguments I might have because I move on very quickly. It is no longer important for me to win the argument or to even argue for that matter. It's more important for me to enjoy my life and live my life fully. You will have to decide which is more important for you as there is no right way.

Another example that can be useful to establish a positive ritual is to have a collection of affirmative statements about yourself that you review on a daily basis. You will be in a ritual of honoring and expressing the best aspects of yourself so that you do not get caught up in negative self-talk. To help engage this process, ask five people who are very close to you to give you a list of adjectives that they think describe you in a positive manner. These should be people that support you and can give an honest assessment of who you are and how you present to the world. These are people who will lift you up and sing your praises no matter what. Once you have these adjectives, you can then create affirmation cards for yourself that you remind yourself of throughout the day. If you find yourself having times or a particular day where you are feeling low and doubting yourself, ask your cheerleaders to remind you of just how special you are. This celebration of ourselves is something we need to engage more often than we do. In our celebration of our loved ones, we create an affirmative sense of self which we can all benefit from. These consistent positive words serve as an antidote to trauma.

One final positive ritual involves thinking about the times that you have felt the absolute best about yourself. What were you doing, wearing, smelling, eating? Think about all of the characteristics of the times you have felt so good and what it would take to recreate them. Write these things down and refer to them when you are feeling down, reminding yourself of what your circumstances were when you were engaging life at its fullest. Understanding and creating this positive mindset gives a template for establishing how you want to live life consistently. Training your brain to engage these variables allows for rewiring the traumatic patterns that may have been dominant previously.

CHAPTER 21

AUTHENTICITY

Extended Thinking to Understand the Self

"Authenticity is when you say and do the things you actually believe"
SIMON SINEK

In this section, we will further understand how we came to be the people we are. There is much that we observed within our family structure that had an impression on how we came to view the world. These core feelings form a basis for the outlook that we have on life and the manner in which we carry ourselves. We often do not consider how we came to carry such emotions and their impact on us. When we are able to understand how our actions have come into being, we can then implement processes to change those actions that no longer serve us.

In this next exercise, I would encourage you to write down what your mother, father, grandmothers and grandfathers taught you about expressing negative emotions such as anger, frustration and sadness. How did you respond to this teaching? Next, consider how were positive emotions like love, happiness, pride and confidence expressed? What did you teach your child children about these emotions? How have they responded?

My paternal grandfather was an amazing man. Robert "Buddy" Smith raised nine children, instilling in them a sense of pride, confidence, and integrity that allowed them to move forward successfully in life. I only recently found out that my grandfather lost his father in the third grade, a traumatic circumstance for any child. Being forced out of school and into work in a racist society was also traumatic. He did not have an opportunity for counseling to help him process his feelings. He likely chose to just find ways to mute his feelings, as would be the case for most in his situation during those times. Maybe he funneled those muted feelings into his work. He was an extremely hard worker and many of his jobs involved labor that would take a toll on your body. His children learned to work in a similar manner from a very young age and this discipline about work served them, their children and their grandchildren. I am one recipient of the valuable wisdom, traits, and characteristics passed down from my grandfather to his nine children and my many cousins and our children. Although I do not engage in physical labor currently, I understand discipline and hard work and have employed these qualities to maintain my own psychology practice. My grandfather was an innovator and created inventions to help make his work easier. Unfortunately, he never got credit for his inventions and in fact, made a lot of money for other people who had the capital to take his inventions. Born in another time and with the proper backing, my grandfather would likely have been an inventor creating things to make life better for the world.

As it was, my grandfather was born in Midway, Alabama, at the height of the Jim Crow south in one of the most racist states in the United States. Life was difficult and he was challenged to think about every action, as any misstep could be a matter of life and death. Growing up

Authenticity

during the depression, he did not have the luxury of tapping into his emotional side. His father died when he was in the third grade and he had to drop out of school and work to help support the family. He did what was necessary at that time, and although he did not have a formal education, he was extremely smart. He was also fearless and did not suffer fools. Given the advantages of high school and college and a truly equal opportunity, my grandfather would likely have been president of some large company. He showed his love through his work and dedication and his ability to provide for his family, not through his words. As a result, my father never heard him say I love you until he was on his deathbed, cancer had ravaged his body. This left an impression on my father, who from that point, began letting me know that he loved me. I made a decision to let my children always hear me tell them that from birth. And this is the way cycles are broken bit by bit, generation by generation, each person building to make things better. To leave them better than they were before while simultaneously appreciating the foundation that has been laid by those who came before and understanding the context of their lives that did not allow them to reach greater heights.

Although faced with the racism and life or death situations prevalent in Alabama, my grandfather did not back down easily and would defend himself if necessary. His defending himself eventually resulted in his needing to leave town and move to a different state, having stood up physically to a white man, the result of his not taking no mess. This fighting spirit I find admirable, and many in our family possess these qualities, including myself. It is that energy that propels me forward writing this book in the forthcoming manner that I have chosen to go about it. I know that he is with me supporting this process and many of the qualities and lessons he exuded are to be emulated. On the other hand, there were aspects of negativity that he learned honestly, but that did not serve him nor his progeny. These are the qualities that we have had to work to change and I would like to believe that we have made a lot of progress. Physical punishment is one example of this and my experiences with physical punishment pale in comparison to my parents. My father and his siblings received all manner of punishments, which were the norm for many families during this time. As stated before, we often do what we were taught, and this form of punishment was predominant amongst our communities at that time. As we think about those things that have been passed down that do not serve us, we must be careful to take into account the context of why those things were present, to begin with. And have compassion for those who lived through unthinkable times. Finding the balance to understand these family dynamics provides another level of healing while also appreciating the sacrifices made by those who survived unthinkable traumas.

Some other questions that can help you think through this process include the following. What are the family antidotes and values and traditions that you were taught? What did your family teach you about the expression of emotions? How were these specific emotions displayed—sadness, anger happiness, joy? Were you allowed to be free in a space of exploration? What did your family teach you about the role of children?

===== EXERCISE =====

Use the following family influence chart for important members of your family who have had a degree of influence on you. Thinking about and organizing this information can help deepen your understanding of who you are and how you became the person that you are.

Authenticity

FAMILY INFLUENCE CHART

Name _____

Positives	Negatives
1.	1.
2.	2.
3.	3.
4.	4.
5.	5.
6.	6.
7.	7.
8.	8.
9.	9.
10.	10.
11.	11.
12.	12.
13.	13.
14.	14.
15.	15.

Answering these questions can help you arrive at a place of authentic understanding and acceptance of your true self. As we are all products of our environments, we should not carry any shame or embarrassment about the people we have become and the traits that we possess that we do not like. We can instead choose to look deeply at these issues and do the work to bring about change.

CHAPTER 22

HEALING WITH COUPLES

**Methods for Avoiding the Convergence of Traumas.
"Clean Around Your Own Front Door Before You Try to Clean Around Mine."**

> *"You come to love not by finding the perfect person, but by seeing an imperfect person perfectly"*
> SAM KEEN

> *"Have enough courage to trust love one more time and always one more time"*
> MAYA ANGELOU

When we have been impacted by trauma and have not done the work to heal from this impact, we bring the symptoms of this trauma with us everywhere we go. It is like an energetic cloud of dust that follows us as we move through the world. If you can visualize the Charlie Brown character Pig Pen who always had a cloud of dust around him, you can get a sense of the energetic cloud of dust that we can carry related to trauma. As we engage in relationships, we bring that energy with us and the unhealthy ways of being that we have cultivated impact our relationships. This is the convergence of traumas referred to earlier in looking at the examples of unhealthy relationships. In healing these traumas, we can create an atmosphere that allows for a positive sharing in the relationship, a necessity if we are going to have a happy and healthy union. Because a healthy family starts with a healthy couple, exploring this area as another building block in overcoming trauma is absolutely necessary.

To ensure that there is a healthy convergence happening when we engage a relationship, the first key would be to ensure that the previously mentioned work has been completed and we are showing up to the relationship with the best version of ourselves. This does not mean that we are showing up with no flaws or without the need for continued work but rather that we have an understanding of who we are and how we show up in the world and are willing to be accountable for our actions and any resulting impact of these actions. It is at this moment that we can fully engage in a relationship without worry that someone will take advantage of us or cause us any undue harm. If we are ready to disengage at the first sign of any difficulty, this may be a sign that the trauma has not been healed. There needs to be a balance between knowing when an issue just needs more seasoning and work to find a space of compromise versus when it is time to end the relationship and move on.

Having an honest conversation at some point about trauma can help both parties to understand each other and how they operate in the world. As there is progression in the development of the relationship, these conversations can help bring forth areas that might be of concern moving forward. To the degree that individuals are at this place of healing where they are free from any judgment or concern about how they will be perceived, then they will be able to share this information free of any worry because they know who they are and what they stand for. So, for instance, if I shared my difficulty with being emotionally vulnerable and the work that I have had to do to correct this area in my life, that then allows the person that I engage with to be a mirror in helping me to remain true to my desire of being more balanced emotionally. It is true that everyone is not worthy of this level of engagement and dialogue. However, if one is doing the work to bring healing to themselves, then they are more likely to attract into their lives people operating on a similar vibration.

Additionally, discussing family histories can help to bring clarity to areas where potential clashes could occur. For instance, if one person has a history of trauma as it relates to discipline, the fallouts of this trauma might impact the way each of them considers engaging in the discipline of their children, which is necessary for parenting. These potential differences can lead to arguments that will cause problems down the line. One might ask about and be willing to share the specific traumas that have been a part of the family history. Although this does not have to be done early on, pending one's level of comfort with engaging in this conversation, it is something that should be broached prior to moving to a more serious phase of the relationship. The same level of intimacy we have as we share our bodies with each other, we should be willing to engage in sharing our emotional traumas as well. This helps us to truly know the person that we are deciding to have this intimate relationship with. Although this is uncomfortable, I believe it is necessary if we are going to engage in a truly authentic relationship. We should have no problem asking someone about their sexual history to ensure that we are not putting ourselves in danger engaging with someone sexually as they might have an STD that could put us at risk. There is a similar parallel when it comes to the conversation about trauma as we do not want to find ourselves in a situation where that puts us at risk.

If I have reached the place where I am in what I consider to be a loving relationship and I am telling my partner that I love them and they are reciprocating in kind, then it is important to consider what this really means. In aligning our actions and values related to this, a person that loves someone and who has been working to heal themselves from any lingering impact of trauma would not engage in saying or sharing things that would cause harm to the person that they profess their love for. If this is the case, then we should be able to say that I am not doing anything to intentionally bring harm to you. The person is not attempting to stab you in the back or hurt you in any conscious way. At this point, we have established that neither party has a desire to intentionally hurt the other one and in fact, only wants to do things that really show love and offer information that we believe would improve our partner. Given this, we should be able to hear whatever it is that comes out of the mind of our partner. Whether we express the thought or not, it is still there. We cannot claim to want to have an honest, authentic relationship and then not want to hear honest and authentic communication. Of course, our conversation should be tactful and the manner in which we share our thoughts should be considered. However, we should be able to express what we think and feel without worry about being perceived incorrectly or accused of attempting to inflict harm when we are coming from an authentic place. When I am in a space of corrective healing from trauma, I am able to listen to the information that my partner brings to me without feeling any angst, as I can trust that they are providing this information from a pure space and it does not have to be "right," I am able to synthesize the information and ponder whether or not it makes sense for me. Sometimes it will and others, it will not. There is not a correct answer, just a willingness to keep moving forward.

Continuing to specifics as it relates to the communication aspect here, it is important to go through and have an extensive conversation regarding thoughts about finances, parenting, long-term planning, and sexuality, to name a few. These are areas that have the highest level of conflict in relationships, and the conflict, often with ties to trauma, can be prevented with the appropriate healing and subsequent discussion regarding the respective perspectives on these issues. If there are differences in how these issues are perceived, work can be done to find a compromise that both parties can comfortably abide by. Two people come to a relationship with millions of experiences and interactions over the course of their lifetime that have shaped who they are and created their personal worldview. None of us have the entitlement to say that our worldview is THE correct worldview. It happens to be the worldview for you that has or has not served you over the course of your life. Combining your worldview with someone else's worldview can thus be challenging as the other person likely has things that they view differently at some point. If we have a healthy respect for these differences as well as a humility that allows us to not make our perspective THE perspective, this allows room for growth and finding common ground.

One of the biggest issues in communication with couples is the concept of relative words. All words have some degree of relativity. How one person defines a word can differ drastically from the definition of another person. These differences can exist even within the family. It becomes essential that as couples discuss a particular topic, they should ensure that both parties are defining what it is they are talking about in a similar manner. For instance, I have found that couples often define the word marriage differently. This can be the case for couples who have been together for 40 years. When asked to individually define marriage and then compare the definitions, the amazement at how different the definition is for each of them makes clear that they are not on the same page. This then allows us to do the work necessary to create a common definition that both parties can abide.

Another example that I like to use is the word affection. A couple can be arguing about affection and the lack thereof. For instance, the wife might say, you are not giving me enough affection. The husband would reply yes, I am. They might go back and forth arguing about this, ultimately getting nowhere. However, if they took the time to ask each other what they mean by affection, they might find that the wife really means that she would like a body massage, to hold hands when they go out and cuddle while watching television. The husband had in mind making sure he gives her a hug and kiss prior to leaving for the day and upon returning home. Neither of these definitions are right or wrong; they are just different. Yet if the couple does not communicate about their specific definition, they can continue arguing endlessly in a circle, not recognizing that their definitions are not the same.

Ensuring that the foundational unit of the family is in sync and working to eliminate any vestiges of trauma provides a healthy foundation for the evolution of the family. From this vantage point, children can be introduced in a manner that allows them to evolve at their best, overcoming historical traumas. We will delve more into this in our next section.

CHAPTER 23

HEALING IN CHILDREN/THE ART OF PARENTING

> *"Your children are not your children. They are the sons and daughters of life longing for itself. They come through you but not from you. And though they are with you yet, they belong not to you. You may give them your love but not your thoughts for they have their own thoughts. You may house their bodies but not their souls, for their souls dwell in the house of tomorrow, which you cannot visit, not even in your dreams"*
>
> Excerpt from On Children by KHALIL GIBRAN

Our children are a reflection of us as parents. We are the first mirror they have in addition to being the first source of comfort, nurturing and sustenance. The indelible bonds created in the initial years of life go a long way to understanding who we are as adults. You have observed the way that a child mimics their parents, often engaging in the same cadence, tone and witticisms. It is because they have heard this dialogue repetitively since birth and this information has become hard-wired in the brain. Our actions also have been cultivated in a similar way. Our mannerisms, facial expressions even the way we walk can be passed down and is clear to people who observe both parties. It is for this reason that we must ask what are the seeds that we are planting into the minds of our children and what kind of crop will those seeds yield in the behavior that the children ultimately engage, and the people that they will eventually become. We must be careful to avoid planting seeds of trauma and instead plant seeds of possibility, seeds of confidence, seeds of joy and happiness, seeds that show the ability to overcome and thrive. It is in the polishing off of our own building that we are then able to break any cycles of trauma and create new and healthier patterns of behavior. This is indeed the most important role of a parent.

One of the most hilarious things I observe with adults is the way we will lie to or in front of our children and then get upset when our children engage in the same behavior. This makes no sense, yet it happens constantly. Tell them I am not home. Tell the teacher our car broke down so you got to school late. Say that you are six, not seven, so that we can get the kid's price on the meal. We can rationalize our reasons for doing these things and come up with some good justifications. This does not underscore the message that is communicated to our children and their subconscious in those moments of lying. Our rationalization is because we want to achieve some goal as a result of the lie. This is no different than the child's goal when they engage in similar behavior. Even though the child may not be able to rationally explain why they are engaging in the behavior, their brain has been able to process the actions that they perceive, and they mimic the behavior they have observed their parents doing.

When we are engaging in this, we are passing down trauma and not even realizing it. Once we become aware of what we are doing, we have to make a hard decision to be accountable for our behaviors and change what it is that we are doing. In this case, our values and actions are not aligned, and our children are observing the contrast in the two. Even if they are unable to explain in words and detail what it is they are observing, they are making an intuitive analysis that allows them to understand and process what is happening.

So, you are driving along in traffic with your children in the back seat, and someone rudely and aggressively cuts you off, causing you to almost have an accident. How do you respond? Honestly. A few choice curse words. Yelling at the car that has now gone on ahead and out of range. Do you try to chase the car down to flip them off or mouth some angry words? Are you thinking about your children observing your reactions? They are paying attention to everything that happens and encoding this information into their brains. What they see you do; they perceive as the correct thing to do. They have not developed the rational and emotional capacity to think for themselves in an introspective manner, and by the time they reach this point, your behaviors have already hard wired them in a way that it will take some concerted effort to undo. Think back to the example of the children in the lynching postcards. They were taught that they should be smiling at the death of a man hanging from the tree. This thus became their normal and a natural way of being. Most people have seen children at a very young age playing indiscriminately with anyone who is their age regardless of background. At a certain point, the adults began engaging in behaviors such as moving their children away or making comments about certain children that begin to influence these children to now make a different choice. This should make it clear that everything we do impacts our children and has the potential to direct their lives positively or negatively. The brain processes information so quickly during those first few years of life and so it is vitally important that we are vigilant about what patterns we allow to be established.

Continuing this line of reasoning, parents often think that their children are not aware of the conflict that is happening in the lives of the parents. Whether it is a mother and father at odds with each other or a parent suffering from the stressors of the workplace, inevitably, the feelings associated with the things we are dealing with become evident to our children, even as they are unable to adequately give voice to those concerns. The case where the parents are clearly engaging in these behaviors in front of the child should obviously be eliminated if we are moving to a space of not passing down trauma. But it is the more subtle behaviors that are harder to address that we have to pay more attention to in order to ensure that we are not unwittingly allowing this energy to spread to and infect our children.

How do we create this healthy environment? We cannot skip any steps and we must first have done the work previously discussed to get ourselves to a healthy space. It is from this point that we can think about the types of seeds we would like to plant into our children that will yield the fruit of positivity. If I want to create a child that is honest, I need to make sure that I am displaying honesty in my actions, words and behaviors. If I want to create a child that is disciplined, I need to show my child what it means to be committed to my task and accomplish things. If I want my child to be focused, I have to create situations where I am modeling meditation and being in silence, even engaging my child in this process so that it becomes the natural way of being.

A large part of undoing generational trauma is ensuring we are not continuing the cycle of generational trauma. Questioning the things that we engage as a parent are important. We cannot be in our feelings as it relates to this if we truly want to provide our absolute best. I encourage people to engage with others in critical conversations about what it looks like to parent from the position of love rather than fear.

Because there is so much trauma inflicted upon the African American community, it is tremendously important that we as parents create an environment that reinforces the inherent strength that our children possess. We have to convey to our children that they are capable of accomplishing anything that they set their minds to. We have to create a force field around them that repels the negative notions that society would hurl upon them. We have to cultivate the genius inside of them and allow it to manifest in a way that knows no bounds. We have to do this intentionally and consistently with much more fervor than the attacks that are certain to come their way, at least for the time being. We have to let our children know that they are loved unconditionally and not engage in manipulative parenting where we make our love dependent upon them behaving, responding or interacting according to the way that we deem appropriate. When we recognize that we each have our own individual path to live out, we can see ourselves as stewards who provide structure and direction for our children rather than controlling their every movement. It is inevitable that they will have challenges that will cause them some degree of sorrow or difficulty. None of us escapes this and we cannot protect our children from this. But we can provide a safe, sacred space for them to grow, evolve and transform into the people that they are destined to become, with as little impact from trauma as possible.

    I previously had an opportunity to practice creating and undoing generational trauma with my son. I had taken a number of youth to Cuba for an educational trip in 2017. There were five teenagers on this trip and I was interested in them learning and appreciating the culture, in addition to having a fun and enjoyable time. After each day, we would come back to our residence and debrief about the day's activities and what we had learned during our various excursions. It became evident to me that these youngest two teenagers were not taking the experience as seriously as I would like. The next morning as we did our briefing before we headed out, I informed the teenagers that I wanted them to be thinking about their activities during the day and when we arrived back that evening to write a one-page paper about their experiences. In my mind, this would be a simple task that could make them more accountable to engaging the process and ensuring that they were getting out of the experience valuable knowledge that could serve them moving forward. As we prepared to leave, my son asked me if he could talk to me in private. We went to my room, and he began to become very emotional. I had no idea what was going on with him and allowed him to take his time in sharing with me what his concerns were. He expressed to me that by giving them an assignment to do when they were on break and having a vacation from school brought back memories for him of my giving him work to do as a child and not allowing him to have as much fun as he would like. He elaborated on his feelings and why this elicited the emotion that it did from him. I listened and did not attempt to diminish his experience. At the end of the conversation, I told him I would think about what he had shared and look for ways to modify what it was that I asked them to do. I reinforced to him that I loved him and appreciated him feeling comfortable enough to express how he was truly feeling. Throughout the rest of the day, I processed with other friends this situation and my thoughts about it. Although I would not change anything about the structure I provided for him growing up, I had to appreciate the impact that these experiences had on his feelings and development. Prior generations may have dismissed his concerns right away as mere folly of youth. While it is true that young people typically are unable to recognize life from the perspective of their parents, this does not mean that what they experience and understand is wrong. We have to be able to hear these thoughts and concerns and process them if we are to engage in a healthy relationship.

When we returned that night for the debriefing, as we were having dinner, I spoke to the group and told them that I was going to recant my earlier assignment and not force them to do the paper. As I was beginning to say this, my son wanted to offer his own thoughts as he had been thinking about it throughout the day as well. He suggested that they could do a poem together and each of them could be responsible for a stanza of the poem and they could present that to the adults in the group. He stated that he would be responsible as the oldest young adult for ensuring that everyone participated appropriately and was optimally engaged. I was ecstatic about this and felt that my ability to hear what he had to share with me allowed us to move to this compromise. Had I not been able to respect his feelings, we might have had a different outcome that would not have been so pleasant and would not have contributed to the further development of our relationship. Additionally, the ability to have this level of conversation also allows for new patterns of interaction to be established in our family lineage. It is my hope that he will take this progress and build on it with his progeny and I believe he will.

Another level to undoing patterns of trauma involves teaching our children to be critical thinkers. In my experience, parents often overthink this process of teaching and work too hard at creating patterns that will prove unwieldy over the long term. We can enhance the fertile minds that are young children who never fail to ask the question why. We should encourage this asking of questions as that is a natural activation of critical thinking. The young mind is attempting to understand the huge world that surrounds it and make sense of patterns and ways of being. We can enhance this curiosity with our own encouragement and teaching things in a manner that is fun and enjoyable. Unfortunately, many parents extinguish this natural curiosity as they find themselves bothered and annoyed by the questions that are incessant. In an age-appropriate way, we can encourage our children to think of what they think the answer might be and allow them to be creative in possibilities. This primes the brain to stay in a place of active searching, always looking for a better way.

Extending this thinking, a cardinal rule I encourage parents to engage is to never let your child utter the words "I don't know." Utilizing this phrase is creating a pattern that stifles the brain and does not challenge the child to exercise the muscles of the brain and extend themselves out of their comfort zone. It is not important that the child come up with the "right" answer. The goal is to challenge themselves to come up with an answer. This will strengthen the ability to think critically and process information in a manner that allows for going beyond the obvious. All great inventions have this as a component, and there are aspects of this process that can be taught.

Even as we work to eliminate passing on trauma to our children, this does not mean that we lower the standards that we set for our children. We are still required to parent and provide the structure and guidance that will allow them to develop into socially competent adults capable of being self-sufficient. There is a picture in my office with a woman with the words running across her dress that says, "no one rises to low expectations." This challenges parents to consider that if they do not raise the bar, in all likelihood their child will not challenge themselves to reach greater heights. They will become content with marginal effort and become one of the many that fall into the category of wasted potential. We have to set the bar of expectations high so that our children can rise up to them, but in a manner that is inspirational rather than dictatorially abusive. I have been pleasantly surprised when I have raised the bar just giving my children something to do and they reach and surpass the bar that has been set. Many of the parents I work with find this to be the case as well. "They are too young to wash their own clothes, they would have to separate the clothes and I don't want them to damage my washer." This ten-year-old child who can work every piece of technology in the house better than the parents suddenly does not have the aptitude to understand whites, light and dark. They don't understand how to press the proper button or turn a knob. Or are we making excuses that will ultimately limit them. Raise the bar, parents.

Our parents in previous generations may have engaged in physical discipline to get the point across and to propel children to do the right thing. Although many adults can laugh or speak fondly about choosing their own switch or withstanding an incredible whipping, this is not something that we should be proud of. If we had not been traumatized by the whipping imposed upon our ancestors, we would recognize the inappropriateness of these actions and choose not to continue to engage in these behaviors that do not serve us. By no means am I suggesting that we cannot have a response and corrective measures for behaviors that are not appropriate. We just need to think about healthier ways to go about doing this. We can be consistent in holding our children accountable without engaging in corporal punishment and causing additional trauma. If they engage in inappropriate behavior, it has to be dealt with every time, not just when we are stressed or angry. This establishes good patterns and allows the child to appreciate the boundaries.

Trauma has impacted the African American community since the inception of this country in a very profound and long-lasting way. For the vast majority of our time in this country, just surviving was the focus. We have reached a place where survival is no longer the only acceptable goal. Now we must move forward with the new purpose of healing the trauma, allowing us to reclaim our genius and move on to greater things.

CHAPTER 24

BLISS

Living Your Life Fully

"Life has no limitations except the ones you make"
LES BROWN

Having engaged in the process of walking your own personal labyrinth and reaching the center, we can enjoy the peace and tranquility that has come with engaging the winding path to healing. We must consider what we will do to maintain the level of peace and happiness that we have been able to maintain. We must also supplement this foundational work with other more specific things that can help enhance our particular need for healing. If we do not make a conscious effort to maintain our progress, we can be assured that the gains will reverse, moving us back into a space of disarray. As such, we must vigilantly protect our mental health once we have done the work to restore a sense of balance and happiness to our lives. Just one intervention alone is not necessarily the answer, but a combination of simple things done consistently can create a reality that rivals your wildest imaginations. It is impossible to move through life without experiencing any hardships, adversities or difficulties. We will know grief and we will experience loss. This is the human condition. However, we can experience these things from a place of strength and stability rather than from a place of weakness and instability.

I am committed to living my life fully for the 86,400 seconds that tick by every single day and encourage everyone I meet to do the same. We should not waste any of our precious time here in this life. I do not intend to suggest that we should adopt some pollyannaish pretend happiness just for the sake of doing so. Rather my hope is that we live our lives purposely, knowing that we are in control of how we choose to respond and conduct ourselves in any given situation. There are times where I feel sadness. I understand it as a necessary human emotion. I allow it to take its place and fulfill its mission and then I continue on with my mission of living my life fully. This is our challenge in life. Determine those things that bring you happiness in life, do them and do them often. Get a massage. Go dancing or dance alone in your home. Call an old friend and catch up. Do something to connect with nature. Try a new recipe. Drive-in any direction until you are almost out of gas. Draw or paint a picture. Travel to a new city. Play a round of golf. Go to the spa.

Imagine that we are playing a basketball game that is divided into four quarters. The first two quarters may be spent trying to establish our game plan. After halftime, we make adjustments and begin the third quarter with a greater sense of urgency. And once we reach the fourth quarter, we have to give our best effort as now the game is on the line. The last two minutes of the game, if we have played well, is crunch time and we do not want to have any wasted possessions. If we consider our life in this manner dividing it into four quarters and thinking about where we are in the game, it may become apparent to you the necessity of living life fully. For instance, if we expect to live for 80 years, once we reach 40 years old, we are halfway through our life. Once we reach 60, we only have one quarter left. We should consider that in life, that last quarter can often be cut in half because of the natural decline that happens as we age. This is exacerbated if we are not taking care of our health. Even at our healthiest, it is likely the case that we will be unable to do many of the things that we previously could do in our life. This is the natural course of aging and is to be expected. Taking all this into consideration, it should be clear that we do not have time to waste. Thinking about it from this perspective really helps us to appreciate the amount of time that we have to engage in the process of living life fully. An added variable that should be obvious is that none of us know for sure that we are going to get 80 years and quite a few of us get much less than that. Even as you read these words, somebody is completing their time here on earth. I have encountered so many people who have expressed remorse about things that they did not do earlier in their lives. Trips that were not taken, phone calls that were not made, adventures that were not undertaken, relationships that were not repaired. Time wasted and the person living in regret. The things that prevent living a full life include worrying about situations that are beyond our control and allowing negative emotions to dominate our life. We can make a choice to live without regret, to do the things that we want to do that equate to living our lives in a manner that we are completely fulfilled.

    Remember that we have to consistently build our muscles of healing to continue creating and maintaining positive change. If we do not put in the positive repetition of doing things differently, we cannot stay free of the negative implications of trauma. The patterns of old behavior have been well entrenched and are always waiting to reestablish themselves if given an opportunity. Do not allow these old patterns to creep back into your life. If we stay committed to a program of positive forward movement in a consistent way, we can be sure that we will reap the benefits of having change and an optimally healthy way of living. When you encounter another traumatic incident, you will have the necessary tools to negotiate this incident in a manner that keeps you from relapsing. Once you have done the work to create that positive self-love you will not put yourself in a position to be in a place to be disrespected or taken advantage of again. You will know who you are and what you deserve and not accept anything less.

When you understand and accept the flow of life, you will ride the wave and not fight it; you will have clarity about what you can control and do the work to ensure that you have done everything in your power in that regard. Those things outside of your control you will release knowing that worrying does no good and is actually energy expended in a wasted manner.

So as we close out this healing of trauma, I implore you to claim or reclaim your joy as we are a people of joy. Refuse to allow trauma to have any control in our life. I invite you to enjoy the ride that life brings you. Smile, breathe, laugh, love, make love, dance, sing, shout. Embrace all of your feelings but do not allow yourself to be captive to them. Do not allow admittance to anyone into your space who does not affirm you, who chooses to disrespect you, or who wants you to dim your light to make them comfortable. Always allow your light to shine brightly, basking in the glow of God that created and resides in you. Pay attention to the signs of the universe, those coincidences and random occurrences through which God speaks and guides us along our path always giving us direction. Know that your efforts today will pay huge dividends for you, your children, grandchildren, great-grandchildren, great great-grandchildren and more. The healing lies within. Remember who you are. And recall it often.

CHAPTER 25

__ THOUGHTS FOR A FUTURE OF FREEDOM FROM THE CHAINS OF TRAUMA __

> *Emancipate yourself from mental slavery none but ourself can free our minds.*
>
> BOB MARLEY

What would happen if we allowed ourselves to dream and open for our progeny 7 generations from now. If we take Alex Haley's story Roots and look backwards we can see that he was the 7th generation that reaped the benefits of the seeds that his multi-great-grandfather planted. Had he envisioned a time where his progeny would be free and capable of creating something that would inspire and change the world? Or did he just plant the seeds hoping that they would yield something different, something better than what he was currently experiencing. The book and mini-series Roots have been worldwide bestsellers and have been translated into 14 different languages. This has brought the family financial success and generational wealth that would not have seemed possible even a few years before it was written. If we allow ourselves to dream forward in this manner, what can we come up with that can similarly change the world.

In another contemporary example, I have a friend who was born into one of the families that first celebrated Kwanzaa. She was born one month before the first Kwanzaa, and because of how young she was, her family did not travel to attend the event, but they did attend every Kwanzaa thereafter. Reflecting on how they were received during those initial years, it's easy to recognize that People saw them as outcasts, as crazy people who were engaging in this ridiculous made-up holiday. However, they were committed to what they were doing and stayed the course of celebrating themselves with the values that reside in the concepts of Kwanzaa. Over the years, the ideology began to spread and soon enough, we were able to see a number of books and other writings on Kwanzaa. Currently, Kwanzaa has now developed into something so large that major corporations recognize the economic impact it has in their capitalistic way swooped in to try to take advantage of this. The irony in all of this is that the core concepts of Kwanzaa eschew any capitalistic aspects whatsoever. But in the American way, when an opportunity to make money is seen, even those who don't agree or even understand the concepts of Kwanzaa will insert themselves to make money off of the concept. The bigger picture for us is to recognize that over the course of 50 years; Kwanzaa was able to move from a very small cadre of families coming together in a sense of self-determination to honor values that uplift and enrich their families to an international event that impacts and inspires millions of people of African descent. This is the power that resides in us all and if we can appreciate and understand the change that happened over this time, we can tap into the same energy and project it forward. Whatever we can envision, we can then work towards. For me, that vision includes complete healing from the trauma that has evolved from the legacy of this country.

The letter in the preface offered some possibilities in this regard to serve as a potential template for us to stretch our visions as we create a new reality. We can create what we believe in with the strength and resiliency of those families who started Kwanzaa. When we plant the seed of a tree, we will not be around to sit in the shade. So for your last exercise, create a vision for your family and community reality free of any remnants of trauma. Dream big and be free. Come dream with me as we heal ourselves and change the world!

BIBLIOGRAPHY

After Earth, Columbia pictures, 2013

American Psychiatric Association: Diagnostic and Statistical Manual of Mental Disorders, Fifth Edition, Arlington, VA, American Psychiatric Association, 2013

Anthony Gene Carey, Sold Down the River: Slavery in the Lower Chattahoochee Valley of Alabama and Georgia (Tuscaloosa, AL: University of Alabama Press, 2011)

Ayi Kweh Armah 2006 The Eloquence of the Scribes, Per Ankh, Popenguine, Senegal change. 2021. In *Merriam-Webster.com*. Retrieved March 28, 2021, from https://www.merriam-webster.com/dictionary/change

Bernice McFadden, (2010) Glorious Brooklyn, NY: Akashic Books.

Cameron McWhirter 201 Red Summer: The Summer of 1919 and the Awakening of Black America, St. Martin's Press, New York.

Frances Cress Welsing (1991) The Isis Papers, Chicago, Third World Press.

Grier, W. H., & Cobbs, P. M. (1968). *Black rage*. New York: Basic Books.

Guthrie, Robert V. Even The Rat Was White: a Historical View of Psychology. Boston, MA :Pearson/Allyn and Bacon, 2004

Harriet Washington, (2006) Medical Apartheid: The Dark History of Medical Experimentation on Black Americans from colonial times to the present, New York, Doubleday.

Ilibagiza, I., & Erwin, S. (2006). *Left to tell: Discovering God amidst the Rwandan holocaust.* Carlsbad, Calif: Hay House, Inc.

James Benson Sellers, Slavery in Alabama (Tuscaloosa, AL: University of Alabama Press, 1950)

John W. Blassingame, The Slave Community: Plantation Life in the Antebellum South (New York: Oxford University Press, 1979)

Kari Frederickson, The Dixiecrat Revolt and the End of the Solid South, 1932-1968 (Chapel Hill: UNC Press, 2001)

Lardner, G (1980 May 21) McDuffie Death: It seemed to be open-shut case. Washington Post.

Leon Litwack, Trouble in mind: Black Southerners in the age of Jim Crow 1998 Alfred A Knopf, New York.

Lisa Cardyn, Sexualized Racism/Gendered Violence: Outraging the Body Politic in the Reconstruction South

Michael J. Klarman, From Jim Crow to Civil Rights: The Supreme Court and the Struggle for Racial Equality (New York: Oxford University Press, 2004)

Michael Tadman, Speculators and Slaves: Masters, Traders and Slaves in the Old South (Madison, WI: University of Wisconsin Press, 1989)

Noelle Matteson, The Freedom Rides and Alabama: A Guide to Key Events and Places, Context, and Impact (Montgomery: New South Books, 2011)

Osho 2007 Emotional Wellness Harmony Books

Paul Ferrini, 2012, The Twelve Steps of Forgiveness: A Practical Manual for Moving from Fear to Love.

Ridley, C. R. (1984). Clinical treatment of the non-disclosing Black client: A therapeutic paradox. American Psychologist, 39, 1234-1244.

Robert H Gumestad, A troublesome Commerce: The Transformation of the Interstate Slave Trade (Baton Rouge, LA: Louisiana State University Press, 2003)

Stewart E. Tolnay and E. M. Beck, A Festival of Violence: An analysis of Southern Lynching's, 1882-1930

Stewart, Nikita (May 30, 2020). "The White Dog Walker and #LivingWhileBlack in New York City". *The New York Times.*

The Social Dilemma, Netflix, 2020

The Wealth of Other Suns: The Epic Study of America's Great Migration (New York: Random House, 2010)

Tom Burrell 2010 Brainwashed: Challenging the Myth of Black Inferiority, Smiley Books, Carlsbad, CA

"Trauma." Merriam-Webster.com 2021
https://www.merriam-webster.com (8 May 2011).

Whaley, A. L. (1998b). Cross-cultural perspective on paranoia: A focus on the Black American experience. Psychiatric Quarterly, 69, 325-343.

Whitten, L. (2020). Stigma matters: An African American psychology professor comes out of the mental illness closet. *Psychological Services.*

BIOGRAPHY

Anthony Smith, Ph.D., is the Executive Director and Founder of Alase Center For Enrichment, a psychology practice in Durham, North Carolina. He has been involved in the mental health field for over 25 years. He is a licensed psychologist and certified health services provider in North Carolina. He previously served on the faculty at the Duke University Medical School as a professor of Behavioral Science in the psychiatry department.

Dr. Smith is passionate about issues related to mental health in the African American community and has been a member of the Association of Black Psychologists since 1992. He has consulted with organizations regarding issues related to diversity and healthy organizational development. He does a podcast, Black Folks Do Therapy, interviewing Black Psychologists around the world.

RESOURCES

Association of Black Psychologists
7119 Allentown Road, Suite 203
Ft. Washington, MD 20744
(301) 449 3082
www.abpsi.org

Association of Black Social Workers
2305 Martin Luther King Ave, S.E. Washington, D.C. 20020
(202) 678 4570
www.nabsw.org

Black Therapy Central
www.Blacktherapycentral.com

Black Emotional and Mental Health Collective
PO Box #27945
Los Angeles, CA 90027
www.beam.community

ALASE CENTER FOR ENRICHMENT
6015 FAYETTEVILLE ROAD, STE 114
DURHAM, NORTH CAROLINA 27713
PHONE: (919) 957-7357.
www.alase.net

Podcasts available on iTunes and Spotify

Black Folks Do Therapy

Naming It

Therapy For Black Girls

Between Sessions

Black Mental Matters

Minding My Black Business

INDEX

A

acceptance, 49, 136, 194, 209, 220, 260, 280
actions-values alignments, 258, 263
   consistency, lack of, 255–256
   exercise, 257–258
   meaning of, 261–262
acute trauma, 31
addiction, 186, 210, 214
admonitions, 110
adversities, 297
   conquering of, 197
   reasons for, 223–224
affection, 286
affirmations, 229–230, 235
   and brain remapping, 230
   collection of affirmative statements about yourself, 272
After Earth (film), 268
alcohol use/abuse, 31, 34, 54, 55, 209, 214, 242, 249
alignment. See actions-values alignments
anger, 20, 50–51, 54, 70, 181, 249–250
   and compassion, 65
   management of, 202
   repression of, 53, 62–63
anxiety, 13, 31, 33, 34, 62, 142
apathy, 41, 83
Armah, Ayi Kweh, 193
army officer, a traumatic incident involving, 183–184
authenticity, 275–280
automatic response, 33, 234

B

balance, 83, 144, 169–170, 271, 278, 282–283
   realistic, 206–207
   restoration of, 195–197, 297
   universal law of, 175
Barksdale, Donna Jean, 45
beauty, images of, 200–201

Index

being judged, fear of, 64–65, 76, 212–213
belief and belief system, 261–263
   and sexuality, 260
   and value, 254–255
Black Folks Do Therapy, 21
Black Graduation ceremony, 100–101
Black Lives Matter, 231
Black Power movement, 230
Bland, Sandra, 178
Blassingame, John, 40
body-mind relationship, 218
brain, 232
   power of, 233–234
   rewiring of, 218–219
brain remapping, 230–231
   and affirmations, 230
   and transformation, 222–223
Brainwashed: Challenging the Myth of Black Inferiority (Burrell), 262
Brown, Michael, 178
Brown, Willie, 56
Burrell, Tom, 262

C

Capitol incident, January 6th, 2021, 184–185
Cartwright, Samuel, 90
Castile, Philando, 178
change(s). *See also* transformation
   commitment to, 242–243
   definition of, 239
   and discipline, 239–241
   motivation to, 241–243
   as New Year's resolution, 239–240
   positive change, 299–300
   resistance to, 261
   stepping outside of comfort zones, 241
Charlemagne the God (talk show), 50
Chauvin, Derek, 19–20
children, 287–295
   behavioral seeds, 287–288
   creating healthy environment for, 289–291
   critical thinkers, teaching to be, 293–294
   disciplining, 85–89, 239–241
   early childhood trauma, 23–25
   impact of divorce on, 118–121
   impact on, 135–136
   parents' role in nurturing, 198–199
   setting the bar of expectations, 294–295
   values and actions alignment of parents, 288–289
choices making, 67–68
chronic trauma, 31
Civil Rights movements, 45
Cobbs, P. M., 47–48
Co-creators, 191, 255
collective trauma, 84, 93–106, 181
colorism, 201
comfort zones, dealing with, 241, 261–262
compassion, 61, 65, 194, 278
complaining, 220, 235, 267–268, 269
complex trauma, 31
concentration difficulty, 31
confidence, lack of, 31
controllable and non-controllable things, 64, 149, 255, 268, 300
convergence of traumas, 145–146, 176, 281–286
Cooper, Amy, 56–57

314

Index

co-parenting, 121
Cosby, Bill, 100–102
Creator. *See* God/Creator
critical thinking, 82, 106, 124, 263, 293
criticisms, worrying over, 212–213
Crutcher, Terrence, 178
cultural paranoia, 47–48

D

depression, 31, 33, 34, 41, 112–113, 214
Diagnostic and Statistical Manual, 30
diet, 33, 87, 117, 209, 266
dimensions of trauma, 32
discipline, and change, 239–241
disciplining, 85–89
dissonance, 61–62, 217, 258–259
distractions, dealing with, 192, 208, 233
divorce, impact on children, 118–121
downfalls and overcoming, 197–198
drapetomania, 90

E

early childhood trauma, 23–25. *See also* children
ego, 120, 125, 144, 263
emotional availability, lack of, 125
emotional healing process, 91–92
Emotional Wellness (Osho), 156
energy, proper channeling of, 268–269
envisioning our lives, 205–206
epigenetic programming, 218–219
equality, struggle for, 44–46, 106
equilibrium, 245–251

"Even the Rat Was White" (Guthrie), 90
experience level with a version of trauma, 29–30
exploration, 14, 215, 263
eyewitness videos, 56–57, 62, 103, 177–179, 184, 188

F

familial patterns of behavior, 245
family and community, creating a vision for, 303
family chart, 246–251
family histories, discussion of, 283
family influence chart, 278–280
family trauma, 25–28, 32, 145–146, 159, 251
fear, 64–65, 76, 210–213, 217
feeling of the absolute best about oneself, 272–273
fight, avoiding, 144
financial trauma, 32
flashbacks, 31, 58
flow of life, 208, 300
Floyd, George, 19–20, 61, 179, 183, 231
Fogg, Master, 144
forgiveness, 70, 82, 150, 159, 175, 269–272
The Four Agreements, 117
freedom riders, 44–46
frustration, 20, 54, 147–148, 182, 186, 234, 270, 275

G

gaslighting, 187–188, 196, 256
generational trauma, 25–28, 159, 251. *See also* family trauma

315

convergence of, 145–146, 176, 281–286
impact of, 13–14
undoing, 290–292
genograms, 246–251
Gibran, Khalil, 287
Glorious (McFadden), 52–55, 74
goals setting, 206–207, 208–209
God/Creator, 152–153, 198, 219, 225, 300
grace, 194
Grant, Oscar, 178
gratitude, 97, 226, 235, 269
Gray, Freddie, Jr., 178
Great American lie, 186–187
Grier, W. H., 47–48
guilt, 213–214
Guthrie, Robert, 90

H

hair and hair texture, 201–202
Haley, Alex, 301
happiness, 15, 84, 192, 198, 215, 224, 297, 298
hard drive analogy, of trauma, 68–69
hazing, 227–228
healing
  labyrinth analogy, 199–203
  power to heal ourselves, 233
  and restoration of balance, 195–196
  and source of trauma, 81
healing process
  self-inquiry, **245–246**
healing/healing process, 191–192, 193, 194–195, 198, 299
  and alignment, 253–263
  and change, 239–244
  commitment to, 244–245

consistency in, 233
  with couples, 281–286
  internalization, 225–226
  readiness for, 220–221
  and rituals, 265–273
  time and effort, 236–237
  writing letter to parents, 226–227
health, taking care of, 299
help seeking, difficulty in, 63–64
hiding feelings and thoughts, 47–48, 59–60
Holiday, George, 177
honesty, 212–213, 224
hopelessness, 20, 63

I

impostor syndrome, 213
inequities, 96, 145, 183, 187, 255–256
infidelity, 53, 110–111, 112–113, 116
innovations, 219, 222
inspiration, 163, 205–215
institutional racism, 99
intensity of trauma, 31
internal evolution, 200
internalized trauma, 179–181, 234
intuition, 68, 71, 82, 207
inventions, 219, 231–232
irritability, 31

J

Jackson, Jesse, 230
Jean, Botham, 178
Jefferson, Atatiana, 178
Jim Crow era, 43–44, 210, 276
Just Mercy (film), 148–149, 181–182
"justice" upon Mr. Brown, 57–58

K

karma, 113, 118, 119
King, Rodney, 177
"know thy self," 226
Kwanzaa, 301–303

L

Left To Tell (Illibagiza and Erwin), 139
liberty and justice, 221–222
life events, conceptualization of, 225
life values, 20. *See also* actions-values alignments
life vision, 208–209
listening skill, 82
living purposefully, 298
Loebeck, Agnes, 56
Lorde, Audre, 16
love, 198, 254

M

Maat (ancient Egyptian concept), 225
marital therapy, 128. *See also* relationships
marketing, 262
Martin, Trayvon, 178
McDonald, Laquan, 178
McDuffie, Arthur, 69–70
McFadden, Bernice, 52, 74
McMillan, Jack, will of, 36–39
media, symbolic reminders of traumatic events through, 181–182
Medical Apartheid, 51
meditation, 119, 207, 208, 266, 270

mental attitude, 197–198
mental health, 13, 30, 33, 297
mental health services, 49–50
microaggressions, 98, 106, 182
mind
    and body, relationship between, 218
    power of, 233
mistrust, 48–49, 51
Monet, Janelle, 178
motivation, lack of, 214–215

N

natural disasters, trauma related to, 32
negative thought, overcoming, 230, 233–234, 236
nightmares, 31
normalization, 33

O

On Children (Gibran), 287
opioid crisis, 214
oppression, 32–33
outcomes of trauma forms of, 31, 62–65

P

panic attack, 142
paranoia, 47–48
parent(s)/parenting, 85–89, 106, 158, 287–295
    and grandparents, teaching about negative emotions, 275–276
    role in nurturing their children, 198–199

Index

role of, 227–228
thinking oneself as, 227
writing letters to, 226–227
Parker, Richie, 219, 222
patterns of trauma, undoing, 293
perseverance, 102, 148, 219–220
personal blueprint, 198, 205–210
   and addiction, 214
   and fear, 210–213
   and guilt, 213–214
   and lack of motivation, 214–215
personal trauma, 84–95, 85
personalities and environment, combination of, 246
physical exercise, 210, 266
physical fitness, 209–210
physical punishment, 89, 90, 278, 295
police violence, 177–178, 186, 196
   army officer, a traumatic incident involving, 183–184
   Floyd, death of, 19–20, 61, 179, 183, 231
political hypocrisy, 187–188
positive change, 299–300. *See also* change(s); transformation
positive rituals, 265–273, 265–273
   affirmations, 272
   balance, 271
   complaining, 267–268, 269
   diet, 266
   energy, proper channeling of, 268–269
   feeling of the absolute best about oneself, 272–273
   forgiveness, 269–272
   gratitude, 269
   meditation, 266, 270
   physical exercise, 266
   prayers, 266
   self-forgiveness, 270–271
   teaching ways, 266–267
positive thinking, 229–237
posttraumatic stress disorder, 30–31
prayers, 140, 266
priorities in life, 257–260
progeny, 301
psychological trauma, 45
purpose in life, 154, 197–198

R

race riots, 56
racial terror lynchings, 42–43
racism, 32–33, 69–71, 98–99
rage, 47–48
realistic, being, 206–207
reckless behavior, 31
relationships
   actions and values alignment, 283–284
   affection, 286
   communication, 284–285
   finding common ground, 285
   honest conversations in, 282
   relative words, 285
religious values, 254–255
reminder alarms, 235–236
repercussions, 52–55
repressed anger, 53, 62–63
responses to trauma, 33–34, 193–194
Rice, Jerry, 243
Rice, Tamir, 178
Ridley, Charles, 48
rituals. *see* positive rituals
Roots (Haley), 301
running, 210

Index

S

sadness, 20, 185, 193, 275
Scott, Walter, 178
self-analysis, 234–235
self-destructive behavior, 31
self-disclosure, 14, 75
self-doubts, 76, 214, 243
self-esteem, 31, 45, 58, 96, 202, 234
self-forgiveness, 270–271
self-healing, 223
self-knowledge, 197–198, 199, 219
self-love, 159, 167, 175–176, 196, 198–199, 235, 256, 300
sexual trauma, 32, 42
sexuality and religion, 260
slavery, 35, 59
   Jim Crow era, 43–44
   and legal policies, 43–44
   lynchings, 42–43
   separation of families, 41–42
   sexual exploitation, 42
   struggle for equality, 44–45
   trauma imposed by, 40–41
   value of life in, 36–39
   whippings, 41
Smith, Anthony J., 82–84
   birth of, 156–158
   childhood years, 85–92
   children custody arrangements, 118–121, 127
   college years, 93–106
   co-parenting, 121
   criminal charges and arrest, 139–144
   disciping by parents, 86–91
   divorce and its impacts, 118–121
   domestic violence, witness of, 130, 141, 143, 166–167, 172, 176
   fidelity challenges, 110–113
   first daughter, health issues at infancy, 114–115, 132–133
   first marriage, 107–118
   first son, health issues at infancy, 109–110
   first two children and second wife, 136–138
   high school experiences, 91–92
   molesting accusation, 146–148
   mother of, 85–86, 156–158
   return of older two children into his life, 152–154
   second marriage, 123–155
   separation from children, 118–119
   spiritual guidance, 82
   third marriage, 159–176
Smith, Robert "Buddy," 276–278
smoking, 209
Social Dilemma (documentary), 262
social media, 76, 212, 262
socialization, 68
societal trauma, 84, 177–188
   collective trauma, 181
   eyewitness videos, 56–57, 62, 103, 177–179, 184, 188
   gaslighting, 187–188
   internalized trauma, 179–181
   media, symbolic reminders, 181–182
   police violence, 19–20, 61, 177–179, 183–184, 186, 196, 231
   political hypocrisy, 187–188
soul, 225
spirituality, 82, 149–150, 221
standards for living, 22

staying safe, 22
Sterling, Alton, 178
stigma, 48, 49–50
stillness, 207, 208
stressors, 32–33
subconscious, 233
survival versus thriving, 22, 33, 145
symptoms, 31
systemic racism, 102
systemic trauma, 222

T

"talk, the," 22, 59–60
talk therapy, 15
Taylor, Breonna, 179
Taylor, Johnnie, 112
temporary escape, 214
terror lynchings, 42–43
Thai Chi, 210
Till, Emmett, 21–22
time, utilization of, 298–299
trained response, 33
transformation. *See also* change(s)
    and actions-values alignment, 258
    avoiding unrealistic expectations, 236
    individual and collective systems, 222
    readiness for, 219, 220–221
    remapping of brains, 222–223
    willingness for, 217–219
trauma, definition of, 29, 30–32
Truth, Sojourner, 197

U

unhealthy relationships, 281
US Public Health Service Syphilis Study at Tuskegee, 51

V

value of life, in slavery, 36–39
values, 253–254
    alignment with, 254–255
    exercise, 257–258, 259–260
vegan diet, 117
voting rights, 149

W

Washington, Harriet, 51
Welsing, Frances Cress, 108
Whaley, Arthur, 48
white privilege, 185
"white women's tears," 56
World Peace, Metta, 50–51
worrying, 300
Wright, Daunte, 179
writing down the thought without any judgement, 234–235

Y

yin and yang, 195. *See also* actions-values alignments; balance
yoga, 210